Folk Heroes of Britain

Rogo, ut omnis lector, qui legerit hunc librum, det veniam mihi, qui ausus sum post tantos haec tanta scribere quasi garrula avis vel quasi quidam invalidus arbiter. Cedo illi, qui plus noverit in ista peritia satis quam ego.

I ask every reader who reads this book to pardon me for daring to write so much after so many others have done so, like a chattering bird or an incompetent judge. I yield to all those who are more expert in these matters than I am.

NENNIUS: *Historia Brittonum*

CHARLES KIGHTLY

Folk Heroes of Britain

with 51 illustrations,
including 9 maps

THAMES
AND
HUDSON

To my godchildren

© *1982 Thames and Hudson Ltd, London*
First paperback edition 1984

*Printed and bound in
the German Democratic Republic*

Contents

Acknowledgments

The author would like to thank the following for their help and advice during the composition of this book:
Peter Addyman, of the York Archaeological Trust; Ian Ball, of Sarn; Bernard Barr, Sue Boorman and the staff of York Minster Library; Anthony Barton; Mrs Margaret Brown; Dr Hugh Chapman, of the Museum of London; Penny Crocker; Francis Felix, OSB; Brian Hartley; David MacLees, of the Royal Commission for Ancient Monuments (Scotland); Mrs Sue Medd, who did the typing; Hilary Moxon; Dr Bill Shiels; Mr Maurice Smith, of York City Library, and his staff; Catherine Stirling and Dominic Twyman, intrepid searchers for the site of Caratacus' last stand; Mr D. Webb, of Colchester; Dr Christopher Wilson; and H. Beauchamp, who did a lot of work at the last stages.

Introduction

Heroes attract myths as inevitably as magnets attract iron-filings: but just as the filings will eventually conceal the magnet, so the hero may at last be totally obscured by the myths. Such a fate has, to a greater or lesser extent, overtaken all the men and women to be considered in this book. Yet all were real people, renowned for real qualities and real deeds: and if we allow them to be devalued into fairy-tale characters we not only insult their memory but also lessen our chances of understanding the great events in which they played leading parts. Surely, then – as the chronicler William of Malmesbury wrote of King Arthur – they are 'clearly worthy, not merely to remain the subject of silly fables, but rather to be proclaimed in truthful histories'.

The aim of this book, therefore, is to discover as much as possible about the careers of several semi-legendary but entirely historical figures. Foremost among them are Caratacus of the Catuvellauni, the guerrilla leader who 'scorned the might of Rome' for eight years; Boadicea, who may or may not have ridden in a scythe-wheeled chariot, but who certainly came close to prising loose the Roman grip on Britain; the real King Cole, far more splendid than the 'merry old soul' of the nursery rhyme; Alfred, who not only burnt the cakes but saved England from Viking domination; King Harold, Wild Edric and Hereward 'the Wake', who strove valiantly but fruitlessly against the Norman invaders; and William Wallace, but for whom Scotland might have become an English province.

We shall see them primarily through the eyes and words of their contemporaries or near-contemporaries: and despite the centuries which divide us from them, it is surprisingly often possible to do so. Surprisingly often, too, these ancient accounts of our heroes will provide new insights: for many of them have been little studied, most are available only in books long out of print, and a number of the most revealing have never before been translated into modern English. But such documents will not tell us the full story, even when carefully interpreted in the light of their authors' often violent prejudices: and the gaps they leave will have to be filled in from a wide variety of other sources, ranging from the reliable to – it must be admitted – the distinctly dubious. Thus archaeology, official archives, poems, genealogies and place-names will all add their pieces to the jig-saw, and so too will local traditions like those which preserved the dim memory of King Cole in Ayrshire for fourteen centuries, or that of Wild Edric in the Welsh March to this day.

7

Why were these men and women so famous in their own time, and so long remembered after it? Originally, perhaps, because all were quite literally 'folk' heroes, the particular champions of one of the constituent peoples of Britain during the long interracial struggles – of Romans against Britons; Romano-Britons against Picts, Irish and Saxons; English against Danes and Normans; and Scots against English – from which the nation emerged in roughly its present form. Frequently, too, they were the champions of the losing rather than the winning 'folk', the memory of whose deeds acted as a much-needed salve for the wounded pride of their compatriots. And though all were warriors, by no means all achieved the goals they fought for: many endured terrible tribulations, some were betrayed to their enemies, and most met with violent deaths. What mattered was not their ultimate victory, but their refusal ever to give in, the dogged perseverance in an apparently lost cause displayed by Caratacus in the Welsh hills, Alfred on Athelney, Hereward amid the Ely fens or the hunted Wallace in Scotland.

Later, when the enmities between the peoples of Britain had begun to fade into the past, our heroes continued to be remembered mainly because their exploits made such good stories. These were told and retold, often coming to incorporate incidents borrowed from the sagas of other, less famous, men: and later still, chroniclers, poets and novelists adapted them to their own times and purposes, turning Wallace into a saint, Boadicea into a Patriot Queen and Hereward into a Victorian gentleman. Thus the legends grew and flourished, but the real people on whom they were based became increasingly difficult to discern: this book, it is hoped, will do something to restore them to their rightful place in history.

CHAPTER ONE

'The Beloved Battle Expert'

Caratacus and the Roman Conquest of Britain

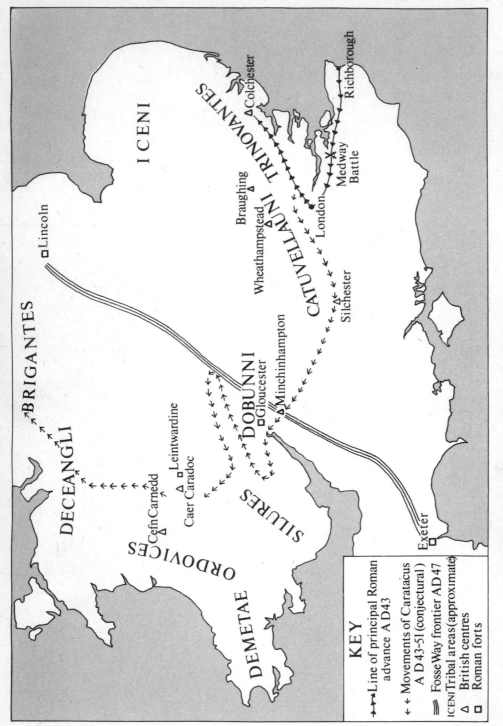

Map 1 *Caratacus' campaigns*

KEY

➤➤➤ Line of principal Roman advance A D 43
← ← Movements of Caratacus A D 43-51 (conjectural)
≣ Fosse Way frontier AD47
ICENI Tribal areas (approximate)
△ British centres
◻ Roman forts

ICENI

BRIGANTES

DECEANGLI

ORDOVICES

SILURES

DEMETAE

DOBUNNI

CATUVELLAUNI

TRINOVANTES

Lincoln

Cefn Carnedd
Leintwardine
Caer Caradoc

Gloucester
Minchinhampton

Exeter

Silchester
Wheathampstead
Braughing
Colchester

London
Medway Battle
Richborough

IF HEROISM IS HEREDITARY – and our Celtic, Saxon and Scandinavian ancestors all fervently believed that it was – Caratacus was off to a flying start, for he belonged to by far the most aggressive and formidable tribe in Iron Age Britain, the Catuvellauni. Archaeologists have yet to decide whether they formed part of the confederation known as the Belgae, 'the boastful ones', who about a century before the birth of Christ spilt over from their homeland in northern France to raid and then colonize south-eastern Britain: or whether, as now seems more probable, they were a much longer-established people, who furiously and successfully opposed the Belgic invaders. But it is certain that by 55 BC they were firmly in control of the Hertfordshire area, and at war with most of their neighbours. Indeed, both their tribal name ('the men good in battle', 'the battle experts') and their subsequent history make it quite clear that, even by the standards of their 'war-mad' fellow Celts, the Catuvellauni were exceptionally addicted to fighting.

Manifestations of this Celtic love-affair with battle are well attested both by horrified but fascinated classical writers and by archaeology. Believing that the soul resided in the skull, the European Celts were undoubtedly head-hunters, offering freshly severed heads in their temples and embalming those of specially noteworthy enemies in cedar-oil, to be kept in a chest, occasionally conversed with, and brought out for honoured visitors. Their British cousins almost certainly indulged in similar practices, borne out by finds like the row of skulls which adorned the gateway of Bredon Hill fort (Herefordshire and Worcestershire) and the widespread ritual heads in stone or metal, including three found in Catuvellaunian territory at Welwyn, Hertfordshire.

Celts took great pains to deck themselves for war, and Caesar tells us that: 'All the Britons stain themselves with blue vegetable dye [woad], which produces an azure colour and makes them appear more horrible in battle. They let their hair grow long, and shave every part of the body except the head and upper lip.' The Welwyn heads, and those on coins issued by Caratacus' grandfather, indicate that the Catuvellauni also retained the European habit of matting their hair with lime-wash, so that it stuck up in bright spikes from the scalp. Fighting naked and shaving the body – as their Highland and Irish relatives occasionally did until the

16th century – were perhaps intended to prevent an enemy getting a handhold, but this precaution was, typically, often negated by the wearing of eminently seizable gold neck-rings or 'torques'. For the Celtic warrior loved martial finery almost as much as war itself, and Celtic craftsmen applied their very considerable talent for decorative art primarily to the embellishment of helmets, swords, shields and chariots.

War-chariots remained an important part of the British armoury long after they had been abandoned in Celtic Europe, providing an unpleasant surprise for Julius Caesar when he first landed in 55 BC. 'This', he wrote, 'is the manner of fighting from chariots':

First they drive about in all directions and throw javelins, and usually the terror inspired by their horses and the rumble of their wheels throws the enemy ranks into confusion. When they have worked their way in between the troops of cavalry, they leap down from their chariots and fight on foot. Meanwhile, the chariot drivers retire a little way from the fighting and place their chariots so that, if the warriors are hard-pressed by enemy numbers, they can easily get back to their own side. Thus they display in battle both the mobility of cavalry and the steadiness of infantry, and by daily use and practice they can control their horses at a gallop even on slopes and steep places, checking them or turning them round in a moment. They can run along the chariot pole, stand on the yoke, and dart very swiftly back into the chariot.

The Roman historian Tacitus, describing chariots still in use during the Scottish campaigns of his father-in-law Agricola in AD 79–84, adds the rather surprising information that it was the aristocrat who drove the chariot, while his retainers did the fighting; perhaps, for once, skill was valued above belligerence.

Scythe-wheeled chariots, so vital a part of modern folklore about the 'Ancient Britons', find no place in the accounts of Roman historians, and the slender evidence for their existence rests entirely on fleeting mentions by a geographer and two poets:

The Britons . . . fight not only on horseback and on foot but also from vehicles and chariots equipped in the Gaulish fashion: they call 'covinni' those on which they use scythed axles. . . .

[Pomponius Mela: *De Chorographia*]

The Belgae, the skilful guides of the beaked [i.e. scythed] chariot . . .

[Lucan: *Pharsalia*]

Even so . . . the native of Thule [i.e. Britain] drives his scythe-armed chariot round the close-packed ranks in battle. . . .

[Silius Italicus: *Punica*]

The last gives us some idea of how such horrendous vehicles might have been used, and they could also have made life very uncomfortable for enemy horses if 'they worked their way in between the troops of cavalry'.

However this may be, it is clear that the chariots described by Caesar were light, scytheless, two-man vehicles, rather like the one whose remains were discovered in a bog at Llyn Cerrig Bach on Anglesey. They were designed, not for concerted chariot 'charges' or disciplined close-formation fighting, but rather for hit-and-run javelin attacks and for the swift transport of picked warriors to the scene of the fiercest fighting. This kind of heroic open warfare, full of sudden rushes and precipitate retreats, was and remained characteristically Celtic: Tacitus, declaring that the 1st-century Britons were as reckless in courting danger as they were anxious to avoid it when it came, is echoed by Geraldus Cambrensis describing the 12th-century Welsh: 'From their first fierce and headlong onslaught . . . they seem most formidable opponents, but if the enemy resists manfully and they are repulsed, they are immediately thrown into confusion. With further resistance they seek safety in flight.' The Britons, then, were not 'steady troops' in either the modern or the Roman sense. Worse still, they were incurably tribal-minded: 'We have no more effective weapon against them', says Tacitus, 'than their refusal to take council together for the common good. It is rare for even two or three tribes to combine against a shared danger: thus they fight singly, to be defeated collectively.' War-mad though his people were, any British leader would thus inevitably stand at a disadvantage against the disciplined and united Romans. Here again, however, heredity was on Caratacus' side, for his family had long and unique experience of yoking together their independent-minded country-men.

Cassivellaunus, perhaps Caratacus' great-grandfather and certainly an ancestor, had been chosen to command British resistance to Caesar's invasion of 54 BC. Even Caesar's propagandist report admits that he used his cavalry and chariots to great effect against the Roman advance through Kent, swooping out of the hills and woods whenever the invaders relaxed their guard and then conducting feigned withdrawals which lured pursuers to their doom. A Celtic enemy would probably have been hopelessly discouraged by these tactics, but the Romans pressed on undeterred to the Thames, where they found the only usable ford – variously identified as at Brentford; near the present London Bridge; or, most probably, at Tilbury – guarded by the Britons and blocked with sharpened stakes fixed in the river bed. The Venerable Bede, writing in the 8th century, makes the almost unbelievable claim that these stakes were still visible in his day, 'cased in lead and thick as a man's thigh'.

Neither Britons nor stakes could prevent the Romans from crossing, and as they neared Cassivellaunus' homeland he fell back on pure guerrilla warfare. Disbanding his main army, he retained a swift-moving force of 4000 chariots, which hung about Caesar's flanks, set upon his scouting and foraging parties, and denied him supplies by driving off the cattle in his path. At this stage, however, the brittle alliance of British tribes fell apart, for Cassivellaunus' neighbours began to see friendship with Rome as an attractive alternative to Catuvellaunian bullying. The first defectors were the powerful Trinovantes of Essex, whose king Cassivellaunus had recently slain, and five other tribes followed, probably including the Iceni of Norfolk and Suffolk. These revealed to Caesar the whereabouts of Cassivellaunus' headquarters (placed by modern archaeologists either at Wheathampstead near St Albans or, most recently, at Braughing in northeast Hertfordshire) which the Romans stormed and captured after a brisk fight. But the majority of Cassivellaunus' fighting forces escaped, and he retained enough prestige with his fellow-Britons to play one final card: he ordered the Kentish chieftains to attack the Roman beachhead near Deal. Had the Britons succeeded in destroying Caesar's transports, the marooned invaders would have had no alternative but to surrender. They failed, and Cassivellaunus himself had to sue for terms. Having forced him to hand over hostages, to agree to pay an annual tribute, and to promise not to attack the Trinovantes, Caesar returned to Europe the triumphant victor.

That, at least, was Caesar's version. Reading between the lines of his account, however, it seems probable that it was he who began the peace moves, and Tacitus subsequently declared that Julius had 'revealed' Britain to his successors rather than actually conquered it. The Britons themselves went further, soon coming to believe that they had decisively beaten the Romans. Caratacus, a hundred years later, is reported to have encouraged his followers with this remembrance, and in time Cassivellaunus became a fully-fledged folk hero, the earliest British historical figure known to have been thus honoured.

The stories told of him have not come down to us in full, but a number of references to them occur in the *Trioedd*, 'Triads of the Island of Britain', a catalogue of ancient Welsh legends arranged in threes according to theme. Here, for instance, is one of those which mentions Cassivellaunus, known by the British version of his name: Caswallawn – 'excellently good':

The Levies that departed from this Island, and not one of them came back:
The first went with Elen of the Hosts and Cynan her brother
The second went with Yrp of the Hosts. . . .
The third levy went with Caswallawn son of Beli, and Gwenwynwyn and Gwanar, sons of Lliaws son of Nwyfre. . . . And those men came from Arlechwedd [in modern Gwynedd]. They went with Caswallawn their uncle across the sea in pursuit of the men of Caesar. The place where those men are is in Gascony. And the number that went in each of those Hosts was twenty-one thousand men. And those were the Three Silver Hosts: they were so called because the gold and silver of the Island went with them. And they were picked men.

Though the oldest surviving Triad manuscripts date only from around the 13th century, some of the Triads themselves may first have been recorded five or six centuries earlier, and the stories they list are certainly of considerable antiquity. Reconstructing these stories from the Triads is as tricky a business as reconstituting the plot of a novel from an exceptionally detailed index, but it is at least clear that the Caswallawn of British legend is a vastly different figure from the Cassivellaunus described by Caesar.

Caswallawn the folk hero has supernatural qualities; his magic cloak of invisibility ensures that only his darting sword can be seen in battle, and among his exploits is the extermination of an invading horde of fairies (or possibly dwarves) from Arabia. He has, on the other hand, some extremely human weaknesses. He is persuaded to allow the Romans to land (one of the Three Unfortunate Counsels of Britain) by the gift of a horse called Slender Grey, and he is Caesar's rival for the love of an exceptionally beautiful girl named Fflur (Flower) whom he goes to seek in Rome disguised as a shoemaker. Having repulsed Caesar, and celebrated with one of the Three Extravagant Feasts, he pursues the enemy to Gascony in France with a mighty army but, as described in the Triad above, not one of his men returns to Britain. It is, perhaps, just possible that this last story preserves the memory of a disastrous counter-raid on Roman Gaul, mounted by Cassivellaunus after Caesar's withdrawal.

Whatever the exact truth about Caesar's invasion may have been, it certainly proved no more than a temporary setback to the aggressive expansionism of the Catuvellaunian 'battle experts'. Tasciovanus, who was probably Cassivellaunus' son or grandson and who reigned from about 20 BC, pushed their tribal boundaries westward into Bedfordshire and Buckinghamshire and southwards into Surrey and west Kent, but their most spectacular advances were made under Tasciovanus' son Cunobelinus – 'The Hound of the Shining One' – whom Shakespeare knew as Cymbeline. Succeeding in about AD 10, Cunobelinus at once overran the Essex Trinovantes and established his capital in their chief town of Camulodunum, later Colchester, and in the following decades he or his family moved into east Kent, Berkshire, Oxfordshire and northern Hampshire. By the end of his thirty-year reign he ruled or dominated virtually the whole of southeastern Britain, and the Roman historian Suetonius called him, not 'ruler of the Catuvellauni', but simply 'King of the Britons'.

The Romans did little enough to impede his progress, for Caesar's successors Augustus and Tiberius rejected military intervention in favour of treaties with both Cunobelinus and Verica of Sussex, the one remaining independent monarch in southeastern Britain, and the invasion planned by the mad Emperor Gaius Caligula in AD 40 turned into pure farce. Drawing up his armies on a Channel beach, he suddenly ordered them to fill their laps and helmets with sea shells, and forthwith returned to Rome with their 'plunder' to celebrate a formal Triumph over the ocean. Nor did the crippled, shambling Claudius, who followed Caligula in AD 41, seem likely to present a threat to anyone.

Caratacus and Togodumnus, who probably succeeded their great father Cunobelinus in that same year, can therefore be forgiven for seeing the Roman Empire as a paper tiger, whose tail could be twisted with impunity. Which of them was the elder brother is uncertain, but it is likely that Togodumnus took over the Catuvellaunian heartland north of the Thames, while Caratacus received the newer lands to the south and west. There, near Guildford in Surrey, one of the very few surviving examples of his coinage was discovered, depicting on one side the head of Hercules or of some British war-god, and on the other an eagle killing a snake. These are not devices likely to be used by a man intent on peace, and it soon became clear that Caratacus had inherited in good measure the warlike traditions of both his tribe and his family. Within two years he had apparently overrun at least part of the Gloucestershire Dobunni, and had certainly completed the Catuvellaunian conquest of the southeast, annexing the hitherto independent enclave of Sussex and driving its ruler Verica into flight. The last was much the more momentous action, for Verica was an ally of Rome, and it was there that he went for aid. To add insult to injury, Caratacus thereupon demanded the fugitive's extradition, threatening to take revenge – perhaps on Roman merchants in Britain – if his wishes were not complied with.

'Reckless of courting danger', like all his race, Caratacus had gone too far. Claudius, despite or perhaps because of his deformity, yearned for real military glory as opposed to the spurious triumphs of his crazy predecessor, and the British insult to Rome showed him clearly where to seek it. Other factors, like reports of Britain's mineral wealth and the hope of wiping out the anti-Roman Druids who were using Britain as a base to stir up trouble in occupied Gaul, were also in favour of decisive action, and by the spring of AD 43 an invasion force of 40,000 men had assembled under Aulus Plautius around Boulogne. It was neither a happy nor a confident army. Rumours about the hazards of campaigning 'beyond the limits of the known world' were rife, and it was perhaps as late as July when they were finally persuaded to embark: crossing the Channel by night, they landed unopposed at Richborough near Sandwich in Kent.

Dio Cassius, the only Roman historian of the invasion whose work has survived, now takes up the story:

They landed on the island, and found none to oppose them. For the Britons, because of reports that had reached them, did not expect the Romans to come, and had not assembled an army. Even when they did muster they would not attack the Romans openly, but lurked in the marshes and woods, hoping to wear down the invaders so that – just as had happened in Julius Caesar's time – they would sail away without achieving anything. Plautius therefore had a great deal of difficulty finding them, but when he finally did so, he defeated first Caratacus and then Togodumnus, the sons of the late Cunobelinus. (The Britons were not independent, but ruled by the kings of other tribes.) When these kings had fled, Plautius received the capitulation of a section of the Bodunni [*sic*], a people subject to the Catuvellauni. Then, leaving a garrison behind, he marched on until he came to a river.

Reading between the lines, it appears that Caratacus and Togodumnus heard about the long Roman delay from their Gallic cousins, and concluded that Claudius' invasion, like Caligula's, was a non-starter. When it actually arrived, they at once adopted Cassivellaunus' guerrilla tactics, shadowing the Roman advance first from the salt-marshes around Sandwich and then from the thick downland woods around Canterbury, and mounting two separate holding attacks to delay its progress while forces came in from the remoter parts of their dominions. Among these, most probably, were the otherwise unrecorded 'Bodunni', whom most archaeologists identify with the newly conquered Gloucestershire tribe of Dobunni, unwillingly conscripted into the Catuvellaunian army and only too glad to go over to the enemies of their oppressors. Their desertion, recalling the break-up of Cassivellaunus' alliance against Caesar, was ominous: if history was not to repeat itself, Caratacus and Togodumnus must abandon guerrilla warfare and halt the Romans by main force before they penetrated any further.

They chose to hold the line of the Medway, doubtless the river towards which Plautius was now reported to be marching, probably following the northern edge of the North Downs and aiming for the ford near the present M2 motorway bridge above Rochester. Plautius' final camp before reaching it was apparently somewhere around Bredgar, near Sittingbourne, where a hoard of Roman gold coins, the latest dating from AD41, was discovered in 1956: they were presumably concealed by a Roman officer who did not survive the ensuing battle.

'The barbarians', continues Dio Cassius, 'believed that the Romans would not be able to cross the river without a bridge, so they camped on the far bank without taking precautions. But Plautius sent across a detachment of "Celts", who were trained to swim the swiftest streams in full armour.' We know from other sources that these 'Celts' were Batavian auxiliaries from the marshy Low Countries, inured by long experience to amphibious warfare.

These took the enemy by surprise, but instead of shooting at the men they wounded the chariot horses, so that even the charioteers could not escape in the resultant confusion. Then Plautius sent across Flavius Vespasian (later emperor) and his brother Sabinus, who was acting as his lieutenant. Their division somehow managed to get over the river, and also took the barbarians by surprise, killing many of them. The remainder of the Britons, however, did not flee, but renewed the action on the following day. The fighting was indecisive for a long time, but Gnaeus Hosidius Geta, after nearly being captured, finally defeated the enemy so soundly that he later received triumphal decorations, though he had never been consul.

Quite the most remarkable thing about the battle of the Medway is that the Britons, though clearly shaken by the surprise Roman river-crossing, did not follow their usual practice of withdrawing in the face of determined opposition: instead they stood their ground overnight, counter-attacking the next day with such vigour that the issue was long in doubt. On no other recorded occasion did a British force stand up to a Roman army for more than a few hours, let alone hold it to a two-day battle. They were, admittedly, not yet inured to Roman invincibility by a long line of defeats, and they enjoyed a considerable tactical advantage over their enemies: but, with subsequent events in mind, it is tempting to attribute the uncharacteristic tenacity of the defenders of Rochester ford mainly to the leadership of Caratacus.

From this position the Britons fell back on the River Thames, which they reached near the point where it flows into the sea and forms a great pool at flood-tide. Being well acquainted with the position of the fords and firm ground, they got across quite easily, but the Romans who tried to follow them were not so successful. The 'Celts' [Batavians], however, swam over as they had done before, and another force managed to cross a bridge a little further upstream, whereupon they attacked the barbarians from several points at once, cutting many of them down. But, pursuing the remainder too incautiously, they found themselves in impassable marshes, and so lost a number of their own men.

Shortly afterwards Togodumnus perished, but the Britons, far from giving in, united all the more firmly to avenge his death. Because of this, and the trouble he had experienced at the Thames, Plautius now became fearful: refusing to advance any further, he decided to guard what he had already won, and to send for Claudius. He had, indeed, been instructed to do so if he met with especially stubborn resistance, and stores of equipment, including elephants, had already been assembled for the imperial expedition.

Caratacus, then, was beaten but not routed on the Medway – Dio mentions no slaughter of fugitives such as normally follows the account of a Roman victory – and retired in good order to the Pool of London, putting the formidable River Thames between himself and pursuit. Plautius, however, contrived by good luck, good management or British treachery to gain control of a bridge, and with the help of the indispensable Batavians he crossed the river and entered the Catuvellaunian heartland. No major geographical obstacle now stood between the invaders and the British capital at Colchester, and Roman losses in the swamps – probably Hackney Marshes – were more than paid for by the death of Togodumnus in a skirmish. The 'battle experts', it is true, were likely to fight fiercely to defend their own territory, but all in all Plautius was doing extremely well. His 'fearfulness', indeed, was almost certainly diplomatic. The British campaign had been mounted principally to gain glory for Claudius, and Claudius, complete with his elephants, must be allowed to gather its fruits in person.

About a month later, allowing for the journey from Rome, the emperor

joined the troops waiting for him near the Thames. Taking over command, he crossed the river, engaged the barbarians who had gathered to oppose him, defeated them in battle, and took Camulodunum [Colchester], the royal town of Cunobelinus. Afterwards he won over many tribes, some by force and others by capitulation. He disarmed the conquered and handed them over to Plautius, who was ordered to subjugate the rest of the country. Claudius himself then hastened back to Rome . . . he had spent only sixteen days in Britain. . . .

Whether Claudius actually saw much fighting is dubious. Suetonius, his biographer, declares that 'he fought no battles and suffered no casualties', and his short stay (nearly half of which must have been spent in travelling) left little room for serious campaigning. On returning home, however, the emperor staged a pageant of 'the storm and sack of a fortified town, with the surrender of the British king', so there was probably at least a token resistance at Colchester. The main event of the 'campaign', nevertheless, must have been the formal submission of the 11 'kings of the Britons' mentioned on the Arch of Claudius in Rome: some of these will have actually been conquered, others (probably including the rulers of the East Anglian Iceni and the northern Brigantes) anxious to make the best possible bargain with the invaders. The ease with which Claudius obtained their surrender – presumably negotiated in advance by Plautius – and the lack of real resistance to his march on Colchester show clearly that, despite all Caratacus' efforts, British tribal disunity had triumphed once again.

Where, meanwhile, was Caratacus himself? Dio Cassius' account of British affairs, which dries up with Claudius' departure in the autumn of AD 43, leaves him by name in east Kent and by implication near the Thames: the surviving manuscripts of Tacitus, which do not take up the story until the autumn of AD 47, rediscover him as an established resistance leader operating in or near south Wales. Given these uncertainties, any account of what happened to him between these dates must be conjectural, though archaeology provides a few indications.

One possibility is that, despite his defeat on the Medway, his inability to hold the Thames crossing, the loss of his brother and the defection of his allies, Caratacus fought on to defend his father's capital. When this too failed, he surrendered to Claudius – in which case he is the 'British king' of the pageant – but later changed his mind and fled. It is altogether more probable, however, that his flight occurred during the period between the death of Togodumnus and the arrival of the emperor. Realizing that the southeastern tribes were turning against him, and that a defeat at Colchester would leave him trapped with his back to the sea, he and his immediate followers withdrew out of the line of the Roman advance, determined to fight another day.

He must, therefore, have gone westwards, but it is most unlikely that he immediately moved as far from the theatre of war as Wales. To do so would imply giving up the struggle rather than continuing it, and a Catuvellaunian prince, coming as a defeated fugitive, would at this stage have little hope of gaining support from Welsh tribes among whom he was presumably a complete stranger. Given Caratacus' need to restore his prestige and the fact that he now probably commanded only his small personal warband, a better policy would be to operate on the fringes of enemy-held territory, particularly in areas where he had ruled before the invasion and where he may still have had friends. There, avoiding engagements with the main Roman forces, he could encourage resistance among wavering British tribes, and launch hit-and-run raids on those which had already gone over to the invaders.

Archaeology provides two hints that this is exactly what he did. A rampart and ditch thrown up soon after the invasion at Silchester in Hampshire, a settlement once ruled by Caratacus but now in the hands of Cogidubnus, Rome's leading British ally, may well have been intended to protect the town against its former owner. Further west, at Minchinhampton in Gloucestershire, a naturally strong position near a crossing point of the Severn and not far from the frontiers of Wales has been reinforced by cleverly sited earthworks similar to those found in Catuvellaunian territory. This, its excavator claims, was Caratacus' base for raids on the neighbouring Dobunni, the tribe whose levies had deserted him before the battle of the Medway. If so, he may by now have commanded a formidable force, for the Minchinhampton works defend an area of some six hundred acres, ample room for a large Celtic army complete with its camp-followers and herds. Tacitus later declares that Caratacus' 'long series of drawn battles and victories had exalted him above all other British war-leaders': some of these victories, there is little doubt, were achieved in the years between 43 and 47.

However successful Caratacus may have been against his British foes, he was nevertheless far from strong enough to take on the Romans themselves. By the summer of 47 an inexorable three-pronged advance had given them control of almost the whole of lowland England, and the frontier of the conquered territory ran from Exeter in a virtually straight line north-eastwards to Lincoln. Defended in depth by forts, and traversed from end to end by the remarkable military road called the Fosse Way, the frontier was clearly intended to be a permanent one: since it passed within a few miles of Minchinhampton, Caratacus must by this time have crossed the Severn into Wales. His position, however, was vastly different from that of four years earlier. No longer a fugitive stranger, he was now a famous resistance leader, whose victories on their borders must have been known to the Welsh tribes and whose prowess preceded him into the mountains.

The Romans, no doubt, were pleased to see him go, for resistance leaders (if you cannot capture or kill them) are safer in exile than at large within your territory. When Plautius ended his governorship in 47 he must have returned to Rome with the sense of a task well performed. His Fosse Way frontier protected the richest and most civilized part of Britain: the remainder, mainly barren uplands inhabited by barbarous pastoral tribes, was probably not worth the trouble of subduing. So long as the frontier held, and the tribes outside remained quiet, there was nothing more to be done but to organize the Romanization of the conquered province. If Plautius had been right, the southwestern peninsula, the west Midlands, Wales and the north of England might never have formed part of the Roman Empire, with incalculable effects on the subsequent history of Britain. He was, however, sadly mistaken, for the frontier did not hold, and the tribesmen did not remain quiet. The man responsible, almost certainly, was Caratacus.

Tacitus, taking up the story at the arrival of Plautius' successor, reports that:

the governor Publius Ostorius was greeted by chaos in Britain. The enemy, not believing that a new commander would take the field against them with an unfamiliar army and with winter already begun, had burst violently into the territory of our allies. But Ostorius, knowing that it is initial results that produce fear or confidence, rushed forward his light troops at once, cutting down those who resisted and chasing off the broken fugitives. Then, to avoid a new rally by the enemy or a precarious and resentful truce which would allow no rest to the general or his army, he prepared to disarm all suspects and subdue the whole area on this side [i.e. the southeast] of the Rivers Trent and Severn.

Caratacus had chosen his moment with care, and administered a severe shock to the Romans and their supporters. Where exactly the attack came from is uncertain, but subsequent events make it likely that it was spearheaded either by the Deceangli of northeast Wales or the Silures of the south. In either case the frontier was broken, and though Ostorius managed to drive out the raiders, he was in no doubt about the extreme seriousness of the situation. The enemy remained unsubdued and, truce or no truce, would certainly attack again: worst of all, their action had put new heart into malcontents within the conquered area, and their next incursion might well set the whole province aflame. There was no alternative but a major change in policy. Waverers must be neutralized, a demonstration must be made against the raiders, and the newly created but unsatisfactory Fosse Way frontier must be abandoned for a stronger one further to the north and west.

Having been forced to adopt this troublesome and expensive new policy, Ostorius found its implementation frustrated at every turn. His disarming of 'suspect' tribes provoked a serious East Anglian rising by the Iceni and their neighbours (of whom we shall hear more in the next chapter) and it was not until the summer of AD 48 that he was able to march against the Deceangli of modern Clwyd and Cheshire, whose lands linked Wales with the powerful Brigantes, the southernmost of the still unconquered peoples of northern Britain.

The countryside was laid waste, and booty was taken on every hand: the enemy dared not attack his army openly, and if they did creep out of their hiding places to ambush the column, their deceit was punished. Ostorius had nearly reached the Irish Sea when a rising among the Brigantes called him back, for he was firmly resolved not to undertake new conquests without securing the old ones.

Whether the governor intended merely to destroy the Deceanglian fighting force, or whether (as the Brigantes clearly believed) he also hoped to drive a permanent wedge between the free Britons of the north and west, his expedition was a failure. Before he could plan a new move, moreover, the Silures ('upon whom neither harshness nor clemency had any effect') launched a new attack from south Wales. The Romans had lost the initiative.

To whatever extent Caratacus had orchestrated the governor's earlier troubles, there is no doubt that he was the moving spirit behind the Silures. His recognition as their leader not only implies a notable victory over tribal separatism, but also testifies to his charisma, his power of binding men to him: it was, perhaps, no mere coincidence that his name – or nickname – means something like 'the beloved one'. For the Silures were very different from his own people. The prototypes of the 'little dark Welshmen' of English folk-memory, these swarthy curly-haired men reminded Tacitus of Spaniards. Their remote ancestors may indeed have come from Iberia: certainly they were aborigines compared to the Catuvellauni, and they knew little of southeastern innovations like towns and coinage. Their wandering pastoral way of life made them far more mobile and difficult to pin down than the more settled tribes of lowland England, and at the core of their territory lay the barren mountains and steep densely wooded valleys between the upper Wye and the southern Welsh coastal plain. They were also quite exceptionally warlike and ferocious, and it is appropriate that among their gods they worshipped a personification of that most savage and stealthy of British predators, the wild cat. They were, in short, a people ideally adapted for guerrilla warfare, and with an experienced resistance leader like Caratacus at their head they would prove a very tough nut to crack.

Quite apart from all these considerations, Caratacus had another and perhaps overriding reason for basing himself among the Silures: their territory faced what was now the most vulnerable section of the Roman frontier. With the Second Legion garrisoned far away at Exeter, the Ninth in Lincolnshire, the Fourteenth around Stafford and Lichfield and the Twentieth in reserve at Colchester, there was no strong force immediately available to prevent Caratacus from crossing the lower Severn and striking at the vitals of the Roman province.

Caught off balance, the unfortunate governor was thus faced with the necessity for another major campaign. This time he meant to be sure of eliminating Caratacus, and his preparations were thorough and pains-taking. First of all, as a temporary measure, he no doubt sent a scratch force of auxiliaries to reinforce the threatened sector, but nothing short of a full legion of 5000 men would suffice to secure it, let alone to invade Silurian territory. Since to transfer any other legion would be to court trouble elsewhere on the frontier, the only possibility was to bring up the Twentieth, and even this would leave the still-restive East Anglian tribes unguarded. A colony of time-expired legionary veterans was therefore established at Colchester, 'to be a safeguard against rebels and to inure the friendly natives to the rule of law'. Later events proved them incapable of either, but in AD 49 their presence enabled Ostorius to move the Twentieth to a new Severn-side fortress at Kingsholm near Gloucester.

Aimed at the eastern entrances to Siluria, along the southern coastal plain or up the Usk valley, they were to be Ostorius' main striking force, but not his only one. Roads were built at this time from Gloucester to the west Midland bases of the Fourteenth Legion, and it is clear that they too were to take part in the campaign, perhaps moving down the Wye valley to attack from the north. There is also evidence that a Roman fleet was now operating in the Bristol Channel, and this could be used to land an out-flanking detachment of the Second Legion in the territory of the pro-Roman Demetae of Dyfed, thus closing the net from the west. Ostorius, in fact, was preparing to turn Caratacus' Silurian stronghold into a trap, and by the summer of AD 50 his preparations were complete.

'Then he marched against the Silures, a naturally ferocious people reinforced by their trust in the prowess of Caratacus.' Though we know no details of the campaign, we can guess that it followed the lines of subsequent actions against the same tribe. 'Engagements, generally fought like bandit wars among the woods and swamps, followed each other in quick suc-cession, and either luck or courage prevailed. Some happened by chance, some by design, some were provoked by anger, some by lust for plunder . . . in all of them the Silures resisted most obstinately.' Before long, however, it became clear to the Romans that something had gone very badly wrong. The trap was closing, but Caratacus was no longer inside it: for all the governor's careful planning, he had got away yet again, slipping through the mountain passes into central Wales. The exasperation and excuse-making that followed this realization are reflected in Tacitus' words: 'But at this time Caratacus, inferior in numbers but superior in his knowledge of that treacherous country, cunningly shifted the war into the land of the Ordovices.'

His decision to do so is not difficult to explain. The whole Roman field force had been committed to the encirclement of Siluria, and to extricate it and regroup it for a new objective would occupy the governor at least until the next campaigning season. Even then the lands of the Ordovices would be hard to penetrate, harder to surround and harder still to police effectively. Covering the whole of central and northwestern Wales from the upper Wye valley to Anglesey, they included some of the wildest and most inaccessible terrain in the whole of Britain, with endless opportunities for ambush and evasion. The Ordovices themselves, tough and primitive hillmen whose tribal name ('the hammer-fighters') suggests that their favourite weapon was the ancient stone-headed axe-hammer, would prove useful allies in their own country, and if really hard-pressed Caratacus could escape via the territory of the Deceangli to join the free peoples of northern Britain.

With these factors in mind, Caratacus' next action is all the harder to understand: for 'after being joined by all those who feared Roman rule, he hazarded everything on a pitched battle'. Having scored all his most brilliant successes in guerrilla warfare, and having now come to the best guerrilla country of all, he was about to precipitate the situation he had striven for nearly eight years to avoid, the very situation in which he had suffered his only wholesale defeat on the Medway. Had he, perhaps, become over-confident? Had his success in thwarting Roman plans caused him to underestimate his enemies, or did the support of 'all those who feared Roman rule' lead him to believe that he was now strong enough to beat them on ground of his own choosing? Had Celtic bravado finally overcome his hard-learned caution and strategic sense? Or was his decision that of a desperate man, weary of running away and plagued by mutinous followers who demanded a clear victory as the price of continued support? Since we have only the Roman version of what followed, we shall probably never know.

The site of the battle was so chosen that approaches, escape routes and everything else were unfavourable to us and most advantageous for his own men. On one side rose steep hills, and wherever there was an easy ascent the enemy had piled up boulders into a kind of rampart. In front of the position flowed a river with an untested ford, and all the defences were bristling with armed men.

The British chieftains, meanwhile, went around encouraging their tribesmen, uplifting their spirits by making light of fear, inflaming them with hope and otherwise inciting them to battle. Caratacus himself, almost flying from one position to another, proclaimed that this day and this battle would mark the beginning either of the recovery of freedom or of perpetual slavery. He also called on the names of their ancestors, who had driven out the dictator Julius Caesar: it was valour alone that had kept them free from the axes of Roman executioners and the demands of

Roman tax-gatherers, with the bodies of their wives and children undefiled. The warriors responded with great shouts of approval, and each man swore by his tribal oath that neither wounds nor enemy weapons would make him give way.

Their obvious enthusiasm for battle dismayed the Roman general, who was already apprehensive about the intervening river, the reinforcing ramparts, the overhanging cliffs, and the crowds of savage defenders who thronged everywhere. But his soldiers demanded battle, crying out that no strong position was proof against courage, while their officers, using the same arguments, spurred them on to still greater zeal. Then Ostorius, having carefully examined the enemy lines to see which points were impenetrable and which might be vulnerable, led his eager troops forward.

They crossed the river without difficulty, but when they got up to the ramparts, and the fight was being decided by the exchange of missiles, the Romans had decidedly the worst of it, and many of them fell. So, after they had locked their shields together into a protective 'testudo', they pulled down the crude and ill-built heap of stones: this turned the combat into a hand-to-hand struggle on equal terms, and the barbarians now retired to the hilltops. Even there they were pursued by both light auxiliary troops and heavy legionary infantry, the former skirmishing with their spears while the latter advanced shoulder-to-shoulder. The British ranks, lacking the protection of breastplates or helmets, were thrown into chaos: if they resisted the auxiliaries they were laid low by the javelins and stabbing swords of the legionaries, and if they turned to face the legionaries they fell to the lances and slashing swords of the auxiliaries. It was a famous victory, and Caratacus' wife and daughter were captured, his brothers being allowed to surrender.

Given that we can accept it as a substantially historical narrative rather than a flight of literary fancy, Tacitus' splendid but impressionistic account provides few details of when, where and by whom the battle was fought. We know, however, that it occurred during the campaigning season of AD 51, and can guess that on the Roman side Ostorius led the greater part of the Fourteenth and Twentieth Legions and their auxiliaries, an army of roughly 15,000 men. The British force was probably smaller, and certainly made up of levies from several tribes. Its heart and soul was Caratacus' own warband – Catuvellaunian veterans who had been with him since before the battle on the Medway and reinforcements picked up during the subsequent years of guerrilla fighting – but the largest contingents must have come from the Ordovices and Silures. The Deceangli, Brigantes and other free tribes may also have contributed, and interspersed among them were little groups of fugitive irreconcilables hunted out of the conquered province: 'all those', in fact, 'who feared Roman rule'.

The site of the battle presents far greater difficulties. It certainly lay in Ordovician territory and, since Caratacus was challenging the enemy to a showdown rather than turning at bay, we should look for it relatively near the Roman frontier and the present Anglo-Welsh border, in eastern Powys rather than in the remote fastnesses of Snowdonia. More specifically

Tacitus' account shows that it was fought on a steep, irregular hillslope, precipitous at some points but ascended at others by trackways blocked with makeshift ramparts. At the foot of the slope ran a fordable river, and at the top was a plateau large enough for a battle and flat enough for heavily armed legionaries to advance in formation. Finally, since its approaches and escape routes favoured the Britons and worked against the Romans, the site cannot be on an isolated hill: it should, rather, be at the edge of a large area of British-held upland, which the Romans could only attack frontally from a river valley below.

The spectacular countryside of the Welsh borders, however, is full of uplands and river valleys, and many places there have at one time or another been 'identified' as the battlefield. Most will not fit the bill. Some, like the Herefordshire Beacon near Malvern, lie well outside Ordovician territory, others are on isolated hills or far from a river, and others again are hillforts defended by formidable earthworks and ditches, with no need of reinforcement by 'ill-built heaps of stones'. The current favourite among archaeologists, a steep-sided block of hills southwest of Caersws in northern Powys, is much more worthy of consideration. Crowned by the Ordovician hillfort of Cefn Carnedd, the massif juts into the Severn valley to challenge an army moving along this principal routeway into central Wales, and is bounded on three sides by the Rivers Severn and Tarannon, one of which would have to be crossed before it could be attacked directly.

But if circumstantial evidence tends to support this site, the oldest recorded tradition places the battle further south. Some three miles northeast of the border town of Knighton, on a hill towering above the Shropshire hamlet of Chapel Lawn, stands a magnificent many-ditched hillfort. When the Welsh antiquarian Humfrey Lhuyd visited it during the early 1560s, 'the inhabitants informed him that the place was called Caer Caradoc, that is the City of Caradoc, and that formerly great battles had been fought there against a certain king called Caratactacus [sic], who at last was conquered and taken by his enemies'. Since Tacitus' unique account of Caratacus, lost during the Middle Ages, was not published in Britain until 1534 and not translated into English until the 1570s, it seems likely that the story preserved a genuine folk-memory, and Lhuyd was 'bold enough to confirm that . . . this must be the identical spot where Ostorius contended with Caractacus'.

We cannot be so certain, but neither can we reject the tradition out of hand: though Caer Caradoc, with its strong permanent defences, cannot itself be the exact site, the battle may indeed have been fought nearby. The surrounding landscape accords well with Tacitus' description, for the hillfort stands on a spur of a flat-topped and steep-sided range of uplands, not far from the Ordovician border with the Silures, and with easy escape routes via the hills to the north and east. To the south the range descends

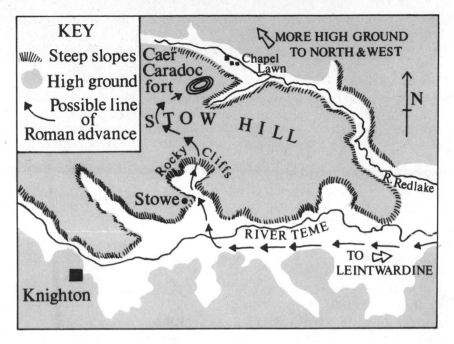

Map 2 Caratacus' last stand

sharply into the Teme valley, forcing a Roman army advancing from the fort at Leintwardine – almost the midpoint of the Roman road from the base of the Twentieth Legion to that of the Fourteenth – to keep to the flat land on the far side of the river. To attack the position, Ostorius would thus need to ford the Teme before fighting his way up the slope, possibly near the hamlet of Stowe, where a number of trackways ascend amid almost vertical cliffs to the summit plateau. After the battle some of the Britons may even have made a last stand at Caer Caradoc, where the non-combatants had already taken refuge: it was there, perhaps, that Caratacus' wife and daughter were taken.

Caratacus himself got clear away. No doubt he had fast horses in readiness, and as soon as he saw the fighting turn irreversibly against the Britons – perhaps even as soon as the Romans reached the hilltop – he made off furiously to the north or the west. He had lost a battle, he had lost his wife, his daughter and his surviving brothers, but, as long as he himself remained at liberty, he had not lost the war. Even at this, his darkest hour, he can have had few doubts as to his next move: he made straight for the land of the Brigantes. Driven out of the southeast, the

West Country and Wales, he now meant to renew the attack from the north.

The Brigantes, who occupied most of the wide lands from the Humber-Mersey line northwards to the Tyne and Solway, were a numerous but loose-knit tribal confederacy. Some of their clans (perhaps those in the Lancashire area) had three years earlier proved willing to resist any Roman threat to their independence, and it was upon these that Caratacus will have pinned his hopes. But the overall ruler of the confederacy, Queen Cartimandua ('sleek pony'), was strongly pro-Roman: she may well have submitted to Claudius in AD 43, and have thereafter maintained her somewhat precarious dominance only with Roman backing. It is therefore hard to believe a remark by Tacitus that Caratacus 'sought her protection'. More probably he tried to stir up the anti-Roman elements of the tribe against her, planning after her deposition to lead the whole confederacy in a fresh assault on the conquered province. Instead he somehow fell into her hands, and was 'handed over in chains to the Roman victors'.

The governor knew that Caratacus was far too big a fish to be dealt with in Britain. His long resistance, and the absence of major wars elsewhere, had left him without rival as the Empire's Public Enemy, and soldiers' tales of his daring raids and hairbreadth escapes will have lost nothing in the retelling, especially among his Romanized cousins in Gaul. The fall of such a hero, and with it the apparent completion of Claudius' long-delayed scheme for the conquest of Britain, could be properly publicized only in Rome. To Rome, accordingly, Caratacus was sent, and his journey there became a kind of triumphal progress:

His fame had spread from the islands of Britain into the neighbouring provinces, and he was well known in Italy itself: everyone was desperate to see the man who had scorned our might for so many years. Even in Rome the name of Caratacus was not without honour, and the emperor, seeking to enhance his own splendour, only made him seem more glorious in defeat. For the people were summoned as if for some magnificent spectacle, while the Praetorian Guard stood to arms on the parade-ground before their camp. There, while Caratacus' lesser retainers were herded past, the neck-rings and other trophies he had won from other British tribes were displayed: next his brothers, his wife and his daughter were put on show, and finally the king himself appeared. Fear made the rest of the prisoners degrade themselves by appeals for pity, but Caratacus sought mercy neither by words nor by downcast looks. Coming to the emperor's dais, he spoke in this manner:

'If my high birth and good fortune had been matched by moderation at the hour of success, I would have come to this city as a friend rather than a prisoner: nor would you have rejected a peaceful alliance with a man of such noble ancestry, the ruler of many nations. But as things turned out, I am humbled, while you are glorified. Once I had horses and warriors, fine weapons and treasure: is it any wonder I was unwilling to lose them? Just because you want to dominate the world, does it follow that everyone else wants to be a slave? If I had been dragged before you after

surrendering without a blow, neither my misfortune nor your triumph would have become famous: if you execute me, both will soon be forgotten. Spare my life, then, to be an everlasting memorial to your mercy.'
The emperor answered by granting pardon to Caratacus, his wife and his brothers.

Tacitus does not pretend to quote Caratacus' speech verbatim – one wonders, indeed, if he really spoke in Latin – but it is clear that, like the 'long and florid orations' subsequently made in the Senate, the whole ceremony was stage-managed to display Claudius as a mighty but merciful victor. We can only guess at the British king's real sentiments; perhaps they are best revealed by a much-quoted remark made as he walked among the magnificent buildings of Rome after his release: 'Why, when you have all this, do you still envy us our poor huts?'

Caratacus and his family, it seems, spent the rest of their days in Italy. Certainly it would have been impolitic to permit him to return to Britain where, despite the fact that decorations had just been awarded to Ostorius for 'completing the conquest', resistance had flared up anew. 'Either because the removal of Caratacus had made the Romans drop their guard in the belief that the war was over, or because compassion for so great a king had stirred up the enemy to avenge him', the Silures went on the rampage again. A few months later, getting the worst of a savage guerrilla war, the governor died 'worn out by anxieties and cares'.

The conquest of Britain would not be completed for another thirty years, and the Romans would have to face many more frontier wars, as well as a bloody and dangerous revolt within the province itself: but never again would they encounter an enemy to match Caratacus. His resourcefulness and strategic ability, his personal triumph over tribal separatism, and above all his steadfast refusal ever to give in, make him well worthy of a place in any list of British heroes.

CHAPTER TWO

'The Bloody Queen'
Boadicea's Revolt against Rome

Despite Caratacus' fame among the men of his day, it is not he who personifies for the modern mind the spirit of British resistance to Rome. That position undoubtedly belongs to a woman who, in the space of under two months, probably slaughtered more Romans and destroyed more Roman property than Caratacus accounted for during nearly nine years of guerrilla warfare. She is now generally known as 'Boadicea', but this version of her name, like the 'Voadicia' and 'Bonduca' favoured by Tudor and Stuart historians, is based on a mistranscription of Tacitus, who called her 'Boudicca'. The correct spelling, according to experts on Celtic languages, is 'Boudica' or 'Boudiga' – 'Victoria', the victorious one.

Who Boudica's parents were is unknown, but she came of the royal house of the Iceni, the tribe or group of tribes inhabiting northern East Anglia. Thus she belonged to probably the most magnificent aristocracy in all Britain, whose great wealth and love of display is vividly demonstrated by the discovery on their territory of many golden torques and arm-rings – notably the hoard from Snettisham in Norfolk – and of elaborate bronze horse-trappings and chariot-fittings. These gilded princes seem to have been comparatively recent incomers from northern France, but the peasantry they ruled were apparently older native stock – a situation which may well have a bearing on Boudica's status within the tribe. Their lands were defended on the north and east by the sea, and to the west by impenetrable fenland, but to the south they bordered with the Trinovantes of Essex and, more crucially, with the belligerent and expansionist Catuvellaunian 'battle experts' of Hertfordshire and Bedfordshire.

By the time Julius Caesar landed in 54 BC these troublesome neighbours were presenting a threat serious enough to convince the Iceni that any enemy of the Catuvellauni was a friend of theirs, and they probably had no part in the alliance which the Catuvellaunian king Cassivellaunus led against the invaders. When Caesar crossed the Thames, indeed, the 'Cenimagni' ('great Iceni'?) were among the tribes which offered him tribute in return for protection against Cassivellaunus, and hastened that king's downfall by revealing the whereabouts of his headquarters. If only as a continued protection against Catuvellaunian aggression, it is likely that the Iceni remained on good terms with Rome during the years after Caesar's withdrawal, and when full-scale invasion came in AD 43 they held aloof from British resistance, formally and voluntarily submitting to the Emperor Claudius at Colchester. Certainly they must have been regarded as favoured and reliable allies for, instead of being subjected to Roman officials, they retained their independence as a 'client-kingdom' within the province, a privilege accorded to only one other British tribe.

It was not long, however, before their special relationship with the victors appeared in its true light. For four years, while other tribes were defeated and overrun, the Iceni must have congratulated themselves on their wisdom. Tales of Caratacus' exploits may have tempted a few young malcontents to talk of fighting, but the British resistance leader was far away and, besides, he was a Catuvellaunian, the hereditary enemy of their people. Then, early in AD 48, began the rude awakening. The Roman governor Ostorius, intent on securing the province before marching against north Wales, ordered the disarming of all 'suspect' tribes, among whom he chose to include the Iceni. The people that had imagined themselves the free and equal allies of Rome – 'a strong people, unbroken in battle because they had joined our alliance of their own free will' – were to be treated like any conquered tribe.

It was not to be borne, and the Iceni at once rose in angry revolt. Joined by contingents from neighbouring tribes, the rebels somewhat unwisely decided to make their stand in 'a position surrounded by a rustic earthwork, with a narrow entrance impassable to horsemen' – doubtless one of the scattered East Anglian hillforts, possibly Stonea Camp near March in Cambridgeshire. Ostorius, who was concerned enough to lead the Roman attacking force in person, surrounded the place with auxiliary infantry and dismounted cavalry, and at a given signal these stormed over the ramparts in several places at once. 'The Britons, with the desperate consciences of rebels and all their escape routes blocked, performed many famous prodigies of valour', but in the end they were overwhelmed and cut to pieces.

Having taught the Iceni a sharp lesson and destroyed much of their fighting force, the governor was disposed to be lenient: with Caratacus and the Welsh tribes threatening the western frontier of his province, he had in any case neither the time nor the troops to occupy their territory – yet. So they kept their 'independence', though it is probable that Ostorius insisted on a change in the tribal leadership, and it may have been now that Boudica's husband Prasutagus came to power – perhaps because he had taken no part in the rising, and could be trusted to follow a pro-Roman line. Thus the unequal alliance was patched up, but the massacre at the hillfort was not easily forgotten. The process which turned the loyal friends of Rome into her most fanatical British enemies had begun.

Roman activities in East Anglia during the next decade did little to encourage reconciliation. The impressionistic accounts of Tacitus and of the less reliable Dio Cassius do not always allow us to judge when – or even in what order – events occurred, but we know that the next step towards disaster was the establishment of a veteran's colony at Colchester in about A D 49.

Its immediate purpose was to free the legion garrisoning Colchester for the campaign against Caratacus, but in addition to forming a 'bulwark against rebellion', the old soldiers were supposed to 'inure the friendly natives to the rule of law'. To this end they were granted estates in and around the old Trinovantian royal capital, which was to be converted into a model Roman city and a shining example of the benefits of Roman civilization. It became instead a byword for Roman rapacity, since the cynical old sweats soon took to augmenting their grants by 'expelling the Britons from their houses and turning them off their farmlands, calling them captives and slaves. The serving soldiers did nothing to curb the veterans' outrages, for they themselves were men of the same character, who hoped in time to do the same kind of thing themselves.'

Colchester's fine new buildings only served to remind Britons of their conscripted fellow-countrymen toiling under harsh conditions in the quarries and tile-works outside the town, and most controversial of all was the great temple to 'the Divine Claudius'. Probably founded after A D 54, when Nero poisoned and succeeded his stepfather and then made amends by honouring him as a god, this shrine to the man who had conquered Britain was naturally regarded by the natives as *arx aeternae dominationis* – the citadel of eternal subjection. To add injury to insult, the Britons – and especially those wealthy men unfortunate enough to be chosen as priests of the new cult – were expected to pay for the objectionable temple themselves: no light expense, for it was by far the largest building yet to be raised in Roman Britain, decorated regardless of cost with rare marbles imported from Italy, Greece, North Africa and even the Middle East.

The new town and temple afflicted the Trinovantes more than their northern neighbours, but the Iceni – if hints in the summary of Dio Cassius can be believed – fell victim to a still more blatant piece of Roman greed and corruption. Along with the other leading British allies of Rome, they had received considerable cash presents from Claudius, but Catus Decianus, Nero's procurator or financial agent in Britain, now demanded that these should be returned, insisting that the gifts had really been loans. Already burdened by Roman taxation – by land-tax and property-tax, customs-dues and corn-levy – the Britons were unable to pay, and were forced to turn to the waiting money-lenders. The chief of these (by a curious coincidence) was Seneca, Nero's tutor and principal adviser, who lent them the vast sum of 40 million sesterces – more than 40,000 times the annual wage of a legionary – at very high rates of interest. With this, presumably, they paid off the procurator, who paid off Nero: Seneca afterwards recalled *his* loan in its entirety, plus interest, and 'resorted to severe measures in exacting it' – no doubt his agents forced the debtors to sell their property and livestock, and some of them must have been utterly ruined. Thus the Britons finished up in a worse financial position than ever, while both Nero and his tutor were much enriched: it is satisfactory to note that the emperor eventually forced Seneca to commit suicide.

The context of this sordid affair is uncertain, but it accords well with the period (apparently early in his reign) when Nero considered abandoning Britain altogether: in these circumstances he would feel able to milk the province for all it was worth, with no need to consider the long-term repercussions on Romano-British relations. By 57 he had decided instead to retain the province and extend its frontiers, but the damage had been done, and when Gaius Suetonius Paullinus took over the governorship late in 58 he found East Anglia simmering with resentment.

Suetonius was not a man likely to lose much sleep over the hurt feelings of provincials. A tough old professional soldier – he was over sixty when he came to Britain – he had made his formidable reputation by a brilliant campaign against the Moors, when he led the first Roman army ever to cross the Atlas Mountains. As an expert in mountain warfare, his task was to prosecute Nero's 'forward policy' by completing the conquest of Wales, and so long as there were no actual disturbances in East Anglia it was upon this that he concentrated all his attention and energies. After two years of successful campaigning in 59 and 60, he was ready by the spring of 61 to march against his main objective, the isle of Anglesey. Rich in cornlands, the island was not only the granary of north Wales but also the headquarters of the fiercely anti-Roman Druid priesthood, a spiritual powerhouse for resistance whose influence spread all over Britain.

Tacitus describes the scene:

Drawn up on the seashore was a dense mass of armed warriors. Among them, bearing flaming torches, ran women with funereal robes and dishevelled hair like Furies, and all around stood Druids, raising their hands to heaven and calling down dreadful curses. This weird spectacle temporarily stopped the Roman soldiers in their tracks . . . but then they advanced their standards, cut down all who stood against them, and pushed the enemy back into their own fires. Afterwards . . . they destroyed the groves sacred to the cruel superstitions of the Druids, whose religion dictated that altars must smoke with the blood of prisoners and the will of the gods be discovered by examining the entrails of men. At this moment news reached Suetonius of a sudden and unexpected uprising in the Roman province.

Three hundred miles away in East Anglia, the simmering pot had at last boiled over.

King Prasutagus of the Iceni, long renowned for his wealth, had died leaving the emperor as joint heir with his own two daughters: he believed that such an act of submission would secure both his kingdom and his family fortune from harm. Just the opposite happened, for both his realm and his household were plundered as if they were spoils of war, the former by Roman centurions and the latter by the procurator's slaves. First of all his wife Boudica was flogged, and his daughters cruelly raped. Then the Icenian chieftains were stripped of their ancestral lands – as though the Romans had been made a present of the whole country – while the late king's relations were treated like slaves. Faced with these outrages, and fearing worse to come once they had been absorbed into the Roman province, the Iceni reached for their weapons. They also incited to rebellion the Trinovantes and others who, still unbroken by subjection, had secretly plotted together to regain their freedom.

The terse account of the outbreak of revolt in Tacitus' *Annals* requires, as usual, a deal of analysis and amplification. When Prasutagus died is uncertain, but it was presumably early in AD 61. That he had managed both to retain his famous wealth and to keep his much-provoked people in check proves him to have been an astute politician, and as such he must have been aware that Icenian independence had little chance of surviving his death. Client-kingdoms were an anomaly in the Roman Empire, and his had been established at a time when Rome found it convenient to have British allies: that time had now passed, and Rome had already shown herself more interested in Icenian gold than Icenian friendship. A personal legacy to Nero himself might, however, flatter or bribe the emperor into leaving the tribe some degree of autonomy, and Prasutagus' family some portion of his wealth.

Nero chose instead to declare himself insulted – even in Rome itself he is recorded to have 'seized the entire estates of those who had shown ingratitude by not bequeathing him enough' – and ordered the governor to annex Prasutagus' whole kingdom, while the procurator confiscated all his property. Suetonius, preoccupied with Wales if not already there, apparently took little interest in the operation, but the Procurator Catus Decianus – already well hated for his part in the loans swindle – involved himself personally with sadistic relish. Tacitus elsewhere names his avarice as a principal cause of the rising, and he and his agents will have helped themselves to many a choice piece of Icenian jewellery which never reached the imperial coffers. Doubtless they met with a degree of immediate resistance, and this may have been one excuse for their vicious treatment of Boudica and her daughters – of which more shortly – but, if subsequent Roman unpreparedness is anything to go by, there can as yet have been no warning of the conflagration to come. Only after Decianus had returned to London did the real British reaction set in, and Tacitus' biography of his father-in-law Agricola gives us an impression of its tenor.

Patient submission, they argued, would gain them nothing but heavier burdens – the result of allowing themselves to be too easily pushed around. Each tribe once had a single king, but now two rulers had been foisted on them, the governor tyrannizing over their lives and the procurator over their property.... The former's centurions and the latter's slaves combined coercion with insults, and nothing was now safe from their greed and lust. In war it was the stronger party who gained the spoils, but now it was mostly cowards and stay-at-homes who were seizing British property, kidnapping their children, and conscripting their loved ones into the Roman army – where, not knowing how to die for their own country, they could die for another's. In any case, what a contemptible number of soldiers the invaders had brought over, if the Britons compared them with their own numbers! ... The Britons would be fighting for their homes, their wives and their families, but the Romans had only avarice and easy living to inspire them: they would run home – just as Julius Caesar had run home – if only the Britons could emulate the valour of their ancestors. Nor should they be disheartened by a single defeat or setback, for suffering would only produce more vigour and greater endurance. Now, at last, even the gods were taking pity on Britain, taking away the Roman commander and keeping him exiled in another island. They themselves were taking council together – which was always the most difficult thing to achieve – and in enterprises of this sort it was more dangerous to be caught plotting than to take the plunge.

Neither Tacitus nor Dio Cassius, however, provide a satisfactory explanation of Boudica's central role in the revolt. Tacitus' *Agricola* simply states that the rebels were 'led by Boudica, a woman of the royal house – for the Britons do not distinguish between the sexes when it comes to military command', and in the *Annals* he makes Boudica claim: 'The Britons were accustomed to female war-leaders, but she did not now come forward as one of noble descent, fighting for her kingdom and her wealth: rather she presented herself as an ordinary woman, striving to avenge her lost liberty, her lash-tortured body, and the violated honour of her daughters.' Dio admits that: 'all this ruin was brought upon the Romans by a woman, a fact which in itself caused them the greatest shame.' Also that: 'The person who was chiefly instrumental in rousing the natives and persuading them to fight the Romans, the person who was thought worthy to be their leader, and who directed the conduct of the entire war was Buduica, a British woman of the royal family. She was, however, possessed of greater intelligence than usually belongs to women.' As members of a severely patriarchal society, both historians found the idea of a woman successfully commanding men repugnant and embarrassing, and their somewhat confused and over-glib explanations suggest that they did not really understand how the situation had come about.

The Roman portrait of Boudica, then, is not entirely convincing. Her intelligence, her commanding personality and the wrongs she had suffered undoubtedly did play their part in placing her at the head of the revolt, but it seems likely that they were not the only factors involved, and it is even possible that she gained her position because of her sex, not in spite of it.

One speculation worth pursuing – though it can only be a speculation – is that the Icenian monarchy was matrilinear. The succession, in other words, would pass from mother to daughter rather than from father to son, and kings ruled only as consorts. This system was a very ancient one, originating in the period before the connection between mating and birth was recognized, and when queens ruled alone as the earthly representatives of an all-powerful and (apparently) self-sufficient earth-mother goddess. When man's role in conception became known, his religious and political status improved, and queens began to take official husbands; first of all for a year at a time – after which the unfortunate king was generally sacrificed – then for longer periods, and eventually for the king's natural lifetime. But the queen, the symbol of fertility, remained the focus of tribal religious life, and she and her daughters were regarded as the only reliable transmitters of the true royal line: the paternity of a child, after all, could never be certain, but its maternity was beyond question.

As invading Indo-Aryan peoples – including the Celts – came to dominate Europe, their sky-father god and consequently male-dominated society generally displaced the earth-mother worship and matriarchal customs of the earlier inhabitants: Robert Graves, indeed, interprets many of the ancient Greek myths as reflections of the struggle between the systems. Here and there, however, the old ways survived in more or less modified forms, probably as a result of local compromise between incomers and aborigines. The Picts of central and northern Scotland, whose culture apparently included a considerable pre-Celtic element, undoubtedly maintained a matrilinear monarchy right up until the mid-9th century, and their lengthy king-lists provide only two possible cases of a son succeeding a royal father. In Ireland the legendary Queen Maeve of Connaught, arch-enemy of the Ulster hero Cuchulainn, is clearly portrayed as a matriarch, for her king-consort is very much her subordinate, and her heir is her daughter, not her son. Nearer home still, the Brigantes of northern England may also have preserved some kind of matrilineal succesion: Queen Cartimandua, the captor of Caratacus, ruled in her own right, and when she fell out with her husband over tribal policy she divorced him and married his armour-bearer.

There is, admittedly, no direct evidence that the Icenian nobility did adopt the matrilinear customs of their older-established peasantry. If they followed the conventional patriarchal system, however, it is somewhat surprising to find Prasutagus leaving half his kingdom to his daughters. Though he may have had no sons, he presumably had brothers, nephews, or at least male cousins, and in view of the precarious political situation at his death he might have been expected to appoint one of these as his successor. But if female succession was the tribal rule he would have been forced to act as he did, and his appointment of Nero as co-heir may have been a futile attempt at compromise, designed to smooth the transition to provincial status via the marriage of his daughters to Roman husbands.

The existence among the Iceni of an ancient and hallowed matrilinear monarchy would certainly account for Boudica's apparently unquestioned leadership of the tribe. It would also render the persons of the queen and her daughters especially sacred, so that their treatment by the Procurator Decianus becomes blasphemous as well as brutal. To flog a king's widow and rape his daughters is unforgivable in human terms, but to flog a sacred queen and rape the bodily guardians of the royal line is to shatter the most unbreakable taboos and spit in the face of the gods themselves. If the loss of their liberty, their pride and their gold provoked the Iceni to rise, the affront to their religion ensured that the revolt, when it came, would be prosecuted with the utmost savagery.

More light is thrown on Boudica's religious role by Dio's description of her appearance at the hosting of the rebel tribes.

She was very tall, and her aspect was terrifying, for her eyes flashed fiercely and her voice was harsh. A mass of red hair fell down to her hips, and around her neck was a twisted gold necklace: over a tunic of many colours she wore a thick mantle fastened with a brooch – this was her invariable attire. Now she clutched a spear to help her strike fear into all beholders, and spoke in this manner. . . . When she had finished, she consulted the will of the gods by letting a hare escape from the folds of her robes: it ran in what they considered to be a lucky direction, and the crowd gave a mighty cheer. Boudica then raised her hands to heaven and said, 'I thank you, Andrasta, and call upon you as woman speaking to woman. . . . I beg you for victory and preservation of liberty. . . . Mistress, be forever our leader.'

Designed though it was to titillate Roman sensation-seekers, this picture has the ring of truth about it. Boudica's golden torque, her brooched mantle and multicoloured – perhaps tartan – tunic all accord with what we know of aristocratic Celtic dress, and Caesar mentions the hare as an animal especially sacred to the Britons. (Long after Christianization, indeed, British witches were regularly credited with the power to turn themselves into hares, and as recently as 1969 the author was assured in a remote Lincolnshire village that a local woman still did so.) The ritual with the hare, the spear, the flashing eyes and harsh voice all combine to give an overwhelming impression of an almost superhuman figure, a great priestess as much as a great ruler. Whether or not she was precisely a sacred queen, it seems more than likely that Boudica's followers saw her as the direct representative of Andrasta, the goddess she invoked.

One further speculation. Andrasta's name seems to mean 'the Invincible One', but Dio later translates it as 'Victoria' – which was, of course, the meaning of Boudica's own name. Pagan Celtic deities frequently had more than one title, and it is conceivable that Andrasta was also known as Boudica. Certainly there *was* a goddess called 'Boudiga', for a Romano-British merchant of York and Lincoln (the latter not so very far beyond Icenian territory) erected an altar to her in AD 237. It is just possible, then, that the Icenian queen's name was not a personal name at all, but an hereditary religious title passed through the female line: after the initial success of the rising, the victorious queen may even have become so completely identified with the invincible goddess of victory that the Iceni believed themselves led, not merely by a representative of the goddess, but by the goddess herself.

There is, at any rate, little doubt about the nature of the invincible Andrasta. She is known only from Dio's account, and unless she is related to the Gaulish 'Andarta' ('Powerful Bear') or the Hampshire 'Ancasta' she may have been a specifically Icenian goddess, perhaps the patron-ancestress of the tribe. But her name, the orgy of human sacrifices later offered to her, and the sexual junketings which accompanied them show her to have been a typical Celtic war-goddess, presiding both over death and battle and over fertility and increase. She has close links, therefore, with Brigantia ('the High One'), the ruling war-goddess of the Brigantes, whom the Romans also called 'Victoria', and with the terrifying Irish Morrigan ('Great Queen'), the triple war-goddess whose three persons were Nemain ('Frenzy'), Badb Catha ('Battle Raven') and Macha ('Crow', whose sacred birds were fed on the stake-impaled heads of the slaughtered).

It is no great surprise to discover evidence of matrilinear monarchy in the lands where these fearsome battle-goddesses were worshipped, or to find that Boudica, like Andrasta, has parallels there. The historical Carti-mandua of the Brigantes fought a long civil war against her husband, while the legendary Queen Maeve ('Drunken Woman'), aided by the shape-shifting Morrigan, led her forces in person during the great War of the Brown Bull of Cooley. The same Irish saga, incidentally, tells of Aifa and Scatha ('The Shadowy One'), two famous woman-warriors who ruled in the 'east of Alban' – that is in eastern Scotland, heartland of the matrilinear Picts.

Perhaps, after all, Boudica was no more than a strong-minded widow, a victim of circumstances who led the revolt because no man came forward to do so. We cannot prove otherwise, and should not minimize the important economic and political motives for the rising. But we should similarly not ignore the strong possibility that Boudica – whether as sacred queen, priestess, or inspired representative – was first and foremost the heiress of the ancient, bloody and orgiastic goddess of life and death, and that the savagery of the rebels was the direct outcome of the Roman insult to that goddess's power.

Who took part in the rising, how large was the rebel army, and when and where did it muster? The prime movers, obviously, were the Iceni, but Tacitus tells us they were immediately joined by the much-tried

Trinovantes and by 'others still unbroken by subjection': this could refer to almost any tribe within the Roman province, but in the geographical circumstances is likely to mean contingents from the Coritani of Leicestershire and Lincolnshire and even from those old enemies of the Iceni, the Catuvellauni of Bedfordshire and Hertfordshire. Dio claims that the rebel army numbered 120,000 at the outset, rising to 230,000 by the final battle, while Tacitus, who says unhelpfully that the Britons 'rose in unprecedented numbers', estimates their casualties in that battle at 80,000. Given an estimated population of 2 million for the whole of Roman Britain, Dio is almost certainly exaggerating considerably, but it is not unlikely that initial rebel numbers really did run into tens of thousands, for Tacitus states that 'men of all ages took up arms'. He also declares that the rising made them neglect the sowing of their crops, which later caused a famine: this seems an unlikely oversight, and moreover would date the outbreak to February or March AD 61, rather too early in the year to coincide with Suetonius' attack on Angelsey, which must have taken place some way into the campaigning season. It was perhaps in May, then, that the Britons hosted, and it is reasonable to suppose that they gathered at Boudica's palace, now generally believed to await discovery somewhere in the Norfolk Brecklands around Thetford.

Their first moves were against the soldiers left behind to consolidate the takeover of the Icenian kingdom, who were 'hunted down in their scattered posts and overwhelmed in their forts'. But the principal rebel objective was that running sore on the Trinovantes, the hated veterans' colony at Colchester.

Nor did the destruction of that city seem to present any problem, for it had not been defended by a wall: the Roman leaders, thinking to make the place pleasant rather than serviceable, had neglected to take this precaution. Just about now, for no apparent reason, the statue of Victory at Colchester toppled down, turning its back as if fleeing from an enemy. Frenzied women went about raving and prophesying doom. Strange howlings in foreign tongues, they said, had been heard in the local senate-house, the theatre had resounded with wailing [*ululatibus*], and a mirage of a wrecked city had appeared in the waters of the Thames Estuary. Even the ocean had seemed to turn to blood, and the ebb-tide had left behind what looked like human corpses on the beach. All these things encouraged the Britons to hope, but struck terror into the veterans.

Suetonius, however, was far away, so they appealed for aid to the procurator Decianus Catus, but he sent them barely two hundred men – and these without proper equipment – to reinforce their small garrison. Relying on the temple of Claudius to protect them, and misled by secret rebel sympathizers who threw all their plans into confusion, the Romans failed to build a defensive rampart and ditch. They did not even evacuate their women and old people, so that only the able-bodied would be left in the place.

As a prelude to their attack, then, the Britons mounted a psychological assault on two fronts. The notoriously superstitious Roman populace were thrown into a panic by the circulation of horrific rumours and the manu-facture of portents – the collapse of the statue of Victory, symbol of the 'Colonia Claudia Victricensis', was doubtless assisted by judicious noc-turnal crowbar-work. The complacency of the city elders, born of long British submission to Roman oppression, was meanwhile encouraged by highly placed fifth columnists who scoffed at danger and frustrated prac-tical attempts to organize defence. It looks as if this war of nerves lasted about a week (presumably while the Britons were mopping up the out-lying garrisons) for the citizens had time to send fifty-six miles to London and receive their derisory reinforcement, probably a ramshackle con-tingent of clerks and other semi-military hangers-on from the procurator's finance office. Archaeological evidence of feverish activity in Colchester armourers' workshops just before their destruction points to last-minute efforts to re-equip both these newcomers and the ageing veterans who made up the bulk of the male population. But little else was done, and:

While they were still acting as heedlessly as if they were living in the midst of peace, they were engulfed by a horde of barbarians. Everything was overwhelmed and burnt in the first enemy assault: only the temple, where the soldiers had rallied, held out for two days before being stormed and taken. Petillius Cerialis, commander of the Ninth Legion, was marching to the rescue when he was inter-cepted by the victorious Britons, who routed him and cut his infantry to pieces: Cerialis and his cavalry managed to escape to their fortress, and took refuge within its defences.

The huge rebel army poured straight into the unwalled city, and those who were cut down at once were probably more fortunate than those who gained the illusory safety of the temple. Since the garrison was relying on its protection, the building may well have been strengthened and provided with food and water, but (even if the soldiers shut out the non-combatants whom they had failed to evacuate) these stores will not have lasted long. Taking refuge as they were in the very 'citadel of eternal slavery', the most hated place in the whole province, the beleaguered Romans could expect no mercy at all from the Britons, and could only hope against hope for relief from outside the city. Perhaps they died in a last despairing sally, taunted by the rebels with the news of Cerialis' defeat.

Cerialis had apparently set out from his base at Longthorpe near Peterborough, some ninety miles away, with about 2000 legionaries (the number of replacements drafted to the Ninth after the revolt) and a regiment of auxiliary cavalry: his route lay down Ermine Street to Huntingdon, then along the Via Devana through Cambridge. Well known as an impetuous commander ('more inclined to underestimate than to fear the enemy') he may well have pushed on without proper reconnaissance, and it has been plausibly suggested that he was ambushed while his troops were strung out in column of march. But whether he was attacked by a detached British task force somewhere in the fenlands (as implied by his flight to his base) or near Colchester by the main rebel army (as implied by 'the victorious Britons') is uncertain, for no trace of the battlefield has yet been discovered.

There is plenty of archaeological evidence, however, for the destruction of Colchester. The conflagration which engulfed the town has left behind carbonized building-timbers and hard-baked clay walls, and in one shop flame-molten glassware from the upper shelves had dripped onto pots stacked on the floor below. A fruit shop (which clearly catered for the nostalgic tastes of Mediterranean colonists) produced charred dates, and other finds include the scorched remnants of a bed and a fire-marked cache of hurriedly buried small change. The temple, too, was apparently put to the torch – perhaps its defenders were eventually smoked out – for blocks of heat-damaged alabaster from its façade were fit only for lining a later drain.

The loot from wealthy Colchester must have been considerable. The 'Hockwold Treasure', five battered silver cups and two bowls found near the Norfolk-Suffolk border, may well be part of it, as may the gladiator's helmet from Hawkesdon near Lavenham in Suffolk – perhaps worn by a British warrior during the revolt and hastily discarded afterwards as incriminating evidence. This last was almost certainly the fate of the life-size bronze head of Claudius found in the River Alde near Saxmundham, Suffolk, in 1907. Roughly hacked off at the neck and lacking its original glass eyes, it had once formed part of a statue, perhaps even the principal statue of the emperor from the temple itself, though its comparatively poor workmanship makes it more probable that it stood in some less important place. It would, at any rate, have been a much-prized trophy of the downfall of the 'citadel of eternal subjection' and its alien 'god' – particularly to the head-hunting Celts.

The bitter hatred which the rebels felt even for the lifeless symbols of Roman domination is also well demonstrated by mutilation of tombstones in Colchester's military cemetery. The effigy of Centurion Facilis was overturned and broken in two, and that of the cavalry officer Longinus, which must have especially infuriated the Britons by showing him riding in contemptuous triumph over a cowering naked barbarian, was still more comprehensively defaced: Longinus' face has been completely chiselled away (later a favourite post-Reformation technique with 'Popish' images), a great gash has been gouged across his memorial inscription, and someone has even smashed his horse's nose.

Such thoroughgoing malice against the dead does not augur well for the living, and it is probable that most of the 15,000 or so inhabitants of Colchester were slaughtered, those that survived the initial massacre being reserved for mass ritual sacrifice. 'The Britons', reports Tacitus, 'took no prisoners and sold no captives into slavery, and neither did they observe any of the other conventions of war. Instead they hastened to slay and to hang, to burn and to torture, almost as if they were revenging in advance the coming Roman retribution.' It is surely more likely that the East Anglian tribes thought their revenge long overdue, and Dio's account emphasizes that their savagery was closely intertwined with religion.

Those who were taken by the rebels were subjected to every conceivable kind of outrage, but the worst and most bestial atrocity was this. They hung up the noblest and most highborn women naked, and then cut off their breasts and sewed them to their mouths, so that the victims seemed to be eating them: afterwards they impaled the women on sharp stakes, which they thrust lengthwise through the whole body. Accompanied by sacrifices, feasts and sexual orgies, these things were done in all their holy places, but especially in the sacred grove of Andrasta. This was their name for 'Victoria', and they worshipped her with particular reverence.

Dio's account has been dismissed as sensationalist fiction, but the sexual overtones and accompaniments he reports would accord well with an offering to a Celtic goddess of war and fertility, and sacrifice by impalement is recorded in Gaul and suggested in an Irish saga. Human sacrifice revolted the Romans, and must have been suppressed in the Icenian client-kingdom, but at this hour of Andrasta's triumph the old custom may well have been revived and the groves have once again drunk human blood.

The Britons, then, had utterly destroyed Colchester, and their morale-boosting defeat of Cerialis had not only demonstrated that they could beat first-class Roman troops as well as clerks and veterans, but had also wiped out the only force in East Anglia capable of threatening them. Their next logical steps would be either to march at once on London – already the largest Roman town in Britain, the seat of the hated procurator, and as completely undefended as Colchester – or to move swiftly northwards against the remainder of the Ninth Legion, thus liberating the whole of eastern Britain from Roman control. In the event they did neither, but delayed around Colchester long enough to allow Suetonius to cover the 270-odd miles from Anglesey and reach London before them.

Several explanations for the delay are possible, each depending on a somewhat different estimation of Boudica's character. The first is that, given the notorious tendency of Celtic armies to run amok after a victory, she simply did not have enough control over the rebels to make them quit their looting. Secondly, it is entirely possible that Boudica and her followers were not at all swayed by logical or tactical considerations, regarding themselves rather as the inspired and invincible servants of the avenging goddess. Andrasta had given them success, and Andrasta would ensure their ultimate victory, but first her sacred groves must be properly honoured, even though these presumably lay some distance away in the land of the Iceni: the resultant delay was irrelevant, for London and

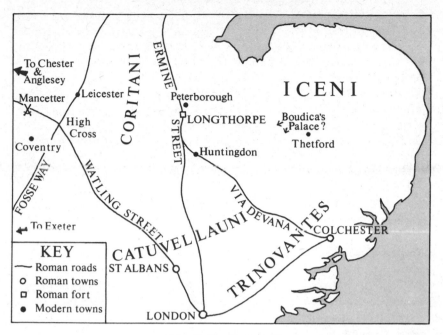

Map 3 Boudica's revolt

Suetonius would then inevitably be delivered into their hands, just as Colchester and Cerialis had been. If, conversely, we see Boudica more as a general than a priestess, the delay may have been a carefully considered ruse of war, designed to lure Suetonius into a hopeless defence of an unwalled town, where he and the principal Roman army would be surrounded and destroyed. This danger, at any rate, clearly occurred to the governor:

Suetonius, displaying remarkable steadiness, pushed straight through enemy-held territory to London – a town not honoured with the status of a Roman colony, but widely famous for its merchants and merchandise. At first he was in two minds about making a stand there, but when he considered how small his force was, and thought of the terrible price paid for the rashness of Cerialis, he decided to sacrifice that one city in order to save the whole province. Neither tears and lamentations nor appeals for help could sway him, and he gave the order to depart, allowing those citizens who were fit to do so to join his column. Those who stayed in London – whether because they were women or feeble old men unfit for war, or because they were too attached to the place to leave – were wiped out by the enemy. A similar disaster overwhelmed the town of Verulamium.

Perhaps not yet fully realizing the gravity of the crisis, Suetonius seems to have pressed on to London with his cavalry alone, leaving his infantry to

45

follow at their steady regulation twenty miles a day. Galloping down Watling Street (now, prosaically, the A 5) he must have run the gauntlet of wandering rebel warbands during the last hundred miles of the journey but – by stratagems and detours we can only guess at – managed to come through unscathed, to find the city in chaos. 'The procurator Decianus Catus, unnerved by the calamity at Colchester and terrified by the hatred of those whom his avarice had goaded into revolt, had fled to Gaul.' Many of the more substantial citizens had doubtless followed his example, and it cannot have been long before the governor also grasped the utter hopelessness of London's situation. His comparatively small force of cavalry was supremely ill-suited for a streetfighting defence of the unwalled town, and few reinforcements could be gleaned from the surrounding demilitarized zone, while the whole rebel army lay between London and the remnant of the Ninth Legion. If Suetonius was to avoid either being caught in a trap or cut off from his main body, he must fall back along Watling Street and fall back quickly, unhampered by a straggling tail of civilian refugees: the 'citizens who were fit to accompany him' will probably have included only those who owned or could commandeer horses. Soon afterwards, perhaps within a matter of hours, Boudica's triumphant army poured into London.

Some notion of what followed can be surmised from archaeological evidence, notably the thick layer of burnt debris – datable to Boudica's period by accompanying pottery – which marks the destruction of wattle-and-daub buildings. This has come to light in Aldgate, where the Britons entered the town on the main road from Colchester, but finds cluster thickest in the area between modern Cannon Street Station and the Bank of England, the core of Roman London. A contemporary rubbish-pit under St Swithin's House in Walbrook produced two great wine-jars, lying in a situation which suggests (according to Ralph Merrifield) 'that someone rapidly disposed of a considerable quantity of wine just before the house went up in flames. There is nothing to show whether the wine-jars were emptied by looting tribesmen, or by the householders, determined to empty their cellar before they marched with Suetonius, or to gain courage while they awaited the arrival of Boudica.' Nearby, at the junction of modern Lombard and Gracechurch streets, stood a large stone building which may well have been the headquarters of the hated procurator: this the rebels apparently demolished – a poor consolation, no doubt, for failing to lay hands on Decianus himself.

Just how many Roman Londoners did suffer British vengeance is uncertain – the contemporary population has been estimated at 30,000 – but there are indications that many of them, as at Colchester, were ritually sacrificed. The bed of the Walbrook stream, which ran through the middle of the Roman city but has long since disappeared underground, has for hundreds of years been producing detached human skulls. The 12th-century romancer Geoffrey of Monmouth had to invent the decapitation of an entire Roman legion to account for the number discovered in his day, and at least fifty-five recorded examples have come to light in Victorian and later times: there are unauthenticated reports, moreover, of 'an immense number' found in Blomfield Street before 1829, 'a mass of skulls' in a sewer in Copthall Avenue in 1851, and 'upwards of a hundred' under Finsbury House about 1905. All known find-spots are in the upper reaches of the Walbrook, around Liverpool Street Station. Exactly when the skulls were deposited has yet to be established, but the cult of the severed head and the worship of running water both played an important part in Celtic religion, and the many coins and trinkets dropped into the Walbrook 'for luck' during the later Roman period seem to show that this stream was especially sacred. It is therefore likely that the skulls were those of human sacrifices to a British river-spirit, and at least possible that they are the heads of Boudica's victims, ritually massacred near Liverpool Street and dedicated to the gods as a thank-offering for the destruction of another Roman town.

'A similar disaster overtook the municipality of Verulamium: for the barbarians, who rejoiced in plunder and shunned hard work, steered clear of fortresses and garrisons and headed for places where the spoil was richest and the defences lightest.' It was not only the prospect of easy plunder, however, that drew Boudica twenty-five miles northwestward to Verulamium. The town, whose remains lie on the outskirts of modern St Albans, was in its way as much a magnet for rebel hatred as Colchester. Like Colchester, it was a model settlement, built in the Roman manner by Roman architects as an example of the benefits of Roman urban civilization: yet it was raised, not for Roman veterans, but as a reward for a group of British 'collaborators' – Catuvellaunians who had rejected both the leadership of Caratacus and their own ancient customs to throw in their lot wholeheartedly with the invaders and adopt their way of life. Traitors to the liberation movement as well as traditional enemies of the Iceni, they could expect but short shrift from Boudica, and it seems unlikely that many stayed to defend the earthwork ramparts round their town. Those that did were slaughtered, and the flames enveloped Verulamium: amid the usual burnt layer, they left for archaeologists an apt memorial of the town, the charred remains of a colonnaded Roman-style parade of shops.

Despite Tacitus' contemptuous remarks, it seems likely that there was also a tactical reason for the move on Verulamium: by marching there, Boudica was following in the tracks of Suetonius' withdrawal, aiming for a final showdown. She could not have chosen a better time, for Roman fortunes were now at their lowest ebb.

'Never before nor since has Britain ever been in a more uneasy or dangerous state. . . . We had to fight for life before we could think of victory.' Thus Tacitus, doubtless quoting the reminiscences of his father-in-law Agricola, then a staff-officer at Suetonius' headquarters. Things looked indeed very black. The three principal cities of the province, including its spiritual capital and its commercial centre, lay in ruins, and the Ninth Legion was effectively out of action. By now, moreover, news of yet another disaster must have come in. The Second Legion, the only remaining sizeable unit in Britain outside the governor's expeditionary force, had refused to march to his aid.

The Second, based at far-off Exeter, was temporarily commanded by Poenius Postumus, who as *praefectus castrorum* was comparable to a cross between a regimental sergeant-major and a senior quartermaster. As such he was unused to high command, and it is conceivable that Suetonius' order rooted him to the spot in panic. There is, on the other hand, some evidence that the southwestern tribes had by now begun to join in the rising, and Postumus may have had good military reasons for holding on to his fortress rather than risking the fate of the Ninth by a long and hazardous march to the governor – who might, in any case, be annihilated before the Second could reach him. Whatever his motives, he was to pay dearly for his mistake after the revolt: 'conscious that he had cheated his legion of its share of glory and broken military law by disobeying his commander-in-chief, Poenius Postumus ran himself through with his own sword.'

The news of the Second's refusal to march, travelling quickly along the tribal grapevine, must have strengthened both Boudica's desire to force a battle and her conviction that the hour of final triumph was at hand: the Romans, it seemed, had lost heart, and once she had overwhelmed the governor the remaining garrisons, isolated and demoralized, could be wiped out piecemeal. Suetonius, conversely, must now have entertained serious doubts about fighting, and Dio reports that he wanted to put off a battle until 'a more advantageous juncture', perhaps until he had been reinforced from Europe: 'but he was running out of food and, with the barbarians advancing relentlessly upon him, he was forced against his better judgement to engage them.' Tacitus, loyal to his father-in-law's old general, admits only implicitly that the Britons held the initiative. Yet the governor still had an important card to play: if he could not dictate the timing of the battle, he could at least select the best place to stand and fight it.

At this time Suetonius, having with him the Fourteenth Legion, together with detachments of the Twentieth and auxiliaries from the nearest forts (about 10,000 soldiers in all) prepared to abandon delay and join battle. He chose a position in a narrow defile, protected to the rear by woods: he was sure there were no enemy forces except to his front, where the open plain was without cover, so that there was no fear of a surprise attack.

Though Tacitus here describes the site of the battle clearly, he gives us no idea of its whereabouts, and this annoying omission has given rise over the centuries to a variety of more or less incredible suggestions, including sites near Chester, others in Essex or even – by Lewis Spence in his *Boadicea, Warrior Queen of the Britons* – under platform 10 at King's Cross Station. More serious considerations place the battle on or near Watling Street somewhere to the northwest of St Albans: the latest and probably the best guess (advanced by Dr Graham Webster in his two books on the revolt) is that it was fought near Mancetter, between Atherstone and Nuneaton in Warwickshire. The area fits Tacitus' description, for Mancetter stands on a ridge of high ground, still densely wooded in places and containing several defiles facing across the plain of the River Anker towards Watling Street and the British line of attack. A few miles to the southeast is High Cross, near Hinkley, Leicestershire, Suetonius' most likely campaign base: there Watling Street, the line of the governor's withdrawal from London and of his infantry's advance from north Wales, meets the Fosse Way (here the B4029) along which the Second had been expected to march from Exeter. Finally, the Mancetter area has recently produced archaeological hints of a battle – a strong double ditch of Roman construction, possibly dug to protect a flank of the governor's position, and a hoard of contemporary small change, perhaps concealed before the fight and never recovered.

Wherever the battlefield was (and we shall probably never know for certain) there is little doubt that it was carefully chosen to enable a small but well-armed and disciplined force to hold off and then defeat a much more numerous but ill-equipped and loosely organized enemy. The high ground and woods which protected it on three sides would prevent an outflanking move by British cavalry and chariots, forcing Boudica to attack on a short and strongly held front. There the Roman heavy infantry could employ their famous infighting tactics to best advantage, while rebel numbers would have the minimum effect – only the front ranks could use their weapons, and the undisciplined hordes behind, with no room to manoeuvre, could only crush them forward onto the Roman swords.

Thus he drew up the legionaries in close order, with the light-armed auxiliary infantry on either side of them and the cavalry massed in readiness on the flanks. The British forces, however, ran riot all over the field in their mobs on horseback or foot. They had never appeared in greater numbers, and they were so full of confidence that they had even brought along their wives to witness their victory, stationing them on wagons arranged round the extreme edge of the battlefield.

To the Britons, such total assurance of victory must have seemed fully justified. They had an unbroken record of almost effortless success, and the Romans had so far fled before them or died at their hands. Now they vastly outnumbered the enemy: many new recruits will have joined their triumphant march from London, and though Dio's statement that they numbered 230,000 is probably exaggerated, it is entirely possible that there were ten British warriors for every Roman. Above all, they were led by the invincible Boudica and her daughters, at once a constant reminder of the sufferings of the British people and – as her followers may by now have seen her – a personification of the avenging mother-goddess. Tacitus, in the set-piece speech he now puts into her mouth, prefers to show her as a wronged woman taunting and encouraging her menfolk.

Boudica, with her daughters standing in front of her, was borne about in a war-chariot from tribe to tribe. 'We Britons', she declared, 'are accustomed to female war-leaders, but I do not now come forward as one of noble descent, fighting for my kingdom and my wealth: rather I present myself as an ordinary woman, striving to revenge my lost liberty, my lash-tortured body, and the violated honour of my daughters. Roman lust and avarice had reached the point where our very bodies – even those of old people and virgins – were no longer left unpolluted. But now the gods are granting us our just revenge: the one legion that dared to stand and fight has been cut to pieces, and the rest either cower in their forts or look about them for a means of escape. The enemy won't even stand up to the shouts and battle-cries of so many thousand men as we have, let alone endure our blows and assaults! Consider our numbers, and the reasons why we are fighting: then you will either conquer or die in this battle. I, a woman, am resolved to do so – you men, if you like, can live to be Roman slaves'.

It is, of course, extremely unlikely that any of Tacitus' informants could have heard (or understood) what Boudica really did say that day; but Agricola, the staff-officer at Suetonius' side, may well have remembered and passed on the gist of his own general's speech.

Suetonius himself did not remain silent at such a decisive moment: though he was confident of his soldiers' mettle, he thought it best to reinforce it with encouragements and entreaties. 'Don't worry about these yelling savages and their empty threats', he cried, 'you can see there are more women than warriors in their ranks. They're untrained and badly armed, and they'll break straight away when they recognize the Roman courage and weapons that have routed them so often. Even when many legions are in the field, it's only a few soldiers that really decide the course of a battle – think, then, what glory each of you will gain, a handful of troops winning the fame of a whole army! Just stick close together: throw your javelins – then push on, knocking them down with your shields and finishing them off with your swords. Don't stop to think about plunder, when you've won the battle you'll have it all.'

Certainly these sentiments were well calculated to appeal to Suetonius' men. Heavily outnumbered though they were, they were still a formidable force, well led and well positioned. At least two-thirds of them were legionaries, the cream of the Roman army: each was helmeted and armoured, uniformly equipped with two seven-foot *pila* or throwing spears, with a great rectangular shield, a short stabbing sword and a dagger. His legions, moreover, were the Fourteenth and the Twentieth, the units which had routed Caratacus a decade before and which now came fresh from a successful campaign in Wales, unscathed from the destruction of the Druid groves: they were not likely to be overmuch concerned by British threats or curses, and their morale will have been relatively unaffected by the reverses in the southeast.

The general's words were greeted with such enthusiasm – for his soldiers, hardened veterans of many battles, could scarcely wait to hurl their spears – that he gave the order to begin the fight without any doubts about its outcome.

At first the legionaries stood their ground, using the narrow defile as a fortress: then, as soon as the attacking enemy had come close enough for them to be sure of their aim, they all hurled their javelins together and burst forward in a wedge formation. The auxiliaries charged in the same way and the cavalry, thrusting with their lances, rode down all who stood to oppose them. The rest of the Britons turned and ran – but found escape difficult, for they were trapped by the ring of wagons round the field. The Romans did not hesitate to slaughter even the British women, and the bodies of the very baggage animals, bristling with spears, added to the heaps of dead. It was a glorious victory, worthy of the triumphs of ancient times: some say that nearly 80,000 Britons were slain, while the Romans lost only about 400 dead and very few more wounded.

Boudica, then, began the battle, launching the tribes at the motionless Roman line: Dr Webster states that they advanced uphill, but this appears to be only speculation. If the Romans followed their normal practice, they will have launched their first great volley of about 7000 *pila* when the enemy were about forty feet away, following up with the second at twenty feet. Having thus thrown the leading British ranks into disorder, the Romans counter-attacked at once and Tacitus – unless he is merely telescoping the action – implies that they were immediately successful. The greatest slaughter, in any event, probably occurred around the wagons, where the victors seem to have given themselves up to an orgy of killing: in the circumstances of the rebellion the British women could not hope for mercy, but the hard-headed legionary did not usually waste a saleable baggage animal. Even so, Tacitus' estimate of the vastly dispro-portionate casualties – admittedly a qualified one – is hard to take: we might, however, remember Agincourt, where another small professional army routed another huge and overconfident enemy force, killing an estimated 10,000 Frenchmen for the loss of a few hundred English.

Dio (writing much longer after the event but apparently quoting a source now lost to us) tells a rather different story. Making no mention of the defile, he has the Roman army drawn up in three divisions, principally (one suspects) so that he can give Suetonius a stylish but not particularly revealing speech for each of them. More credible is his assertion that the fight was a long and hard one, with Boudica hurling in chariot-charges and the governor countering with auxiliary archers: not until the end of the day did the Romans finally triumph 'killing many around the wagons and in the woods, and taking many others alive'.

Boudica was not among them. Tacitus simply states that 'she ended her life with poison': he does not say where or when, though the context implies that she died some time after the battle rather than actually on the field. According to Dio, however: 'no small number of Britons escaped from the disaster, and were preparing to fight again when Boudica fell ill and died. The Britons, mourning her greatly, gave her a costly funeral: then, feeling that now at last they really had been defeated, they scattered to their homes.'

In the light of what we know or can surmise of Boudica, the suicide story seems the more credible. Her victorious career had suffered a shattering and quite unlooked-for reverse, and there was little hope of raising another British army before Suetonius was reinforced, still less of winning a guerrilla war once those reinforcements had arrived. Conditional surrender was unthinkable: even if she herself could consider such a course, the governor would never negotiate with a woman who (according to Tacitus, apparently quoting an official report) had slaughtered some 70,000 Romans and allied Britons, the great majority of them defenceless non-combatants. But most insupportable of all, for a leader who had believed herself the instrument of divine vengeance, were the implications of her defeat: either Andrasta had cruelly deceived her worshippers, or the once-invincible goddess had quailed before the stronger gods of Rome. Perhaps, indeed, Boudica did not need the poison-cup, but willed herself to sickness and death because she could not bear to live with the knowledge that her goddess had failed.

Generations of writers have speculated about the site of Boudica's grave. One 17th-century antiquarian even claimed that no less a monument than Stonehenge was raised to mark it, and many Victorians firmly believed that it was covered by the prehistoric burial-mound in Parliament Hill Fields, north London. The queen's restless ghost is summoned up to reinforce the claims of other sites: it is said to wander about the Essex hillfort of Ambresbury near Epping, where 'according to tradition' she and her daughters poisoned themselves, and as recently as the 1950s it allegedly appeared, driving a chariot out of the mists, near the Lincolnshire village of Cammeringham. None of these places, however, lie within Icenian territory, where her 'costly burial' seems most likely to have taken place. As a prime target for Romans seeking posthumous vengeance or Icenian gold, its exact position may well have been kept a close secret, and it is just possible that it awaits discovery undisturbed somewhere in the East Anglian Brecklands.

Wherever Boudica's body lies a-mouldering in the grave, her fame has survived many changes of image over the centuries. To the 6th-century monk Gildas, nostalgic for the lost stability of the Roman Empire, she was 'a treacherous lioness', who 'slaughtered the governors left to give fuller voice and strength to Roman rule'. Thereafter she disappears from literature until the discovery of Tacitus' manuscript, to re-emerge under the first Elizabeth as a minor national hero, a remote precursor of the Virgin Queen. The 17th-century, dominated by kings and parliaments, thought less well of her: despite its title, Fletcher's indifferent play *Bonduca* (1610) accords her a subordinate role to her 'cousin' Caratach, alias Caratacus, while Milton's *History of Britain* (1670) dismisses her as a 'distracted woman, with as mad a crew at her heels'. The most familiar view of Boudica, as 'the warrior patriot Queen', really got under way in the late 18th century, when Cowper's *Ode on Boadicea* made a Druid prophesy the downfall of Rome and the rise of the British Empire:

> Then the progeny that springs
> From the forests of our land
> Arm'd with thunder, clad with wings
> Shall a wider world command
> Regions Caesar never knew
> Thy Posterity shall sway
> Where his eagles never flew
> None invincible as they

In this guise, and with her atrocities forgotten or glossed over, she became immensely popular during the empire-building reign of her namesake Queen Victoria, and in 1902 her massive chariot-borne statue was erected on the Thames Embankment, not far from the city she once wiped out in blood and fire. Finally, with empires and Patriot Queens grown out of fashion, Boudica is now in the process of being annexed by the supporters of Womens' Liberation.

Murderous rebel, Patriot Queen, Liberated Woman: each succeeding period has tailored Boudica to its own preoccupations. In some sense, perhaps, she was all these things. But this chapter has tried to show that she may also have been something else, something far less comprehensible to any age or any society other than her own – the last fighting champion in Britain of the ancient and once all-powerful goddess of life and death.

The events that followed Boudica's defeat need be recounted only briefly. Suetonius, reinforced by drafts from Germany, lost no time in embarking on a relentless and comprehensive campaign of revenge, harrying not only the tribes that had actually rebelled but also those which had merely shown signs of wavering. This naturally provoked desperate local resistance, and virtually the whole province might have been laid waste but for Julius Classicianus, the procurator now dispatched to succeed

Decianus. Either (as Tacitus suggests) out of personal animosity towards the governor or (more probably) because he realized that a ravaged land could produce no revenue, Classicianus complained to Rome, calling for Suetonius' replacement by a governor 'who, free from the bitterness of an enemy or the pride of a conqueror, would show more mercy to those who surrendered'. His protests were heeded, and after an Imperial commission of enquiry and a decent interval, Suetonius was retired. His term of office was at any rate drawing to a close, and a further pretext was made of his loss of some ships and their crews 'on the shore' – perhaps during an unsuccessful amphibious operation against Icenian die-hards on the East Anglian coast.

It seems likely that the Iceni never fully recovered from the punishment he inflicted on them. Although their energetic revolt had given the Romans a severe shock, they paid for it by the loss of probably an entire generation of their menfolk and the disappearance or impoverishment of their once-magnificent aristocracy. Thus they became one of the least important of the peoples of Britain, and though a tribal capital was eventually built for them at Venta Icenorum (Caister-by-Norwich) it was among the smallest of Roman towns, a mere provincial backwater. Significantly, and un-usually, it was raised on an entirely new site, far from Boudica's Breckland palace: there were to be no reminders of former glories.

Suetonius' successors – among the most notable of them Cerialis and Agricola – continued to expand the boundaries of Roman conquest. But, realizing that 'military victories achieve little if they are followed by injustice', they followed a much more conciliatory line towards the con-quered, whose gradual Romanization they sought through encourage-ment and example rather than terror and compulsion.

To ensure that men who, because they were uncivilized and lived in isolated dwellings, were easily roused to warfare, should grow used to peace and leisure [Agricola] would encourage them personally, providing public grants to build temples, forums and town houses. The obedient were praised, the sluggish censured, and so a competition for honour replaced coercion. Indeed, he took in hand the provision of a liberal education for the sons of nobles. . . . The next stage was that Roman dress became fashionable, and the toga was often to be seen: little by little, there was a relapse into demoralizing luxuries like colonnades, hot baths and sumptuous dinners. 'This', thought unsophisticated Britons, 'is civilization', but really it was a mark of their servitude.

Insidious though all this was, it was surely preferable to the naked extortions of Catus Decianus and the bullyings of the Colchester veterans. The revolt, then, was not entirely in vain: by teaching the Romans tact, it paved the way to a peaceful merging of conquerors and conquered – perhaps the very last thing that Boudica would have wished.

CHAPTER THREE

'Old Coel the Splendid'
The Real King Cole

Old King Cole was a merry old soul
And a merry old soul was he
He called for his pipe and he called for his bowl
And he called for his fiddlers three
Then fiddle-diddle-dee, diddle-dee went the fiddlers
Fiddle-diddle-diddle-diddle-dee
There's none so rare as can compare
To King Cole and his fiddlers three.

To move from the darksome and bloody career of Boudica to the cheerful monarch of the nursery rhyme seems at first sight to descend from the epic to the merely frivolous. Yet, as this chapter hopes to show, there is good reason to believe that the nursery rhyme preserves a flickering memory of one of the neglected heroes of Britain, and that Old King Cole – known to his contemporaries as Old Coel the Splendid – was once a famous and honoured figure. That he has been excluded from the pantheon of British heroes is scarcely surprising, for his kingdom and his people were long ago swallowed up by alien invaders, the stories of his exploits are all but lost, and the scant and chance-preserved records of his very existence are preserved in the obscurest of sources. To reach him we must sift through sixteen centuries of legends and half-truths, chasing whole shoals of red herrings and meeting in the process such diverse figures as the original of Sweeney Todd, the sainted discoverer of the True Cross, and the poet Robert Burns.

The rhyme itself sounds as if it was originally a drinking catch or a song-with-actions from a Mumming play rather than a nursery jingle: it did not apparently get into print until 1709, when the following version was quoted in William King's *Useful Transactions in Philosophy*:

Good King Cole
And he call'd for his Bowl
And he call'd for Fiddlers three:
And there was Fiddle Fiddle
And twice Fiddle Fiddle;
For 'twas my Lady's Birth-Day:
Therefore we keep Holy-day
And come to be merry.

56

King's book was a satire on the would-be learned 'philosophical' pamphlets fashionable in his day – his chapters include 'A new Method to teach Learned Men how to Write Unintelligibly', 'Whether a Woman, according to Justice and any Principles of Philosophy, may lay a Child to an Eunuch', and 'A Historical and Chronological Account of Consecrated Clouts'. So we need not pay too much attention to his suggestion that the rhyme was composed by 'Bardoulius, Poet Laureat to King Ludd' or by 'Bardocox-combius, who bore the same dignity under Bouduca [Boudica]'. He does, however, make it quite clear that by 1709 the verse already enjoyed a reputation for great antiquity, and that speculation about the identity of the original 'King Cole' was already rife. Two rival candidates were advanced, one being 'the same prince that built Colchester', and the other 'the same as some think denominated Cole-brook [now Colnbrook, Buckinghamshire] for he was a worthy clothier of Reading who . . . happened to be drowned there'.

This 'worthy clothier' (whose cause was also favoured by many Victorian folk-song collectors) was Thomas Cole of Reading, the hero of Thomas Deloney's rambling Elizabethan novelette, *The Six Worthy Yeomen of the West*. According to Deloney, Thomas was one of the richest cloth-merchants in 12th-century England, and a close friend of King Henry I: but he was chiefly notable for the manner of his death. When travelling to London, he would always put up in Colnbrook at the 'Cranes Inn' – allegedly still standing as 'the Ostrich' – leaving large sums of money in the overnight safe-keeping of the landlord and his wife. Unbeknown to him, however, this pair were in the habit of murdering wealthy guests, whom they accommodated in a specially-prepared room:

the part of the chamber whereupon this bed and bedstead stood was made in such sort, that by pulling out of two yron pinnes below in the kitchin, it was to be let downe . . . in manner of a trap doore: moreover in the kitchin, directly under the place where this should fall, was a mighty great caldron, wherein they used to seethe their liquor when they went to brewing. Now the men appointed for the slaughter were laid into this bed, and in the dead time of the night, when they were sound a sleepe . . . downe would the man fall out of his bed into the boyling caldron . . . where being suddenly scalded and drowned, he was never able to cry or speake one word.

The bodies were then thrown into a nearby river or, according to more sensational reports, made into 'pies and penny pasties'.

Though warned off by a series of blood-curdling omens, poor Thomas was boiled alive in his turn. In the best traditions of melodrama, however, his horse escaped from the inn stable, to be identified by a loyal servant who brought the murderous couple to justice. 'And some say that the river whereinto Cole was cast did ever since carry the name of Cole, being called the River of Cole, and the Towne of Colebrooke.'

57

Thomas Cole of Reading may or may not have really existed. There is no evidence that he did, and it seems more likely that Deloney either invented the whole business or adapted an existing tale – of a type common in English folklore – made up to account for a place-name. The story, at any rate, soon became immensely popular (it was reprinted no less than six times between 1598 and 1632) and the wicked innkeeper is clearly recognizable as the ancestor of that favourite Victorian villain Sweeney Todd, the 'Demon Barber of Fleet Street' who razored his customers' throats, tipped them into his cellar, and turned them into sausages. It is altogether more difficult to see how the clothier could possibly have given rise to the nursery-rhyme hero. He was admittedly nicknamed 'Old Cole', but there the resemblance ends, for his story was by no means conducive to merriment: nor, most crucially, could he in any way be called a king.

King Cole, 'the prince that built Colchester', seems a much stronger candidate, and it is he who is now generally accepted as the prototype of the nursery-rhyme monarch. Traditions dating back at least eight hundred years make him a figure of very considerable importance – he was not only the ruler of all Britain but also the father of the revered St Helena, and through her the grandfather of Constantine the Great, the first Christian emperor of Rome. Whether these traditions really can be believed is quite another matter. But certainly they are worthy of detailed examination, and it will be best to begin with a summary of the comparatively few undisputed historical facts of the case.

The story starts in AD 286, when Carausius, the popular and successful commander of the Roman Channel Fleet, rebelled against the authority of Imperial Rome and established an independent 'empire' in Britain and northern France. For the next seven years he contrived to retain his authority by a mixture of diplomacy and warfare, but in 293 he was driven out of France by an imperial general named Constantius, and soon afterwards he was assassinated by Allectus, his own finance minister. This Allectus then ruled Britain until 296, when Constantius launched a two-pronged attack, his own fleet making a diversion in the Straits of Dover while his second-in-command Asclepiodotus landed near Southampton. Allectus, who had been deceived into massing his forces in the wrong place, quickly turned to intercept him, but was defeated and killed near Silchester in Hampshire: Constantius meanwhile entered London in time to save it from plunder by stragglers from the beaten army, and was apparently given an enthusiastic welcome. Britain was thus restored to the Roman Empire.

Constantius – nicknamed Chlorus, 'the Pale-faced' – was very much the up-and-coming man in that empire. A native of what is now Yugoslavia, he had risen entirely by his own efforts, and after his return to Europe in 297 he continued to do so, eventually becoming emperor in 305. Early in his career he had contracted some form of marriage with a lady named Helena, by whom he had a son called Constantine: by 289, however, he had divorced her, marrying for political reasons the adopted daughter of the Emperor Maximian and fathering several more sons. Yet Constantine seems to have remained his favourite. He brought him on his next visit to Britain in 306 and when, after a triumphant campaign against the Picts, he fell sick and died at York, his army immediately proclaimed Constantine his successor.

It was some considerable time, however, before Constantine managed to dispose of all his many rivals for the throne. Shortly before his great victory at the Milvian Bridge near Rome in 312, which gave him control of the Western Empire, he experienced a dream or vision of the Cross, and from then on he espoused the cause of Christianity, whose devotees had hitherto suffered official persecution. In 313 he granted them freedom of worship in his domains, and in 324, when he finally came to rule the whole Roman world, the empire effectively became Christian.

His mother Helena, who was now granted the title of *Augusta* or empress, had meanwhile become an enthusiastic convert to the new religion, and in about 326 she made a pilgrimage to the Holy Places around Jerusalem, where she assisted in the building of a number of churches, including one on the site of Christ's Nativity. When she died four years later, at the age of 80, she seems already to have been honoured as a saint. Constantine himself died in 337, after the longest reign of any Roman emperor save Augustus, and was buried in his magnificent new city of Constantinople. Called 'the Great', 'the Victor' and 'the Equal of the Apostles', he was destined to become the model and symbol of Christian authority for at least the next thousand years.

This much is history, but the stories which began to circulate after Helena's death are not so easy to verify. These centred round the holiest and most dramatic of all Christian relics, the 'True Cross' on which Jesus Himself was crucified. In 346 St Cyril, Bishop of Jerusalem – who should have known – declared it to be common knowledge that the Cross had come to light in his city during the reign of Constantine, though he does not say how or by whom it was found. Forty years later, however, St Ambrose categorically stated that it was Helena who discovered it:

Helena went to visit the Holy Places, and the Spirit came upon her, urging her to seek the wood of the Cross . . . then she laid open the ground and cleared away the rubble: she found three crosses jumbled together, concealed by debris and thus hidden by the Devil – but he could not wipe out the glory of Christ. Now she hesitated, for she knew that two robbers had been crucified with the Lord: but the Holy Spirit inspired her to investigate further, and she therefore sought out the cross which had stood in the middle. Yet the crosses might by chance have become mixed up in the rubble, and have changed places. Turning to the Scriptures, however, she found that the midmost cross had been distinguished by a label attached to it, 'Jesus of Nazareth, King of the Jews'. Thus the truth was established, and the true Cross of Salvation was revealed by its label. . . . She also sought the nails with which the Lord was crucified, and found them. She caused a bridle-bit to be made from one of these nails, and set another in a diadem . . . and these she sent to her son, the Emperor Constantine.

The third nail, incidentally, eventually found its way to Britain: it was set into the pommel of Constantine's sword, which was given by Duke Hugh of the Franks to King Aethelstan of England in 926.

There seems little doubt that the True Cross (or at least what was universally believed to be the True Cross) really was venerated in Jerusalem during the 4th century – in 385 the pilgrim Etheria recorded the care taken to ensure that those who kissed the relic did not surreptitiously bite off pieces as personal souvenirs – and it is quite possible that Helena really did find it, perhaps while watching the digging of foundations for her son's church of the Holy Sepulchre. What is certain is that St Ambrose's comparatively prosaic account of its discovery did not long satisfy a miracle-hungry public, which soon came to believe – among other marvels – that the True Cross had identified itself by curing a dying woman (or a dead man) laid upon it, and that the Holy Nails had been miraculously pin-pointed by a shaft of heavenly light. The empress herself, moreover, came to be credited with finding not only the True Cross but also (according to the 15th-century Englishman John Capgrave) 'the crybbe that our Lorde was leyed in and part of the heye [hay] therein, our Ladye's smock', and 'the bodyes of the Thre Kynges'.

In Roman Britain, closely associated with both her one-time husband and her son, tales of Helena must have found an especially enthusiastic audience among the local Christians. Some of their churches may well have been dedicated to her, while at York, the scene of Constantius' death and Constantine's proclamation, the now-demolished church of St Helen's-on-the-Walls was (according to a highly suspect local tradition) built over Constantius' tomb, 'where was found a lamp burning in the vault of a little chapel, and Constantius was thought to be buried there. Lazius tells us that the Ancients had an art of dissolving gold into a fatty liquor, and preparing it so that it would continue burning in the Sepulchres for many ages.' Recent excavations at the church found no such eternal flame, but did uncover a 4th-century mosaic of a Roman lady, just possibly a portrait of Helena from an early church. The saint's British popularity certainly survived the fall of the Roman Empire and into the Anglo-Saxon period, when comparatively large numbers of churches – mainly in Yorkshire and Lincolnshire – were consecrated in her name, and accounts of her discovery of the Cross appeared in English collections of saints' lives.

Then, about half a century after the Norman Conquest, the legend of Helena acquired both a new significance and a new association – a link with someone called Old King Cole. The document that apparently started it all was written at Colchester in about 1120, being an account of the foundation of a monastery there twenty-five years earlier by Eudo the Steward, the Norman sheriff of Essex. 'Colchester', the relevant passage begins, 'is a city in the eastern part of Britain. . . . The tradition is that Helena, the mother of the one-time emperor, was born and brought up in this city: her rank and power was such – or so they say – that Constantius the father of Constantine the Great besieged the place for three years, but could only win it by marrying Helena.'

The sensational news that the famous St Helena was actually a native of a well-known English town seems to have spread quickly, and in 1129 the chronicler Henry of Huntingdon produced a much more detailed version of the story in his *Historia Anglorum*.

Constantius . . . took to wife the daughter of the King of the Britons of Colchester, whose name was Coel: that is to say he married Helena, whom we call Saint Helena, and by her he had Constantine the Great. This same Constantius, the mildest and most civilized of men, died in Britain at York. . . . Constantine, Flower of the Britons, reigned for thirty years and ten months. He was indeed British both by birth and by ancestry: neither before nor since has Britain produced anyone to match him. . . . Helena herself, that noble child of Britain, caused London to be girt about with a wall, which still stands, and embellished Colchester with fine buildings. Among other works, she also greatly restored Jerusalem, clearing away idols and adorning it with many great churches.

This King Coel seems to have appeared out of the blue – but where did Henry obtain his information? His account sounds extremely authoritative and circumstantial, and some of it (Constantius' death, the length of Constantine's reign, and Helena's Holy Land churches) is indeed quite genuine history, derived from Roman sources via the writings of the Anglo-Saxon chronicler Bede. The rest – the previously unknown parts – is less easily traced, but may well be based on the same local traditions drawn on by the Colchester abbey annalist.

Thus the legend of Coel of Colchester was under way, and within a few years it acquired a great deal more publicity on the appearance of Geoffrey of Monmouth's *History of the Kings of Britain*. This mammoth work, a 'history' of Britain from its foundation by the mythical Trojan prince Brutus until the Saxon takeover, purported to be a translation of 'a certain very ancient book in the British language . . . brought from Wales'. It is probably more accurately described as the first British blockbuster historical novel, for though Geoffrey (or his alleged source, if it ever existed) had a general idea of the chronological order of events and used the names of genuine historical figures where possible, these tend to find themselves playing somewhat surprising roles. Thus Carausius is rightly declared to have usurped the 'kingship' of Britain, but his murderer Allectus (really his finance minister) becomes a general sent from Rome, while Asclepiodotus (who really *was* a general sent from Rome) becomes a

British 'Duke of Cornwall' who slays Allectus and rules in his stead for a decade. Then, declares Geoffrey:

Coel, Duke of Kaercolim, that is to say Colchester, started a rebellion against King Asclepiodotus. He killed the king in battle and took the royal crown for himself. When this was announced to the [Roman] Senate, they rejoiced at the death of a ruler who had done so much damage to Roman power. Mindful of the setback they had suffered when they had lost the kingdom, they sent as legate the Senator Constantius, a wise and courageous man. . . .

When Coel, King of the Britons, heard of the coming of Constantius, he was afraid to meet him in battle, for the Roman's reputation was such that no king could resist him. The moment Constantius landed in the island, Coel sent his envoys to him to sue for peace and promise submission, on the understanding that he should retain the kingship of Britain and contribute nothing more to Roman sovereignty than the customary tribute. Constantius agreed to this proposal. . . . Coel gave him hostages and the two signed a treaty of peace. Just one month later Coel developed a serious illness which killed him within eight days.

After Coel's death Constantius himself seized the royal crown, and married Coel's daughter. Her name was Helen and her beauty was greater than that of any other young woman in the kingdom – for that matter, no more lovely girl could be discovered anywhere. Her father had no other child to inherit the throne, and he had therefore done all in his power to give Helen the kind of training which would enable her to rule the country the more efficiently after his death. Following her marriage with Constantius she had by him a son called Constantine.

Geoffrey's blend of 'history' and romance caught the imagination of his contemporaries, and his book became wildly and enduringly popular. Nearly two hundred copies of his Latin manuscript still survive, and it was soon translated into Norman-French (the everyday language of the contemporary upper classes) reaching a still wider audience with the appearance of English and Welsh versions during the 13th century. His stories were also incorporated piecemeal into the works of other chroniclers, and before long Coel, Helena and Constantine had become an established and indispensable part of British history. It is easy to understand why their legend exercised such an appeal, for it enabled patriotic Britons to claim as compatriots not only a famous saint but also (as Henry of Huntingdon took particular care to emphasize) the immensely prestigious Constantine, the father of the medieval Church and State. During the 15th-century ecclesiastical councils of Constance and Basle, indeed, the English delegation claimed precedence over all others on the grounds that Constantine was their fellow-countryman, 'born of Helena, who was of the royal house of England'.

The story, as stories will, changed somewhat in the retelling. Its first English translator, Layamon, who was a West-Country man, even tried to shanghai Coel to Gloucester:

> In Gloucester was an earl of noble kin
> The highest-born man that dwelt in Britain
> Coel was his name . . .

While in Wales St Helena became hopelessly confused with the legendary Elen Luyddog – Helen of the Hosts – who allegedly dwelt at Caernarfon, where she supposedly married the historical Roman Emperor Magnus Maximus (383–88) and was mother to a son named, infuriatingly, Constantine. The fact that this boy must have been born at least a generation after the Emperor Constantine's death in 337 did not deter Welshmen from claiming them to be one and the same person, and the mix-up remains to this day massively commemorated in stone. For when Edward I took Caernarfon in 1283, in the course of his conquest of Wales, he conveniently found there 'the body of Maximus the prince, father of the noble Emperor Constantine', and proceeded to emphasize the Britishness of the noble emperor by building Caernarfon castle in a style deliberately imitating the city walls of Constantinople.

Despite all this, Colchester clung tenaciously to both Coel and Helena, and by the 14th century some local patriot had composed for the city records the most precise and comprehensive of all accounts of their doings, accompanied by an impressive array of dates, nearly all of them wrong. Here are the relevant entries:

AD 219   Coel, Duke of the Britons, began to build the city of Kaircoel [Colchester]

238   Coel, Duke of Colchester, began to reign over Essex and Hertford

242   Helen, daughter of Coel, is born at Colchester

260   Constantius, sailing to Britain, besieges the city of Colchester for three years

263   The siege of Colchester was raised by the marriage of Helen, daughter of Coel

265   Constantine, son of Constantius, is born in Colchester of Helen

290   Asclepiodotus the tyrant having been slain, Coel Duke of Colchester reigned over all Britain, subject to the Roman tribute

297   Coel, most powerful King of the Britons, died at Colchester in the third month

299   The Emperor Constantius died at York in the 16th year of his Empire

319   St Helen, on the 5th day of May found the Cross of our Lord

322   St Helen, being over 80 years of age . . . fell asleep in the Lord in Britain . . .

330   Constantine the Great, most Christian emperor, flower of Britain, citizen of Colchester . . . died in Nicomedia.

This chronicle obviously diverges from Geoffrey's story at several important points, and its mention of the three year siege, which also appears in the earlier Colchester abbey manuscript, may well indicate that both accounts drew on the same local tradition. Such a tradition was also perhaps responsible for the claim (subsequently accepted by national historians) that King Coel not only lived at Colchester but actually founded the place, naming it 'Coel's fortress' – Kaircoel in British or Welsh, Coel's Chester or Colchester in English. The chronicle's most startling assertion, however, is that buildings raised by Coel and Helena were still to be seen after the Norman Conquest. 'In 1076 Eudo the Steward built the castle of

The large seal of Colchester.

Colchester on the foundations of the palace of Coel, formerly king, and renovated the chapel of St Helen which, it is said, she built herself and dedicated to St John . . . which chapel was dedicated on St Katherine's Day 1239, in honour of St Katherine and St Helen, by Roger Bishop of London.'

Whatever the truth about these buildings – and this will be discussed shortly – there was certainly no lack of reminders of Coel and Helena in medieval and later Colchester. Helena's rough-hewn True Cross became the city's coat-of-arms, and she herself appears on the corporation's seal and, with her father, in the initial letter of its earliest surviving charter. Influential citizens joined the Guild of St Helen, the sick and aged were tended at the Holy Cross Hospital, and until the 19th century the inhabitants of the High Street drew their water at 'King Coyle's pump': while curious visitors would be shown 'King Coyle's Castle' – in fact a Roman gateway – and 'King Coyle's Kitchen', a local chalk-pit.

In the world at large, meanwhile, the legend continued to be generally accepted as gospel throughout the Tudor and Stuart periods. In 1641 the Jesuit Michael Alford even used it as the basis of a Latin propaganda treatise (*Britannia Illustrata: or the Fatherland and Religion of Lucius, Helena and Constantine*) urging his erring fellow-countrymen to return to the Roman Catholic faith of their earliest Christian forebears. But with the growing availability of original Roman sources – none of which mentioned Coel at all – an element of doubt began to creep in: Gibbon's famous *Decline and Fall of the Roman Empire* (1782) curtly dismissed him as fictitious and Gough's 1806 edition of Camden's *Britannia* roundly declared: 'All that has been advanced about this Coel rests on such weak authorities, that it can hardly pass for truth in any degree'. Yet Coel still found his defenders. Philip

64

2 The face of the loser – one of the very few surviving coins of Caratacus, found near Guildford, Surrey.

3 And the winner – Roman gold coin of Claudius, showing a triumphal arch: minted to celebrate his victory 'over the Britons'.

1 'The Celts were certainly head-hunters . . .' (p. 11). Head-trophy in the stone doorpost of a Celtic temple, Roquepertuse, France. 3rd–2nd centuries BC.

4 'At the core of Silurian territory lay barren mountains . . .' (p. 22). The Brecon Beacons, Powys, Wales.

5 The site of Caratacus' last stand (p. 26)? The Iron Age hillfort of Caer Caradoc, near Clun, Shropshire, defended on three sides by precipitous slopes and on the fourth by multiple ditches (top).

6 Roman soldiers attacking a fortress, from Trajan's Column, Rome. The legionaries (right) lock their rectangular shields into a 'testudo', while auxiliaries (centre) charge on the flanks.

7 'A much-prized trophy of the
downfall of Colchester . . .' (p. 43).
Severed head of a statue of Claudius,
found near Saxmundham, Suffolk in
1907.

8 'Around Boudica's neck was a
twisted gold necklace . . .' (p. 39).
Icenian gold torques and bracelets,
found at Snettisham near Hunstanton,
Norfolk.

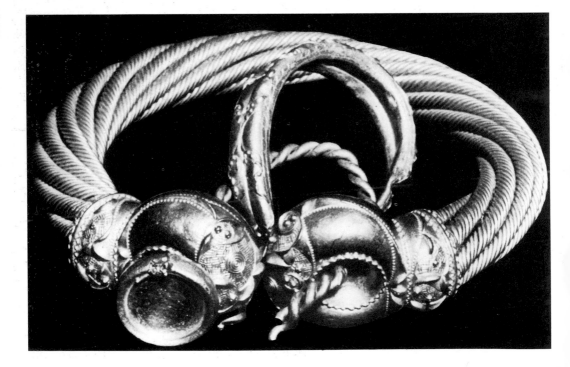

9 'The invincible goddess of Victory . . .'
(p. 40). Brigantia, 'the High One', ruling
war-goddess of the Brigantes. Romano–
British relief from Birrens, Dumfries and
Galloway.

10 'The bitter hatred the rebels felt for
the symbols of Roman domination . . .'
(p. 43). The tombstone of Longinus from
Colchester, mutilated by Boudica's
followers.

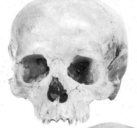

11 Boudica's victims, ritually massacred near Liverpool Street? (p. 47). Decapitated skulls, one damaged by a weapon, from the Walbrook stream, London.

12 'The Warrior Patriot Queen'. The Victorian idealization of Boudica, embodied in her statue on the Thames Embankment, London.

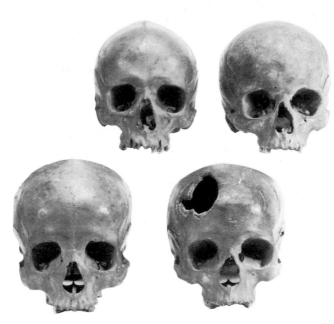

13 (*Below*) 'The conflagration which enveloped the town . . .' (p. 43). Charred dates still lying in the foundations of a Roman fruit shop at Colchester.

14 King Cole's daughter, or 'the landlady of the lowest kind of inn'? The Empress Helena, mother of Constantine and alleged discoverer of the True Cross.

15 The Emperor Constantine, 'the Great', 'the Victor', 'the Equal of the Apostles' and, according to English legend, King Cole's grandson.

16 The medieval view of Cole and Helena: the Colchester charter of 1413. The inscription round Helena reads, 'St Helena, born at Colchester, mother of Constantine and finder of the True Cross' – which also appears in the town's arms.

17 Hadrian's Wall near Housesteads, Northumberland. The northern frontier of Roman Britain and later perhaps one of the bulwarks of Coel's kingdom.

18 The stronghold of one of Coel's subordinates? The Mote of Mark, Galloway, a rocky outcrop fortified by the Britons in the 5th century.

19 'Viking attacks became a full-scale invasion . . .' (p. 98). The Danish Great Army landing, from a 12th-century *Life* of their victim, King Edmund.

20 (*Above, right*) 'Alfred had me made' (p. 103). The Alfred Jewel, given by the king to the monastery he founded near his refuge on Athelney.

21 The Viking chieftain turned Christian king. A contemporary drawing of Cnut presenting an altar-cross to the New Minster at Winchester.

HARO E·D·REX·INTERFEC TVS·EST

22 The death of King Harold, from the Bayeux Tapestry. Is he the figure struck by an arrow, the one cut down by a knight, or perhaps both? (p. 109).

BVS · VI · PREPARA — RENSE · VI · RILI·TER

23–26 (*Above, left*) Norman knights, from the Bayeux Tapestry. Invincible in open country, such troops proved ineffective among the fens and forests where Hereward lurked. (*Left*) The towering ruins of Croyland Abbey, Lincolnshire, where, according to one version of his legend, Hereward lies buried. (*Above*) Hereward's most formidable but most honourable enemy: William the Conqueror, from a contemporary coin. (*Below*) The only surviving remnant of the 'trackless swamps' which surrounded Ely in Hereward's time (p. 130): the National Trust reserve at Wicken Fen.

27 The Wallace Monument on Abbey Crag at Stirling, whence the Scots
descended to defeat the English in 1297. The bridge is later.

28 Letter from William
Wallace and Andrew
Moray (whose names
appear top left) to the
mayors of Lubeck and
Hamburg (p. 167): the
original was lost during
World War II.

29 (*Above*) Early 14th-century English knights. Heavily armoured troops like these, riding chargers trained to attack their opponents (centre) helped to defeat Wallace at Falkirk. (*Below*) But the men who sealed the fate of the Common Army were Edward I's archers, seen here among other foot-soldiers. From the Holkham Bible Picture Book.

30 Hexham Priory Church, Northumberland, where Wallace intervened to save the canons from his unruly followers (p. 170). Shown here is the south transept.

31 (*Below*) 'The Key of Scotland'. Stirling Castle, guarding the vital crossing of the Forth which linked the northern and southern halves of the kingdom.

Morant's patriotic *History of Colchester* (1815) launched a sweeping counter-attack on his behalf, and there were plenty of others reluctant to give up belief in the British king who was father of a British saint and grandfather of a British emperor – 'if only', as one late-Victorian bishop preached, 'because the idea behind the story is a beautiful one'.

Beautiful or not, is the story true? The statements in dispute, briefly, are that a certain Coel founded Colchester in the 3rd century and named it after himself; and that the undoubtedly historical Helena was his daughter. The first statement is easily dismissed, for we have seen in previous chapters that Colchester in fact originated as a pre-Roman British settlement during the 1st century BC, and that it was re-founded as a Roman town in about AD 49, being initially a 'colonia' of veteran legionaries. It is thence that its modern name really derives, for the Romano-Britons called it Caer Colun (Geoffrey's 'Kaercolim') and the early Anglo-Saxons called it Colenceaster, both meaning the 'fortress of the colonia', and not 'the fortress of Coel'.

So Coel neither founded nor named Colchester. Could he have been a British prince who simply ruled there? Not a prince, certainly, for there was no place for native rulers in the heart of a 3rd-century Roman province. Could he, then, have been a leading Romano-British citizen or official, who was implicated in the separatist movement of Carausius, but who managed to make his peace with the victorious Constantius? This is Geoffrey of Monmouth's context for the marriage of Helena and the birth of Constantine, which must therefore have occurred after 296: if so, however, Constantine would have been proclaimed emperor when less than nine years old, and achieved his greatest victory before he was fifteen.

So the details, at least, of Geoffrey's tale are wrong: for we know that Constantine was really born in the 270s, and that Helena and Constantius had separated by 289. Thus, if the marriage and birth truly did happen in Britain, they must have taken place during a much earlier visit by Constantius: and though both the Colchester town chronicle and Coel's 19th-century defenders posit such an earlier visit, there is absolutely no evidence that it actually occurred.

Nor, moreover, is there any real evidence that Helena was nobly born or even British, let alone that she came from Colchester. Eusebius, Constantine's contemporary and biographer, unfortunately says nothing at all about her origins, although he presumably knew of them, but later 4th-century authors state that she was of 'obscure' or 'very low' birth. St Ambrose, indeed, asserted that she had begun life as a *stabularia* – a word which Lewis and Short's standard Latin dictionary interprets as 'the landlady of the lowest kind of inn . . . a stopping-place for animals or persons of the lowest class', adding darkly that 'such pothouses were the usual abode of prostitutes'. Writers since the 16th century have politely modified the description – some claiming that she was called *stabularia* because her father was constable (*comes stabuli*) of Constantius' household, and others explaining that she was so called because she was Constantius' 'hostess' when he stayed at Coel's palace. But the clear implication is that Helena originated as (at best) 'a waitress of questionable morals' or (at worst) the madam of a brothel.

The whereabouts of this dubious establishment are uncertain, but it seems most likely that Helena came from Drepanum in the province of Pontus, now part of Turkey: she is known to have spent large sums of money on beautifying the place, and Constantine subsequently changed its name to Helenopolis ('Helena's city') in her honour, all of which points to it as her home town. Constantine himself, incidentally – on the evidence of a contemporary astrologer, who was naturally interested in nativities – was born at Naissus, now Nish in modern Bulgaria.

So 'Old King Cole' was not a British prince, nor was he the founder of Colchester: Helena – who probably never even set foot in Britain – was not his daughter, nor was Constantine his grandson.

How, then, did the legend arise? We must assume that the early-medieval inhabitants of 'Coleceastre' (as it was called by 1067) can have known little or nothing about the real origins of their town and its name: oral tradition had long since forgotten the Roman colonia, and no history books were available to tell them the facts. Yet the great ruins all around proved that the place was ancient, and *someone* must have founded it. Since its name seemed to mean 'Cole's fortress', they can surely be forgiven for guessing that this founder must have been a 'King Cole'. If this thesis seems far-fetched, consider the parallel cases of Gloucester and York, which were actually founded by the Romans as legionary fortresses called Glevum and Eburacum respectively. Their medieval citizens, nevertheless, believed them to have been originated by mythical figures named Glovi (from whom Gloucester was allegedly named 'Glovi-cester') and Ebraucus (allegedly a British king 'who reigned about the time King David ruled Judaea').

Once invented – and developed by Henry of Huntingdon and Geoffrey of Monmouth – 'King Coel' could be credited with previously inexplicable ruins, rather in the same spirit as an 8th-century Saxon poet attributed the ruins of Roman Bath to 'the work of giants'. We have seen that a Roman gateway was thought to be 'King Coel's Castle': in the same vein 'King Coel's Palace', around whose massive foundations Eudo the Steward built his great Norman castle, was in reality that most impressive of all Colchester's Roman buildings, the temple of Claudius.

It is far less easy to see how Helena became King Coel's 'daughter', and perhaps the only clue is the other building 'restored' by Eudo, the chapel of St Helen. The original chapel was clearly regarded as already very ancient when Eudo rebuilt it. Could it have been founded by the great Anglo-Saxon King Offa (757–94), who was reported to have had a particularly high regard for St Helena? Could it even – as is claimed of the church at York – have been built by Romano-British Christians to honour Constantine's sainted mother? In either case, could its great antiquity have given rise over the centuries to the belief – quoted by the town chronicle – that it was not merely dedicated to St Helena but actually built by her, and hence that she had once lived in Colchester? From this point it would have been but a short step for someone – perhaps Henry of Huntingdon – to relate Helena, the 'royal Colchester lady', to the town's royal 'founder', and thus to complete the legend.

So King Coel of Colchester probably never existed at all, though for seven centuries it suited both English national pride and Essex local patriotism to believe that he did. If we could be sure that the nursery-rhyme really was based on him, our investigation would have to end here.

But we cannot be sure, and it is not even certain that the rhyme originated in England: it may well have come from lowland Scotland. Without doubt it was well known there, and some of the earliest recorded versions – those published in 1776, 1797 and 1806 – are specifically Scottish. The 1806 version ends with the lines, 'There never was a man in merry Scotland/That was half so happy as he', while the first stanza of the 1797 version (which closely resembles that of 1776) runs as follows:

> Our auld King Coul was a jolly auld soul
> And a jolly auld soul was he
> Our auld King Coul fill'd a jolly brown bowl
> And he ca'd for his fiddlers three
> Fidell didell, fidell didell quo' the fiddlers
> There's no a lass in a' Scotland
> Like our sweet Marjorie.

This version was collected for the *Scots Musical Museum* by Robert Burns, who wrote to its editor that 'I have met with many different sets of the words and music'. The poet was ideally placed to hear them, for he spent much of his life in the district of Kyle around Ayr in southwestern Scotland, and this area abounds with stories about a 'King Cole' who is quite distinct from the Colchester hero.

The entire district of Kyle (recorded as 'Cul' in 1153) is allegedly named, indeed, after this Scottish King Cole. Within it, on the river called the Water of Coyle, is the village of Coylton. According to the *Old Statistical Account* of 1798, 'it is believed, very ill-founded, that Coylton derives its name from a King Coilus who was killed in battle in the neighbourhood and buried in the church of Coylton', while Fergus Loch, a mile or so west of the church, 'is supposed by some to take its name from King Fergus, who defeated Coilus King of the Britons in the adjacent fields'. Another tradition, however, locates Coilus' death and burial four miles further north, in the parish of Tarbolton, where Burns had his 'Bachelors' Club' and where, 'within the grounds of Coilsfield House, is a place which the country relates to have been a field of battle, and a stone held in veneration as the monument of old King Coil'. This stone (in fact several large granite blocks) crowns a circular burial mound which, says the *Topographical Dictionary of Scotland*, 'is called King Coil's tomb . . . and is universally stated to be the depository of the remains of Coilus King of the Britons, slain here in an engagement with the Picts and Scots'.

These traditions are traceable back at least as far as the 1520s, when the Scots cleric Hector Boece wrote his Latin *History of the Scots from the Origins of the Race*. His interweaving of fact and downright fantasy gives it a strong family resemblance to Geoffrey of Monmouth's book. Like its famous precursor – from which it borrows heavily in places – it soon became extremely popular, and within a decade it had been translated into Scots-English verse and prose. Boece claims that the original Scots were descended from, and named after, an Egyptian Pharaoh's daughter called Scota. After long wanderings in Africa and Spain they settled in Ireland, whence they colonized the west coast of Scotland from Ayrshire to Argyll. Not long afterwards a fleet arrived from Scythia (the Black Sea area) carrying a host of wandering bachelor Picts, whom the Scots permitted to settle on their borders, giving them Scottish virgins as their wives on condition they chose their future rulers from the female line.

All this allegedly occurred in about 330 BC, when the Britons who inhabited the southern part of 'Albion' were ruled by a king named Coil or Coilus. These Britons (whom the chronicler equated with the English, and thus viewed with hostility) regarded the agreement between the two invading races with horror, and conspired to turn one against the other and so to destroy both. In the irresistible words of the 1535 verse translation:

> The belleall [traitorous] British full of melancolie
> With viperos vennum and odious invie
> With great dissait [deceit] assalit has ane cast [made an attempt]
> To brek that bond the quhilk [the which] was bund so fast
> Ane king thai had wes callit Coilus
> Doggit [dogged] and dour, mad and malicious
> Quhilk with the Pechtis [Picts] made ane quyet tryst [a secret meeting].

As a result open war broke out between Picts and Scots, and the latter sent to their Irish cousins for reinforcements. These were led by King Fergus, who quickly discovered the true cause of the discord and made a new and firmer alliance with the Picts against their British mutual enemy. Boece continues:

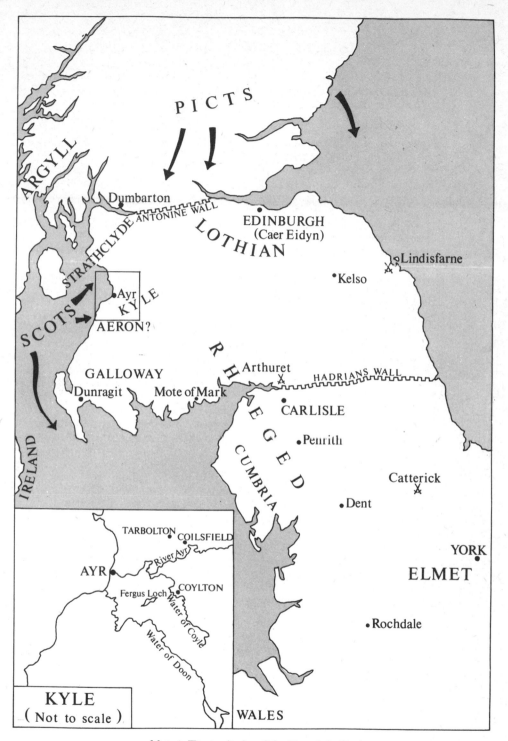

Map 4 The territories of the Men of the North

When this became known to Coilus King of the Britons (who dwelt at York, then the chief city of Britain) he was much troubled in his mind, for he feared the growing strength of these hated neighbours. . . . Therefore, seeking to provoke a new war between them, he launched hit-and-run raids to pillage the Pictish borderlands. Then, when redress was demanded, he denied all knowledge of these crimes and laid the blame on the Scots, declaring that it was they and not the Britons who were stealing the Picts' cattle. The upshot of this, however, was that both Picts and Scots came to hate the Britons and began to attack their frontier, slaying the inhabitants and carrying away their goods.

These attacks infuriated Coilus, who decided to attempt by open warfare what he had been unable to achieve by deceitful conspiracies. Quickly assembling all the necessities of war, he gathered his forces and invaded those lands of the Scots bounded by the Atlantic and the Irish Sea [i.e. Ayrshire and Galloway]. There, after ravaging the countryside with fire and sword and causing tremendous damage, he encamped with his forces by the Doon river [which flows from Loch Doon to the sea near Ayr] sending out parties to slaughter any Picts and Scots they could find.

Meanwhile, as soon as King Fergus heard that war had broken out, he ordered that all cattle and moveable goods should be removed from towns and villages into the high mountains, and that women and children should take refuge among the crags and natural fastnesses: he himself, with the armies of the Picts and Scots, would remain in a fortress prepared in advance. By these means the Britons would in time be weakened by lack of supplies, while his own forces would remain strong, ready when the moment came to issue forth at once and use their weapons stoutly. These plans, however, were betrayed to King Coil by a Scottish deserter, whereupon he sent out 5000 Britons to drive the cattle from the mountains onto the plain. At first light the next morning he intended to set out with his whole army against the enemy base.

When these British movements were made known to the Picts and Scots by their scouts, everyone in their camp grew apprehensive, and Fergus consulted his counsellors as to the best course of action. Some of them, terrified by the numbers and fierce spirit of the Britons, advised him against fighting, but others urged him to battle. . . . So various plans were discussed, and eventually it was agreed that Fergus and his Scots should attack the British camp from in front during the early part of the night, while the king of Picts and his forces would ford the Doon and make their way through country so wild that it had been left unguarded: then, when they heard the war-cries of the Scots, they would fall on the enemy from the rear. The rest they would entrust to fortune.

Shortly afterwards, Fergus launched a surprise night-attack on the British camp, killing the sentries and storming the rampart before Coil knew what was happening: then, while the Britons were trying to fight off the Scots, the Picts raised a terrible shout and suddenly attacked them from behind. Thus the Britons, barely awakened from sleep and unable to rally round their standards or their leaders, were routed. Some, concealed by the dark night, found safety in flight: others, not knowing the country, wandered among twisting glens and steep drops until they were either hunted down or swallowed up by bogs. Among these last was Coil himself: abandoned by his bodyguards, he was sucked under and smothered, leaving his name of Coil (now somewhat altered to 'Kyle') to the place as a perpetual memorial for posterity.

Much of this is, of course, total fantasy. The Picts (whatever their original homeland or marital status) certainly inhabited Scotland long

before the Scots who, far from arriving in the 4th century BC, are not known
to have raided Britain until the 3rd century AD or to have settled there much
before about AD 400. King Coil's 'capital' at York, moreover, did not exist
until three centuries after the alleged date of his death. His 'grave-mound'
at Coilsfield only adds to the confusion, for when it was excavated by
'zealous local antiquaries' in 1837 it was found to cover cremation cist-
burials of a type datable to the Middle Bronze Age, that is around 1400–
1000 BC.

It might well seem, therefore, that Coil of Ayrshire is as fictional as Cole
of Colebrook or Coel of Colchester and that, like them, he was invented to
account for a place-name. 'Kyle', 'Coylton' and the rest, it has been claimed,
actually derive from a Gaelic word meaning – as in Kyle of Lochalsh or the
Kyles of Bute – a narrow arm of sea dividing two pieces of land.

But there is no such geographical feature in or near the Ayrshire Kyle;
while there are, as we shall see, good reasons for believing that the rest of
Boece's tale may contain an element of truth. The principal problem,
clearly, is the impossibly early date, doubtless a product of the chronicler's
natural desire to exalt the antiquity of his nation. If, however, we transfer
the story to the 4th or 5th century AD, many of the difficulties disappear, for
it was during this period that the Scots really did come from Ireland to
colonize western Scotland, and a persistent tradition, recorded in annals
dating from the 7th century onwards, names their leader as Fergus. More
important, there is firm independent evidence that southern Scotland and
northern England really were ruled in about AD 420 by a great British king
named Coel.

Before considering this evidence, we shall need to look briefly at its
historical backdrop, the fluctuating fortunes of the northern borderlands of
Roman Britain. After penetrating deep into Scotland during the 80s of the
1st century AD, the Romans withdrew to the line of the Tyne and Solway,
where Hadrian raised his wall in the 120s. Soon afterwards, however, they
expanded northwards again to annex southern Scotland, establishing their
new frontier on the Antonine Wall, built around AD 143 across the narrow
neck of land from the Firth of Forth north of Edinburgh to the Firth of Clyde
north of Glasgow. But this proved impossible to hold, and by the early
decades of the 3rd century a new arrangement had been made. The Roman
forces retired, this time permanently, to Hadrian's Wall, and the British
tribes of the area 'between the walls' – the modern regions of Lothian, the
Borders, Dumfries and Galloway, the southern half of Strathclyde (including Ayrshire) and Northumberland – were bound by treaties: henceforth
they were to rule themselves but, in return for Roman protection and
Roman gold, they were to act as a buffer between the frontier of the province
and the hostile unconquered Picts of southern and central Scotland. The
policy worked well for both parties, and by the later 4th century the

distinction between Romans and Britons seems to have been dissolving. The undermanned Roman army, hard-pressed by Saxon and Irish attacks on the south, east and west of the province, was heartily glad of the alliance with the northern borderers, while among the borderers we find chieftains with Roman names like Paternus and Tacitus, long-standing allies of the *Dux Britanniarum*, the Roman general who commanded the Wall and the northern garrisons from his great fortress at York.

Exactly what happened in the borderlands when the Roman Empire finally relinquished control of Britain in AD 410 is far from certain, but it is clear that the landward frontier against the Picts held, splitting into a mosaic of independent British princedoms whose lands extended both north and south of the now abandoned Wall. Sometimes in alliance, sometimes at each other's throats, nominally Christian in religion but increasingly Celtic rather than Roman in culture, they flourished for two centuries, until the early 600s. Then, despite heroic resistance, all but the strongest of them – the kingdom of Strathclyde in southwestern Scotland, centred on Dumbarton rock – went down before the conquering English of Northumbria.

Little material trace of these Romano-British borderers has so far come to light in their own lands, where it has been all but obliterated by successive layers of settlement by Angles, Norsemen and medieval Scots, but they did not pass away entirely without a memorial. For they were remembered by their unconquered British cousins in Wales, who knew them as the *Gwr y Gogledd* 'the Men of the North' or the *Combrogi* 'fellow-countrymen' – hence, significantly, both Cymry, the modern name for the Welsh, and Cumbria, once part of the territories of their northern compatriots. Their deeds are recorded in the oldest known Welsh literature, and it is there that we shall find the evidence for Coel's existence.

His name appears first of all in a series of poems which (though their earliest surviving manuscripts date from the early Middle Ages) most scholars believe to have been originally composed by the bards of the Men of the North around the turn of the 6th and 7th centuries. In the *Gododdin*, which laments a disastrous attack on the Anglian stronghold of Catraeth (probably Catterick, north Yorkshire) in about 600, the British leaders are referred to as the 'sons [i.e. the descendants] of Coel', and in another poem, which tells of a British victory over the English chieftain called 'Flame-bearer', 'one Saturday morning in Argoed Llwyfein' (perhaps Leven Forest, in Cumbria) a British prince proudly calls himself 'a whelp of Coel's breed'. An early Welsh Triad also names one of the three invincible armies of the north as 'the Three Hundred Spears of the Sons of Coel', three hundred being the traditional number in a British princely warband.

These poetic references show that Coel was well-known and honoured among the Combrogi, some of whose princes were proud to claim him as their ancestor. Much more can be gleaned, however, from the genealogies or family trees of these princes, probably compiled in the 9th century from earlier sources and commissioned by Welsh rulers who claimed descent from the Men of the North. Thirteen princely lines are traced – all of them save that of Strathclyde ending, significantly, at the time of the final English triumph over the northern Britons – and no less than eight of them originate with *Coel Hen Guotepauc*. *Hen*, in Welsh, means 'old', and *Guotepauc* or *Godebog* seems to be an early form of *godidog*, meaning 'excellent' or 'splendid': thus we reach the name of 'Old Coel the Splendid'.

Many of the forty or so people mentioned in the pedigrees are merely names – we unfortunately know nothing more, for instance, of Pabo 'the Pillar of Britain', Cynfelyn 'the Scabby' or Gorwyst 'Half-bare'. But the later princes are somewhat less obscure, for poems or early Welsh annals frequently tell us when they died and enable us to guess at the areas where they ruled. Gwenddolau, reputedly Coel's great-great-grandson, was killed at the battle of Arthuret, fought in A D 573 near the old Roman fort of Castra Exploratorum north of Longtown in Cumbria: he may well have been defending his capital, for the fort lies by the hamlet of Carwinley, a name probably derived from *Caer Wenddolau* – 'Gwenddolau's stronghold'. His killers were his own cousins Gwrgi and Peredur 'Steel Spear', the sons of Eliffer 'of the Great Warband', who were slain in turn in 580 by an English leader improbably named Eda 'Big-knees'. They too may have ruled in Cumbria, but later tradition associates them with the city of York. Another cousin, Dunawt 'the Stout', is believed to have given his name to Dent on the Yorkshire-Cumbrian border, and Guallawc, a more distant relation, may have held the kingdom of Elmet, round Leeds and Sherburn-in-Elmet in south Yorkshire.

The lands of another group of Coel's descendants were apparently much further north. Those of Clydno Eidyn were almost certainly centred on Edinburgh (once Caer Eidyn), while those of his brother Catrawt 'of the Chalk Hill' may have been around Kelso in the Borders, and those of one Morcant either in Lothian or Dumfriesshire.

The best remembered of all the 6th-century 'sons of Coel', however, were Urien and his son Owain, the last rulers of Rheged. Probably centred on Carlisle and the Solway Firth, this was apparently one of the largest British princedoms, stretching perhaps as far north as Dunragit (Dun Rheged) in Galloway, or even to Ayrshire, and as far south as Rochdale (once Reced-ham) in Lancashire: it certainly extended eastwards across the Pennines to include Catterick in north Yorkshire. These heroes of many Welsh folk-tales, Urien and Owain, were subsequently absorbed into medieval Arthurian legend, where Owain became 'Sir Yvain, son of King Urien', the owner of a flight of magic ravens and of an invaluable pet lion. He was also probably the original of 'Ewen Caesarius', a giant said to have lived near

Penrith in Cumbria and to be buried beneath the 'Giant's Grave' there. If he really was known as 'Owen the Caesar', the Men of the North were still using Roman titles some two centuries after the end of Imperial rule in Britain.

The enduring fame of Urien and Owain reflects the testimony of the early sources. There they appear as the leaders of the last great fight against the Northumbrian Angles, whom they defeated in Argoed Llwyfein and whom (at the head of a British coalition including their cousins Morcant, Guallawc and Dunawt) they eventually all but swept into the eastern sea. In about 590 they trapped the enemy on the island of Lindisfarne off the Northumbrian coast, but on the verge of final victory Urien was assassinated on the orders of Morcant 'out of jealousy, because his skill in warfare surpassed that of all the other kings'. Owain fought on, but Rheged, beset by the renascent Angles and betrayed by its fellow-countrymen, collapsed soon afterwards. Within 50 years its faithless British neighbours, weakened by their own treachery, had gone the same way.

What does this tell us about Coel himself? First of all it shows that, by the late 6th century, his descendants ruled from Edinburgh to Yorkshire and Lancashire. Indeed, save only for the Clydeside lands of the dynasty founded by one Ceredig or Coroticus, they apparently held all the old Roman frontier zone. It is reasonable to suppose that Coel had once ruled all their territories as a single unit, and that during the five or six generations covered by the pedigrees this unit was divided between the various branches of his family. If we allow the conventional 30 years for each of these generations, Coel would appear to have been alive about 180 years before AD 600: that is, in the early decades of the 5th century. This date, moreover, is supported by the fact that an alleged son-in-law of Coel, called Cunedda, is thought to have flourished in about 430, and that his great-grandson Merchiaun or Marcianus may well have been named after a Roman emperor who reigned in the 450s.

Coel, then, seems to have ruled the Roman frontier zone, and to have ruled it at the very time when Britain finally passed from Imperial control. Some scholars, notably the late Dr John Morris, have therefore speculated that he was in fact the last *Dux Britanniarum*, the last Imperially appointed commander of Roman troops in northern Britain; that his name was Coelius or Coelestius; and that when Imperial power failed he turned his command into an independent hereditary kingdom. Other Roman generals in other outlying parts of the tottering 5th-century empire are known to have done precisely this, and there would have been no one in contemporary Britain strong enough to stand in Coel's way. On his death, so the theory runs, his single kingdom began to split into smaller states, ruled either by men who really were his sons and grandsons or by subordinate commanders whom the later genealogies treated as his descendants. As supporting evidence, Morris cites the names of Coel's alleged wife and daughter: respectively Stradweul, which he claims means 'Wall Road', and Gwawl, which he translates as 'Wall' (though it could also mean 'brightness'): odd names for ladies, certainly, and better regarded, he says, as reminders of the Dux's authority over Hadrian's Wall. We might add that Boece's story (for what it is worth) places Coel's capital at York, which once really was the Dux's headquarters.

This version of the story does not account, however, for all the available evidence. There is, for example, absolutely no proof that a *Dux Britanniarum* was still holding office when Britain became independent in 410: such indications as remain, indeed, suggest that by now there were no Roman generals and precious few regular troops left in the province. It is entirely possible, therefore, that by Coel's time frontier defence had devolved solely on the British border chieftains; that Coel himself was the strongest of these chieftains; and that he took advantage of the power-vacuum to expand into the northern English lands vacated by the Roman garrisons. His name, after all, could as easily be British as Roman – and though an admittedly rather dubious pedigree (which purports to trace his descent from a marriage between the pagan god Beli and Anna 'whom they say was the Virgin Mary's cousin') gives his ancestors in the fourth and fifth generations the Roman names of Urban and Grat[ian], his immediate predecessors have purely British names.

Whether Coel was really a Roman general or a British prince, he was clearly an important leader whose main preoccupation must have been the defence of his lands – roughly the section of Britain from the Humber and Mersey to the Forth and Clyde – against invasion by the Picts from the north or the sea-borne Irish 'Scots' from the west. That he succeeded is plain, for though the Picts frequently raided the old Roman province south of Coel's territory, they are always reported as landing from their boats and carrying their plunder home by sea. They presumably did so because they could not penetrate the land-frontier, and there is no evidence from documents, archaeology or place-names to show that they ever annexed any significant part of the lands of the Men of the North. The 5th- and 6th-century Irish colonies on the west coast of Scotland, moreover, are in Argyll, well to the north of the British-held lands, and it was not until several hundred years after Coel's death that the Scots managed to settle south of the Clyde estuary.

Coel, then, maintained the political integrity of his territories, handing them on to descendants who honoured him two centuries later. How he did so is not entirely clear, but there are clues. One is the fact that, somewhere around Coel's time, Anglo-Saxon mercenaries were given lands in east Yorkshire, while others, according to one tradition, were settled in the lands 'about the Wall'. Their descendants were eventually to prove the downfall of the Men of the North, but originally they were doubtless employed to defend the coast against the more immediately dangerous Picts and Scots.

Other, less creditable, British methods are revealed in a blistering letter written by St Patrick to the soldiers of 'the tyrant Coroticus', apparently during the 450s. This Coroticus (or Ceredig) ruled the British kingdom of Strathclyde on the northwestern fringe of Coel's lands, and must have been his near-contemporary. Though he and his subjects regarded themselves as 'fellow-citizens of the holy [i.e. Christian] Romans', they were accused of acting like 'the fellow-citizens of demons . . . the accomplices of the apostate Picts and Scots', for, more precisely, they had been indulging in the highly profitable practice of slave-raiding, carrying off Patrick's Irish converts – some still in their baptismal robes – and selling them to the Picts and Scots. Coel's compatriots were thus not above making agreements with the 'alien peoples ignorant of God' when it suited them to do so: they may even have tried playing one race off against the other, as Coel himself is said to have done in Boece's tale.

It is time, perhaps, to look again at Boece's version of events in the light of our improved knowledge. The essential elements of his story – that Coel was 'King of the Britons'; that he feared an alliance between the Picts and the Scots and tried but failed to divide them by diplomacy and undercover operations; and that he eventually fought them in Ayrshire but was defeated and killed in a surprise attack – now appear quite credible. There are still problems, however, for we know that in Coel's time Ayrshire was not 'in the land of the Scots', but in the realms of the Britons, being almost certainly identifiable with the princedom of 'Aeron' mentioned in several British poems. Coel, this would imply, was not invading enemy territory, but defending his own.

Nor is it likely that his opponent was really 'King Fergus': for Fergus mac Erca, the traditional founder of the Scots kingdom of Dalriada in Argyll, died in about 500, so cannot have been Coel's contemporary. His enemy may rather have been the Irish King Nath-I, who lived during the first half of the 5th century and who is credited with devastating Strathclyde and winning a great victory there. As in Boece's story, he may well have come in support of a group of Scots colonists, made an alliance with the Picts, and established himself in a 'fortress' somewhere in Ayrshire. Where this was, and where Coel's last battle was fought, is uncertain. Boece sites it by the Water of Doon, but local tradition prefers Coylton on the Water of Coyle or Coilsfield on the River Ayr – whose name, incidentally, seems to derive from the Welsh *aer*, meaning 'battle' or 'slaughter'.

One further speculation is worth considering. Is it possible that the Coyle place-names do not merely commemorate Coel's death? Is it possible, in fact, that Kyle *was* named after him – as Glamorgan (*gwlad Morgan*, 'Morgan's land') was named after its most famous ruler – because it was his original homeland, his own special kingdom among his wider territories?

There is a further good reason why Coel's memory lingered so long in the Ayrshire region: for, of all his lands, southwestern Scotland was the very last to remain in the hands of his British fellow-countrymen. Beating off Pictish and Scottish raids, such as the one in which Coel may have died, the Britons of Strathclyde not only weathered the 7th-century Anglian assault which destroyed their compatriots in Lothian and northern England, but also maintained their independence for four hundred years thereafter. Sometimes in alliance, sometimes at war with the surrounding English, Picts and Scots, with the Britons of Wales and Danish or Norse Vikings; sometimes beleaguered in their fortress of Dumbarton and at other times expanding to reoccupy the old British lands in Cumbria, they held out until, in 1018, Strathclyde was peacefully absorbed into the growing kingdom of united Scotland. Within that kingdom their distinctive customs and Welsh language survived, perhaps, until the 14th century. Local folk-memories of Coel persisted longer still, providing Boece with an incident (however confused by ignorance of the facts and propagandist motives) for his chronicle and honouring the fading memory of 'Coilus King of Britons' until Burns' time, or indeed until the present day.

The English-speaking descendants of the Strathclyde Britons may also have produced the famous rhyme. It is likely enough that they did, though it is also conceivable that they simply annexed to their own special hero an English song about a fictitious Coel of Colchester. The original rhyme may even have referred to a third person, or to no person at all.

Perhaps, indeed, it would be best if we could forget the wretched little rhyme altogether, for it has done the real King Cole – Old Coel the Splendid, founding father of the Men of the North – a great disservice. There is, after all, as much, or rather more, genuine evidence for his existence as there is for that other defender of post-Roman Britain, 'King Arthur'. Yet because his name has happened to pass into nursery rhyme, he has become merely a figure of fun, for too long deprived of his rightful place among the historical heroes of Britain.

CHAPTER FOUR

'Sons of Woden and Champions of Christ'
The Heroes of Anglo-Saxon England

THE SIX HUNDRED and fifty years that separate Roman Britain from medieval England saw the three greatest upheavals in the country's history. First and most momentous was the Anglo-Saxon onslaught between the 5th and the 7th centuries, which utterly destroyed the old Romano-Celtic order and laid the foundations of England, Scotland and Wales; then came the Viking attacks between the 9th and the 11th centuries, almost overwhelming Saxon England and leaving it profoundly changed; and finally the Norman Conquest of 1066–9, giving England a new ruling class and transforming it into a feudal, 'medieval' state. And since heroes are commonly born of crises, it is scarcely surprising that this turbulent period has produced a heavy crop of them. Some – like Alfred, Canute and Hereward the Wake – are still household names, while others – like St Edmund of East Anglia and Wild Edric – now enjoy only local fame, and others again are all but forgotten.

Among these last are numbered most of the heroes of the long wars between Briton and Saxon. We have aleady met some of the British champions of the struggle, and Coel's descendants Owain and Urien had their counterparts in the southlands, like them now commemorated only in Welsh verse or confused legend. Men such as Gereint of Devon, who died fighting the Saxons, apparently near Portsmouth in the 480s:

> Before Gereint, the foe's affliction
> I saw white horses shinned in red blood
> And after the battle-cry, bitter graves
> At Llongborth was Gereint slain
> Heroes of the land of Devon
> Before they fell, they slew.

Or Cynddylan of Shropshire, 'the bright buttress of the borderland' and the last British prince to rule east of Severn, slain by the Mercian Angles who sacked his stronghold in the 650s:

> Stand out maids, and look on the land of Cynddylan,
> The court of Pengwern is ablaze; alas for the young who mourn their brothers . . .
> The hall of Cynddylan is dark tonight,
> Without fire, without bed; I weep awhile and then fall silent . . .
> The eagle of Eli, loud his scream tonight,
> Sated with gory drink; the heart's blood of Cynddylan the Fair . . .

About them all – as about the greatest of them all, 'the incomparable Arthur' – hangs an atmosphere of noble defeat, of a fight against hopeless odds and a cause lost. For by the end of the 7th century only Wales, Cornwall and Strathclyde remained British: the rest of southern Britain had passed to the peoples whom history books call Angles, Saxons and Jutes, and whom the Scots and Welsh lump together as 'saesneg' or 'sassenachs' (Saxons), but who soon came to call themselves simply 'the English'.

These English, of course, had heroes of their own: indeed, they were positively obsessed by them, and hero-tales long dominated their culture, serving at once as entertainment, inspiration and instruction. Tacitus reports that the only kind of history known to their 1st-century Germanic ancestors was 'ancient songs about gods and heroes' – if the two were really distinguishable – from whose 'descendants' they habitually chose their rulers. So too did the English, the dynasty of the East Saxons claiming descent from the war-god Seaxnot while the kings of the Northumbrians, Mercians, East Angles, Kentish and South and West Saxons all traced their pedigrees from sky-father Woden – who, through Henry I's Saxon queen, must thus be the 'ancestor' of the present royal family.

Pagan gods apart, the earliest English settlers brought with them tales of semi-historical heroes like Offa, a 4th-century ruler of the Anglian home-land in southern Denmark, whose construction of a famous boundary line may have helped inspire his namesake and descendant Offa of Mercia (757–96) to build his great Dyke along the Welsh border; and Beowulf the monster-killer, whose saga still survives, and who may have ruled in Sweden during the early 6th century. Soon, too, the invaders had heroes of their own, the chieftains who had led them across the North Sea and conquered the Britons: and though their deeds are now known only from hints preserved in later annals, there is little doubt that Hengest, Aelle, Cerdic and Ida – respectively the traditional founders of Kent, Sussex, Wessex and Northumbria – were once celebrated in songs declaimed in the mead-hall or chanted on the road to battle.

The sagas of these great men are forgotten, but a host of lesser heroes of the English conquest may well be unwittingly commemorated daily, whenever a place-name is mentioned. For while the Celts of the north and west almost invariably called their settlements after a natural feature or a Christian centre – as in Inverness (mouth of the River Ness), Rhayader (waterfall) or Llangollen (St Collen's church) – the incoming pagan English often named theirs after the first of their race to live there. Many such names, like Tottenham (Totta's *ham* or 'homestead') have no deeper significance than the modern 'Smith's farm' or 'Jones's place': but others, generally occurring in the southern and eastern counties first occupied by the English, apparently perpetuate the name of the leaders of the small groups of early settlers – perhaps no more than a single boatload – which collectively made up the greater kingdoms.

These are the place-names containing the element *-ing*, meaning 'the followers, dependants, people or dynasty of . . .' a certain chieftain. Thus the followers of Haesta ('the violent one'), the Haestingas, gave their name (and indirectly his) to Hastings in Sussex, while the folk of Reada ('the red') named Reading (Berkshire) and those of Berica named Barking (Essex). Thus, too, we have names like Welling*borough* (Northampton-shire), Bassing*bourn* (Cambridgeshire), Redling*field* (Suffolk), Chidding-*fold* (Surrey), Manning*ford* (Wiltshire), Mading*ley* (Cambridgeshire), Kensing*ton* (London) and Bobbing*worth* (Essex): the 'fortified place', 'stream', 'open land', 'sheep-fold', 'ford', 'clearing', 'village' and 'enclos-ure' of the people of Wendel, Bassa, Raedel, Cidda, Manna, Mada, Cynesige and Bubba. In a very few cases we know something about these men: Cissa, for whom the old Roman town of Noviomagus was renamed 'Cissa's-ceaster', Chichester, was allegedly a son of Aelle, founder of Sussex; while Icel, who gave his name to Icklingham (Suffolk), Ickleton (Cambridgeshire), Ickleford (Hertfordshire) and Hickling (Norfolk and Nottinghamshire), was traditionally an ancestor of the dynasty of Mercia, and the first king of the continental Angles to settle in Britain. For the most part, however, their doings are as obscure as those of Beorma and Snotr ('the wise'), whose folk founded Birmingham and 'Snotingaham', now Nottingham.

Whether or not the descendants of Snotr's original followers told stories about the man who had given them their name, tales of pagan heroes certainly remained unshakeably popular long after the English had been converted to Christianity, and in the late 8th century even the holy monks of Lindisfarne were reproved for their addiction to them: 'Let the Word of God be read in the refectory. There the scriptural reader should be heard, not the harper; the sermons of the saints, not the songs of the heathen; for what has Ingeld to do with Christ?'

Within a hundred years of this rebuke, however, Ingeld and his fellow-pagans were rapidly being supplemented, though by no means entirely supplanted, by the Christian heroes of the English struggle against the heathen Vikings. Beginning as isolated hit-and-run raids during the 780s – one of the first scattered the hero-loving Lindisfarne monks – Viking attacks became a full-scale invasion in 865, when the Danish 'Great Army' of Ingvar the Boneless began the systematic plunder of England. After ravaging Northumbria and the north Midlands, in November 869 they rode their stolen horses into East Anglia, whose young King Edmund they defeated and captured at 'Haegelisdun' – either Hellesdon by Norwich or somewhere near Hoxne in northeast Suffolk.

According to Abbo of Fleury's account, which allegedly derived from the eyewitness report of Edmund's own armour-bearer, Ingvar then demanded that the king should share his treasure with the Vikings, and henceforth rule as their puppet. When he refused to submit to a pagan master, they tied him to a tree, flogged him, and shot him full of arrows 'like the spines of a hedgehog or the prickles of a thistle'; next they cut the 'blood-eagle' on his back, hacking and bending the ribs away from the spine – a recognized form of ritual sacrifice to Odin; and finally, while he still called on Christ, they hewed off his head and threw it into a dense thorn-thicket. Thus his mourning followers were subsequently unable to find it, until a voice from the bushes was heard to call 'Here, Here, Here': it was the head itself that miraculously spoke, and the searchers discovered it clasped between the paws of a massive white wolf, which had piously guarded it against desecration and which shadowed them until head and body were reunited.

The fame of St Edmund of East Anglia, king and martyr, was widespread within a generation of his death, and his uncorrupted body (a sure sign of sanctity) eventually came to rest at the place now known as Bury St Edmunds, where a great abbey grew up around it. The special protector of sailors and the precursor of St George as the patron of all England, he was no saint to trifle with, as the Danish King Sweyn Forkbeard found out in 1014: a few hours after refusing to exempt Bury from tribute, Sweyn died suddenly and in agony at Gainsborough in Lincolnshire, crying out that Edmund had pierced him with a spear.

Still more famous, and a great deal more successful in worldly terms, was Alfred of Wessex, whose kingdom the Great Army attacked in the year following Edmund's martyrdom. Born at Wantage in Berkshire in 849, Alfred had all the hereditary qualifications of an English hero, being allegedly the fourteenth in direct descent from Cerdic, founder of Wessex, twenty-second from Woden and (to lend his family Christian respectability) thirty-ninth from Noah and fiftieth from Adam himself. His grandfather Egbert, moreover, had made Wessex the dominant English kingdom, while his father Aethelwulf had in 851 won a famous victory over 350 shiploads of Vikings 'with the greatest slaughter of the heathen men that ever we heard tell of'.

His parents' favourite son, Alfred was marked out for special distinction at the tender age of four, when he figureheaded an embassy to Rome and was not only confirmed by the Pope in person but invested with an honorary Consulship – a ceremony which the English mistook for a special kind of coronation, though as yet three elder brothers stood between Alfred and the throne. But by the time the Vikings invaded Wessex in the late autumn of 870 two of these had died childless, and the third, King Aethelred, was already ailing, with Alfred, then about 20 years old, acting as his lieutenant.

Following its usual custom, the Great Army established itself in a heavily fortified camp, near Reading, intending to ravage the surrounding country until it was massively bribed to go elsewhere. But the West Saxons were made of sterner stuff than their neighbours: after scattering a raiding party they unsuccessfully assaulted the enemy stockade, and when the Vikings moved to Ashdown in Berkshire, Aethelred and Alfred marched to assail them again. It was Alfred's battle. For while his brother stayed praying in his tent, refusing to cut short his morning Mass, he led an uphill charge and held the Great Army in desperate battle round a stunted thorn tree until the king's troops arrived to even the balance and eventually turn the tide: by the evening the Danes were in full flight for Reading, leaving one of their kings and five of their earls dead on the field.

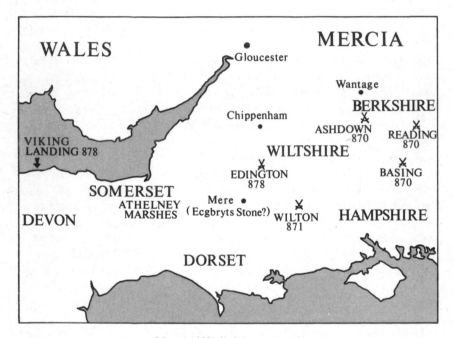

Map 5 Alfred's Wessex campaigns

The Army had suffered its first real reverse since coming to England, but it was by no means ready either to admit defeat or to leave Wessex. Two weeks after Ashdown it sallied forth to rout the royal brothers at Basing in Hampshire, and early in 871, after another victory, it was heavily reinforced by a new 'Summer Host' fresh from Scandinavia. At this critical juncture Aethelred died and Alfred became king: mustering what small force he still could, he attacked the combined Viking array at Wilton in Wiltshire, only to be defeated yet again by their favourite tactic of the 'feigned flight'. The exhausted West Saxons could do no more: worn out by nine full-scale battles in less than a year, 'besides forays innumerable', they at last agreed to pay the customary bribe, and the Army rode away to consolidate its hold over the rest of England.

Before long, indeed, Wessex was the only English kingdom free from Viking sway: elsewhere parties of the invaders were preparing to settle down permanently, and it was a considerably smaller Great Army – now commanded by Guthrum – that late in 875 renewed the assault on Wessex. During the next two years, therefore, Alfred could press the invaders so closely that they achieved little, and in autumn 877 he hustled them, unbribed, out of his kingdom to Gloucester in Mercia.

Alfred's perseverance, it seemed, had triumphed, but the worst crisis was yet to come. For, early in January 878, Guthrum launched a sudden surprise attack on Chippenham in Wiltshire, where the king had apparently been spending Christmas with only his family and immediate retainers: his soldiers, scattered all over Wessex, were also keeping the feast comfortably at home, and since the Army had never before been known to operate in midwinter, their relaxation was perfectly justified. But this was no ordinary raid: it was specifically designed to eliminate Alfred, the essential mainspring of West Saxon resistance, and then to colonize rather than merely plunder his kingdom. And in this it all but succeeded, for though Alfred himself narrowly managed to escape capture, the greater part of his subjects promptly capitulated to the Danes or fled despairingly overseas.

The last surviving English king, meanwhile, 'accompanied by a handful of noblemen and a small band of soldiers and servants, was dwelling amid the woods and swamps of Somerset in great tribulation and anxiety. For they lacked the bare necessities of life, and had to subsist entirely on what they could carry off during their frequent raids on the pagans, or even on those Englishmen who had submitted to the enemy.' Then, at this darkest hour, came a good omen: a Viking party, landing on the north coast of Devon – which perhaps intended to take Alfred's Somerset refuge from the rear – was cut to pieces by local levies, and the magic heathen banner called 'the Raven' (probably the very one that had led the original Great Army to Britain) was captured.

Heartened, Alfred began preparations to turn his raids into a full-scale counter-attack: at Easter 878, taking a leaf from the enemy's book, he built himself a fortified camp on Athelney, 'the island of the princes', in the midst of the then impassable marshes south of Bridgwater. From here, while continuing to harry the Vikings, he sent out messengers to the loyal

English of the nearby shires; and when seven weeks later he rode to the mustering place at 'Ecgbryt's Stone' (somewhere near Mere) he was rapturously greeted by the men of Somerset, Wiltshire and western Hampshire, 'as if – after so many troubles – he had come back from the dead'. With these he marched northwards to attack the Danes at Edington in Wiltshire: we know no details of the battle that followed, but it proved to be the decisive English victory of the war. At the end of it the beaten Vikings fled back to their fort at Chippenham with Alfred hot on their heels, and after a two-week siege – 'worn out by hunger, cold, fear, and at last by total despair' – they begged for peace. Not only did they swear to leave Wessex, offering an unlimited number of hostages without taking any in return – terms they had never been known to offer before – they also agreed to something far more revolutionary: their leaders accepted baptism, and Alfred himself stood godfather to Guthrum. Henceforth, the pirate chief would be a Christian king, bound by the same rules as his English neighbours.

Thus, in less than six months, Alfred's tenacity had completely turned the tables on his enemies. But his wars were very far from over: during the remaining twenty years of his reign he had to cope with two fresh Viking armies, and fight a long and arduous campaign which lasted from 892 until 896 and ranged from Kent through East Anglia to the Welsh borders. Its high point was the capture of an entire Danish fleet, trapped in the Hertfordshire Lea by a fortified boom stretched across the river. Meanwhile, to ensure that Wessex could never again be overthrown by a sudden land attack, he initiated a planned scheme of national defence, so that eventually no village from Devon to Sussex would be more than twenty miles from a permanently garrisoned stronghold. To guard his coasts against casual raiders, moreover, he designed ships which could take on and beat the Vikings at sea: longer, swifter and steadier than the enemy vessels, 'they were built neither after the Friesian nor the Danish pattern, but as it seemed to the king that they would be most serviceable'.

Small wonder, then, that 'all the English peoples gave him their allegiance, save only those that were in captivity to the Danes'. By showing that the hitherto invincible Vikings could be beaten, he united not only West Saxons and Mercians, but even the suspicious Welsh against the common enemy; and when he died in 899, Christian England, though still on the defensive, was no longer in danger of total submergence.

In the Viking lands, where he was seen principally as a formidable general and an unrivalled war-leader, Alfred was surnamed 'the Mighty'; and since at least the 17th century British historians have frequently called him 'the Great'. But his older nickname of 'England's Darling', recorded by Layamon in the 12th century, is perhaps more revealing than either of these formal titles. For contemporary Englishmen did not only revere him as a great and mighty king, they also loved him as a good and wise man, and the *Life* written by his friend Bishop Asser – the earliest surviving biography of a British monarch – helps us to see why. From it we learn that, despite his heredity, Alfred was not cast in a physically heroic mould: he seems indeed to have been rather frail, and was beset all his life by illness, exchanging the painful and humiliating piles of his youth for a mysterious disease, perhaps some form of anxiety neurosis, which baffled his physicians, but 'from whose agonies, or the gloom thrown over him by fear of their approach, he was never free for a single hour'.

Yet neither 'the daily afflictions of his body' nor the demands of war and government could distract him from the pursuit of knowledge, which had been his passion since the day when, as a small boy, he had won a volume of Saxon poems from his mother by learning its contents by heart. Not content with reading his own language, a rare enough ability in a layman, he set himself with the aid of the scholars he gathered around him to learn Latin, an accomplishment almost unknown even among contemporary churchmen, for the once-famous culture of the English had suffered a catastrophic decline during the Viking onslaught. Determined upon its revival, Alfred therefore began at the age of forty-five to translate five 'most necessary' Latin books on history, geography, philosophy and the duties of priests into the tongue used by his subjects: in its own way the task was every bit as daring and heroic as any of his campaigns, for no one had ever before attempted to use English prose for the transmission of anything more than the simplest of ideas. Copies of his translations were then sent out to all the major ecclesiastical centres in his dominions, accompanied, to emphasize the preciousness of the knowledge they contained, by an ornate golden *pugillarius* or pointer.

The 'Alfred Jewel', found in 1693 at North Newton in Somerset, near the monastery the king founded at Athelney in thanksgiving for his deliverance from the Danes, is most probably the terminal of one of these pointers. Exquisitely decorated with a personification of Sight and Hearing, it is inscribed 'Alfred had me made', and may well have been designed by the king himself. Certainly Alfred's extraordinary range of expertise was by no means confined even to soldiering, translation and warship-building, and Asser reports that he not only instructed his goldsmiths, falconers and kennel-masters in their crafts, but also devised 'new kinds of mechanical engines' to help build the towns, palaces and fortresses which he raised or restored 'in nobler and more splendid form than his ancestors had dreamt of'. His most famous inventions, indeed, were the product of his need to regulate an astonishingly crowded life: for it was Alfred who first hit on the idea of telling time by burning marked candles of standard size and, when draughts made these 'candle-clocks' burn irregularly, of enclosing them in boxes of finely-planed transparent horn, the prototypes of the horn-lanterns familiar until the 19th century.

It is not surprising, then, that folktales about Alfred's wisdom persisted until long after the Norman Conquest. So too did memories of his just laws; and William of Malmesbury, writing in the 1120s, relates the charming but unlikely story that when the king had golden arm-rings hung up at public crossroads to demonstrate the strength of his peace, no one dared to steal them. He also reports that illiterate countrymen could still proudly point out the scenes of Alfred's exploits, and legends naturally clustered thickest about Athelney. It was there, according to Malmesbury, that St Cuthbert appeared in a vision to promise the king ultimate victory, backing up his assurances with a miraculously plentiful catch of fish; and thence, shortly before the battle of Edington, that Alfred set out disguised as a wandering minstrel, to penetrate the Danes' camp and learn their secret plans. This last story had, ironically enough, previously been told of the Norse-Irish Viking Olaf Cuaran – who is said to have used a similar disguise to spy on the English before the battle of Brunanburh in 937 – and it would later be attached to several other heroes.

But the most famous of the Athelney tales, and indeed the best known of all the legends of Anglo-Saxon England, belongs to Alfred alone. When hiding from the Danes, it relates, he took shelter one day in the hovel of a cowherd, where

the woman of the house, the cowherd's wife, was preparing to bake some cakes. While the king sat by the hearth, busy tending his bow and arrows and other weapons of war, the cakes began to scorch: seeing this, the wretched woman ran quickly in and snatched them from the fire, scolding the indomitable king and saying, 'Hey fellow, can't you see the cakes are burning? Why didn't you turn them over? You'll be quick enough to swallow them when they're ready.' The miserable woman little thought she was speaking to the famous King Alfred, who had fought so many battles against the pagans and gained so many victories over them.

Another early version makes the owner of the hovel a pigman, and shows Alfred obediently turning over the cakes at his orders.

Though this story was apparently not written down until the 11th century (when the version given above appeared in the *Annals of St Neots*) it may well have been orally current in Alfred's lifetime. It may even have been one of the anecdotes which, says Malmesbury, the king himself enjoyed telling his courtiers during his later years, and it is not difficult to imagine this very humble and human figure playing down his own heroism with a self-mocking tale about the mighty king who could not manage the simplest of domestic tasks. Certainly it reflects the special place that Alfred has always had in English tradition, for it is a story that could only have been repeated about a hero who inspired love as well as reverence or

'*King Alfred when sheltered by the Neat Herds Wife
abused for letting her Cakes burn.*'

admiration: it could never have been told about Boudica, Hereward, or even Robin Hood. For all his great achievements, therefore, it is perhaps fitting that Alfred should now best be remembered for burning some cakes.

Operating from the strong base which Alfred had created in Wessex, his successors – notably his son Edward the Elder, his daughter Aethelflaeda (the formidable 'Lady of the Mercians'), and his grandson the magnificent Aethelstan – went over to the offensive against the invaders: and by the reign of his great-grandson Edgar (959–75) the kings of Wessex had reconquered the Viking-occupied territories and become undoubted kings of all England. But the land they ruled was now not so much English as Anglo-Danish; for all the north and east of it, from the Tees to Watling Street, had long been settled by the descendants of the Viking armies. Within this 'Danelaw', and especially in Yorkshire and round the 'Five Boroughs' of Derby, Nottingham, Leicester, Lincoln and Stamford, where Danish colonization had been most intensive, Scandinavian influence and Scandinavian law and custom prevailed over English.

There, too, tales were told of specifically Scandinavian folk heroes, and Alfred and the Christian English champions of the Viking wars had their pagan Danish counterparts in men like Ragnar Leatherbreeches and his

equally notorious sons, the leaders of the first Great Army and the mur-
derers of St Edmund:

> Ingvar and Ubba, Beorn was the third,
> Leatherbreeches' sons, hated of Christ.

The by now Christian Anglo-Danes, however, compensated for the pride
they took in their heathen ancestors by awarding them suitably horrible
and exemplary deaths: Beorn, for instance, was allegedly swallowed up by
the earth, horse and all, as he rode away from raping a whole convent-full
of nuns.

The rank and file of the Great Army, like the earliest English colonists,
are commemorated all over the Danelaw by place-names, the Scandinavian
'thorps', 'bys' and 'tofts' ('outlying hamlets', 'villages' and 'homesteads')
which mark their settlements. Nothing more than their names is known of
most of them – Sweyn of Swainsthorpe in Norfolk, Thormod of Thormanby
in Yorkshire, or Knapi of Knaptoft in Leicestershire – but legends still
survive about the originators of a few Danelaw towns.

The brothers Thorgils Skarthi ('the Hare-Lipped') and Kormak Fleinn
('the Javelin'), for example, the traditional founders of Scarborough and
Flamborough in Yorkshire, are recorded in the Old Norse *Kormak's Saga*
as 'the most splendid of men. They fought in Ireland, Wales, England and
Scotland . . . and there was no one in all the Army to match Kormak for
strength and courage.' By the time 'Scardyng' appears in the 14th-century
chronicle of Robert Mannyng of Bourne, however, he has become a
British giant. Another figure, Grim, honoured on Grimsby's seal as the
founder of the ancient Lincolnshire borough, represents a less piratical
aspect of the Scandinavian settlement. According to the medieval *Lay of
Havelok the Dane*, he fled to England with the infant Havelok, heir to the
Danish throne, built a house from the wreckage of his ship – round which
the town grew up – and lived there as a fisherman and salt-trader.

Medieval legend – and Shakespeare's *Macbeth* – also remembered the
mighty Danish Earl Siward, who ruled turbulent Northumbria in the
decades before the Norman Conquest; and though he endowed churches
like a Christian nobleman, there is no doubt that Siward was at heart a
stark Viking warrior and quite unreformed, one of the last of his breed in
England. A giant of a man, it was said that his grandfather was a great
white bear, and that his father concealed bear's ears beneath his helmet:
in his youth the earl had slain dragons in the Orkneys, and he fought
beneath a magic raven banner called 'Landwaster'. His attitude to death,
too, was completely Viking. Hearing that his son had fallen in battle, he
remarked only that he rejoiced that the boy's wounds were all in front:
and when his own time came, scorning 'a cow's death' in his bed, he
struggled up and armed himself, to die on his feet with mailshirt on back,

shield on arm and sword in hand. History records that he was then buried
in church, but local tradition maintained that he was laid in a mound like
a heathen king, and still points out a prehistoric barrow near York as
'Siward's Howe'.

Siward, like many of his 11th-century Anglo-Danish contemporaries,
was not a descendant of Alfred's opponents, but part of a second and
reinforcing wave of Scandinavian incomers. For the reign of the unpopular
and incompetent Aethelred Unraed – not, as the name is usually translated 'the Unready', but 'the No-counsel', the Foolish – saw a new series
of Viking attacks, culminating in the full-scale invasion (1013–16) which
displaced the Wessex dynasty and annexed England to the northern
empire of the great Danish King Cnut. These wars also produced new
heroes: foremost among those of the English was Byrhtnoth, the huge old
ealdorman of Essex – when his headless body was exhumed at Ely in 1769,
he was estimated to have been six feet nine inches tall – who fell opposing
a Viking landing at Maldon in 991, his faithful thegns dying to the last
man around him. Their heroism is commemorated in the finest of Anglo-
Saxon battle poems, where one of them declares:

> Thoughts shall be the braver, hearts the bolder
> Courage the keener, as our might lessens.
> Here lies our leader, all for-hewen
> The hero in the dust. Long may he mourn
> Who thinks now to turn from this battle-play.

Many tales were told, too, about Aethelred's son Edmund Ironside, who
fought long and bravely, if inconclusively, against Cnut. In the end he
suggested settling the fate of England by single combat: according to
contemporary sources Cnut refused, but Henry of Huntingdon and other
post-Norman Conquest writers believed that the duel was actually fought,
and drawn, on an island in the Severn. Certainly the two kings eventually
agreed to divide the country between them, but a few months later, in
November 1016, Edmund died in the prime of life, and his rival took all.

Edmund's sudden and premature end – about which we have no
reliable information – was soon blamed by legend on one of the now-
unsung villains of British history, Edric Streona – Edric 'the Grasping',
the Shropshire-based Earl of Mercia. This 'artful dissembler', 'the refuse
of mankind and the shame of the English', had already changed sides at
least twice during the war (generally in the middle of battles) and had
without doubt murdered several of his fellow-noblemen. William of
Malmesbury heard that he had bribed Edmund's servants to 'drive an
iron hook into the king's posterior, as he was sitting down for a necessary
reason', while Huntingdon relates that Edric's own son 'lurking by night
in the king's house of evacuation', did the deed with 'a very sharp knife'.

Most extraordinary of all, however, is the account of the 12th-century Norman writer, Geoffrey Gaimar.

> Edric had an engine made
> A bow which could not miss . . . if anything touched the string.
> Where this bow was prepared, he built a new hut
> A privy house they called it: for that reason men went there
> The king was directed there in the night . . .
> As soon as he sat on the seat, the arrow struck him in the fundament
> It flew as far as the lungs, so no man could see even the feathers.

It is pleasing to learn that Cnut subsequently had Edric executed: one story tells that, having promised to set him higher than all the English, he stuck his head on the highest tower in London.

Cnut himself, now the best-remembered figure of the period, became a hero not only of the Anglo-Danes but also of the English, for though he gave much land to his Scandinavian followers he proved a just king and a good friend to the Church. Ballads about the splendid wedding of his daughter to the German emperor were still popular in the 13th century, but the characteristic that the favourite tale underlined was not his great power as ruler of England, Denmark and Norway, but his Christian humility. Here is the earliest known recorded version, that of Huntingdon:

When Cnut was at the height of his glory, he ordered his throne to be set on the sea-shore as the tide was rising, and said to the incoming sea: 'You are at my command, and the land where I sit is mine: there is none who dares resist my power. I therefore order you not to come up onto my land, nor to presume to wet the limbs or clothes of your lord.' The tide, however, rose in its usual manner, and without reverence soaked the king's feet and legs. He, jumping back, then declared, 'Thus may all the inhabitants of the earth see how vain and worthless is the power of kings. Indeed, I am not even worthy to bear the name of king before Him at whose behest heaven, earth, and sea obey the eternal laws.'

Therefore King Cnut would never afterwards allow a golden crown to be put on his head: rather he would always place it on that of the image of Christ which hung on the cross.

Gaimar sites the story on the Thames at Westminster, while later sources (which attribute Cnut's action to a desire to rebuke the endless flattery of his courtiers) place it at Gainsborough in Lincolnshire – probably due to confusion with Cnut's proclamation as king there after his father Sweyn had fallen foul of St Edmund.

Cnut's two sons followed him in turn, but both died without issue; and in 1042 Alfred's dynasty was restored, by popular acclaim, in the person of Aethelred's only surviving son, Edward the Confessor, a king revered as a saint rather than a hero. When he too died childless in January 1066, however, the succession stood wide open. Edward's own declared choice was undoubtedly his second cousin Duke William of Normandy, the ruler of perhaps the most aggressive and expansionist race in contemporary Europe, but there were also two Scandinavian claimants, both of whom regarded themselves as the true heirs of Cnut. One, Cnut's nephew King Sweyn Estrithson of Denmark, was temporarily too preoccupied by troubles at home to press his claim, but the other, the formidable King Harald Hardrada of Norway, was only too ready to enforce his by invasion, as indeed was William of Normandy. Faced with this double threat of renewed foreign domination, the English noblemen round the Confessor's deathbed acted quickly. Passing over the young and untried Edgar Atheling, Edmund Ironside's grandson, they immediately 'elected' as their king the most powerful man and the best war-leader in England, Harold Godwinson. Though he had not a drop of royal blood in his veins, and though he had (perhaps unwillingly) sworn allegiance to William two years before, Harold was crowned on the very day of Edward's funeral.

Both William and Hardrada at once began preparing invasion fleets, and Harold, judging the Normans the more dangerous threat, spent the summer of 1066 watching the Channel coast. The chances of wind and weather, however, dictated that Hardrada would arrive first, sailing up the Yorkshire Ouse and routing Earl Edwin of Mercia and Earl Morcar of Northumbria in a bloody fight outside York on 20 September. Meanwhile, Harold was marching at top speed from the south, and five days later he suddenly attacked the unprepared Norsemen at Stamford Bridge in the East Riding, cutting them to pieces and slaying Hardrada. Then, forty-eight hours later, the wind changed direction, carrying William's ships to an unopposed landing at Pevensey in Sussex on 28 September. Harold cannot have heard the news until at least 1 October, when he was almost certainly still at York, yet by the 6th his victorious but battered army had, amazingly, covered the 190 miles to London. On the 11th, having waited only for the most immediately available reinforcements, he set out again for the Hastings area, where on the evening of the 13th his worn-out soldiers encamped on the hill of the 'Hoar Apple Tree'. He clearly hoped to surprise William as he had surprised Hardrada, but the next morning the Normans struck first, apparently before the English were properly arrayed: all day long there was 'great slaughter on both sides', but by nightfall Harold's men were dead or in flight.

Harold himself fell – either pierced through the eye by a chance arrow or cut down by mounted knights – at a spot later marked by the high altar of Battle Abbey. Almost at once legends began to cluster about him. Contemporary Norman chroniclers declare that William refused to give Harold's body to his mother, though she offered him its weight in gold, and instead had him buried on the sea-shore, under an epitaph mocking his ill luck with the winds:

> Here, by the duke's command, lies Harold the king
> So that he may stay to guard the coast.

The canons of Harold's recently founded church of Waltham Holy Cross in Essex, however, maintained that his mutilated corpse had been made over to them, though they were able to find it only with the help of his mistress Edith 'Swan's-neck', who identified it by 'certain secret marks'. They then bore it off to Waltham, where Harold's tomb is still shown: perhaps his body was really transferred there from its sea-shore grave.

Soon after the battle, however, and certainly within a century of it, a quite different story began circulating about Harold's fate: that he did not die at Hastings, but survived for many years in obscurity. The fullest version, written around 1216, relates that he was carried badly wounded from the field to Winchester, where he was secretly tended for two years by 'a Saracen woman most skilled in surgery'. Having recovered (though, like the pagan god Woden, lacking an eye) he travelled to Germany and Denmark fruitlessly seeking allies against the Normans, and then became a penitent pilgrim in expiation of his broken oath of allegiance to William. After long incognito wanderings through Kent and the Welsh borders, he was directed by a heavenly voice to St John's church at Chester, where he died at a great age following a deathbed confession of his true identity. A Welsh chronicle, moreover, declared that his incorrupt body was discovered at Chester in 1332, while a 15th-century annalist heard that he had conversed there with Henry I in 1121, when he would have been close on a hundred years old. The whole story is, of course, pure fantasy, the product of a sudden and unexpected defeat and a refusal to believe in the death of heroes which has many parallels elsewhere. Just so, for instance, did many 16th-century Scots refuse to believe that their hero-King James IV had really fallen on the disastrous field of Flodden, holding instead that he had been rescued by four horsemen, to dwell in hiding until happier times.

The Norman Conquest of England, of which Hastings was the beginning rather than the end, continues even now to stir up violent emotions. Since at least the Civil War – when some Parliamentarians blamed all the social ills of England on the 'Norman Yoke', the feudal system imposed by William the Conqueror – and particularly in the High Victorian period, many have championed the 'Saxon' cause. Pre-Conquest England, they hold, was almost an ideal nation, the abode of a high-minded, liberty-loving and (somehow) Protestant people, who were unfairly defeated and cruelly enslaved by tyrannical Norman lackeys of the Pope. Others, fewer and more recently, maintain that pre-Conquest England was a decadent, even moribund state, an old-fashioned Scandinavian backwater riven by the squabbles of English and Anglo-Danes and of over-mighty noblemen, in sore need of reform and modernization by the forward-looking

Normans. The truth probably lies, as usual, somewhere between these two extremes, but that it lies nearer the latter seems to be borne out by the national collapse that followed William's victory, a collapse reflected in the mournful phrases of the demoralized Anglo-Saxon Chronicler: 'but always, when some initiative should have been taken, there was delay from day to day until matters went from bad to worse, as everything did in the end . . . for God would not remedy matters because of our sins.'

The southern English magnates at first reacted to the news of defeat by proclaiming young Edgar Atheling their new monarch: but as William marched virtually unopposed round London, devastating a wide sweep of countryside and taking towns without a blow, their resolve swiftly turned to capitulation, and on Christmas Day 1066 the duke was crowned King of England in Westminster Abbey. By the following spring he felt secure enough to return to Normandy, leaving his new realm in the care of his half-brother Odo and his friend William Fitz Osbern: his 7000 or 30 Normans had, it seemed, conquered England by a single battle. As yet, however, he actually controlled only the southeast, the district whose morale and fighting capacity had been most damaged by Hastings: but the men of the north were beginning to recover from their mauling by Hardrada, while those of the western shires and of the remoter parts of East Anglia had scarcely had time to become involved at all in the whirlwind campaigns of autumn 1066. It was from these last areas, during the next four years, that the resistance to the Normans was to come. Had such resistance been somehow orchestrated into one concerted and unanimous movement, William might well even now have been pushed back across the Channel. Instead it was sporadic, local and uncoordinated, and thus foredoomed to failure: yet its leaders were long remembered.

It began, significantly, in the one part of England which had experienced Norman landlords in the years before 1066, the Welsh border counties of Herefordshire and Shropshire. There, during the latter part of his reign, the Confessor had settled a few Norman knights, encouraging them to build castles at Hereford and elsewhere as bulwarks against the ever-troublesome Welsh. These alien fortresses, the first of their kind in England but soon to become the widespread instruments and symbols of Norman oppression, were much resented by the local Mercian English, and still more so was the high-handed behaviour of their 'foreign' garrisons who, according to the *Anglo-Saxon Chronicle* for 1051, 'inflicted all the injuries and insults they possibly could on the king's men [the English] in that region'.

By 1066 the most powerful of these border Englishmen was 'Edric surnamed "the Wild" [*guilda*]' – which the chronicler latinizes as *Sylvaticus*, 'the Forester' – 'the nephew of that pestilential magnate Edric Streona, that is "the Grasping"'. This Edric 'Salvage' is recorded by *Domesday Book* as having held manors all over both counties, but his lands were concentrated in the steep and barren hills of southwest Shropshire – the Long Mynd, Stiperstones and Clun Forest ranges – and in neighbouring northwest Herefordshire, around Wigmore: he also apparently owned the adjacent and still more inaccessible Welsh upland district of Maelienydd, west of Knighton in modern Powys. His stronghold, indeed, was the very area where Caratacus probably made his last stand a thousand years earlier.

According to the Shropshire-born Norman chronicler Ordericus Vitalis, Wild Edric was one of those who formally submitted to William immediately after his coronation, being honourably confirmed in his estates. If this is true Edric must quickly have changed his mind, for the Worcester version of the *Anglo-Saxon Chronicle* records that in 1067 'Edric the Wild and the Welsh rose in revolt and attacked the garrison [*castelmenn*] of Hereford and inflicted heavy losses on them.' Florence of Worcester provides more details:

There lived at this time a very powerful thegn, Edric called 'the Forester', the son of Aelfric brother of Edric Streona. Because he scorned to submit to the king, his lands were frequently ravaged by the garrison of Hereford and by Richard Fitz Scrob: but whenever they raided his territories, they lost many of their knights and men-at-arms. Therefore, having summoned to his aid the princes of the Welsh, namely Bleddyn and Rhiwallon, this same Edric, about the feast of the Assumption of St Mary [15 August 1067], devastated Herefordshire as far as the bridge over the River Lugg and carried away much plunder.

It looks, then, as if Edric refused from the outset to accept William's rule, and his attitude may well have been encouraged by a long-standing rivalry with pre-Conquest Norman settlers like Richard Fitz Scrob of Richard's Castle near Ludlow. These Normans, emboldened by the success of their fellow-countrymen elsewhere, therefore attacked his lands, but suffered a number of bloody reverses. Not content with this, Edric called in his Welsh neighbour Rhiwallon of Powys and Rhiwallon's brother Bleddyn of Gwynedd in northwest Wales, both former allies of King Harold, and counter-raided Norman-held lowland Herefordshire, penetrating as far as the Lugg bridge at Leominster or even to that near Hereford, though there is no evidence that he sacked the city itself before retiring to his upland fastness.

Nor is there any direct evidence about what happened next, though it is clear that Edric remained defiant, and that the Normans were thoroughly alarmed by the alliance between their English and Welsh enemies. The king's return from Normandy in December 1067 allowed his regent William Fitz Osbern – whom Ordericus calls 'the first and greatest of the oppressors of the English people', and who had already been made Earl of Hereford – to devote his energies to the borders. Attracting free-lance Norman adventurers to his service by offers of generous pay and promises

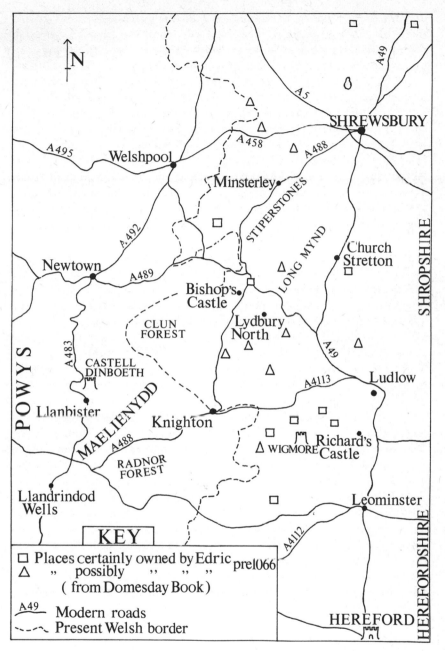

Map 6 The Edric country

of a maximum fine of 7 shillings for even the gravest offences, he used them to garrison a chain of new castles along the fringes of the hill country, including one at Wigmore, on the very edge of Edric's lands and perhaps intended as a base for their conquest.

In the autumn of 1069, however, the Normans were distracted by a far more serious threat. The men of Northumbria, having twice rebelled and twice been defeated, decided at last to offer the crown of England to King Sweyn Estrithson of Denmark. When his fleet – 300 shiploads of Danes, Norwegians, Poles and even pagan Lithuanians – appeared in the Humber it was enthusiastically greeted by a great force of English and Anglo-Danes, and the combined host marched to the taking of York. William moved northwards at once, but as he did so the news from York sparked off revolts behind him. Somerset and Dorset, Devon and Cornwall were up in arms, the Mercians rose at Stafford, while in the borders, says Ordericus, 'The Welsh and the men of Cheshire besieged the king's castle at Shrewsbury, aided by the townsmen under Edric the Wild, that powerful and warlike man, and other fierce English.'

Ignoring the Herefordshire fortresses, Edric had issued forth onto the Shropshire plain in support of his old Welsh allies, now reinforced by the still-unconquered Anglo-Danes of Chester and by the oppressed Shrewsbury townsmen. The besiegers may also have hoped for support from the rebels at Stafford, some thirty miles away, but William turned aside from his march to crush these in person, while Fitz Osbern hurried to the relief of Shrewsbury castle. Before he reached it, however, the attackers had burnt the town and dispersed.

Though he had failed in his objective, Edric at least remained undefeated and at liberty. But the southwestern rebels were routed in the field, and much worse was in store for the northerners. First – according to Florence of Worcester – William bribed Jarl Asbiorn, 'to his utter disgrace', to withdraw the Danish fleet to the Humber: we shall hear more of its doings later. Then he utterly and systematically devastated all the northern counties, burning cattle, corn and even ploughs, so that some survivors turned to cannibalism and those who could sold themselves into slavery for food. In the early months of 1070 he turned southwards, still burning and ravaging, into the northwest Midlands, taking Chester and building new castles there and at Shrewsbury and Stafford. By the time he reached Winchester at Easter there was very little fight left in the English; and although Edric's lands were not directly affected it is scarcely surprising that he lost heart in the face of this overwhelming display of strength. At about mid-summer, therefore, 'Edric the Forester, the most vigorous of men . . . was reconciled with King William.'

Two years later, when William led an expedition against Scotland, Florence records that 'he had in his retinue [*in comitatu*] Edric the

Forester'. Possibly Edric was still considered too dangerous to leave in England, but the sense of the words is that his surrender had been favourably received, and that he became a trusted member of the king's bodyguard. It is surprising, then, that by the time *Domesday Book* was compiled in 1087 all his lands had passed to Norman lords, and notably to Ralph Mortimer of Wigmore castle. It may be that Edric had died childless by then (though later legend gave him a son, albeit fathered in very strange circumstances), but it is perhaps more likely that his estates were forfeited after some new revolt against the Normans. Such, at any rate, is implied by the Mortimer family chronicler:

Sir Ralph Mortimer, the most active of warriors, fought in the borderlands, and especially against Edric, the Earl of Shropshire and Lord of Wigmore and Maelienydd, who refused to submit to the Conquest. After long labours he managed to besiege this Edric in the said [Wigmore] castle, obtaining his lands and others on the border by the power of his sword and of fortune . . . Edric he handed over in chains to the king, who condemned him to perpetual imprisonment . . . Mortimer then refortified the stronghold of Dynetha in Maelienydd [perhaps Castell Dinboeth, near Llanbister, Powys] which Edric had built.

If this story refers to the events of 1070 it presents a number of difficulties, for it is hard to understand why or how Edric could have been defending Fitz Osbern's castle of Wigmore, and why his surrender was not then followed by perpetual imprisonment. It is possible, therefore, that it describes a later revolt in 1075, when Fitz Osbern's son Earl Roger suddenly rebelled against William, whom he hoped to depose with English and Danish help: his rising was speedily crushed, and Mortimer, who helped to crush it, was rewarded with many of Roger's estates, including Wigmore. Did Edric join the revolt, did he try but fail to hold Roger's castle of Wigmore, and was it now that he finally lost both lands and liberty? But this is no more than guesswork, and Edric's ultimate fate remains obscure. The Wigmore tale, apparently not recorded until the 15th century, may indeed have been devised merely to glorify the Mortimers by making them triumph over a famous local hero.

A hero, and a remarkably long-lived one, Edric undoubtedly did become. The earliest fable we have about him appears in *De Nugis Curialum*, the 'Book of Courtier's Trifles' compiled in the 1180s by the Herefordshire-born wit and gossip-writer Walter Map.

This is the story of Edric Wild, that is the Forester, so called from his nimbleness of body and his merry words and deeds: a man of great prowess, Lord of Lydbury North [near Bishop's Castle, in southwest Shropshire]. Accompanied only by a page, he was returning in the middle of the night from hunting in the woods when he lost his way. Then he came to a large building on the edge of the forest, which seemed to be the kind of drinking-den which the English have in every parish, and which they call 'Guild-houses'. Coming closer, he noticed lights inside it, and looking within he saw many fine ladies dancing: they were most beautiful to look upon, provocatively clad only in elegant linen shifts, and were taller and nobler than human women. One among them struck the knight especially, for she was outstanding among all the others in face and figure, more desirable than the mistress of any king ... Seeing her, he was wounded to the heart, and could scarcely bear the love-fire kindled by Cupid's darts ... Though he had heard heathen fables about the troops of night-demons and companies of wood-nymphs, and of how they took sudden revenge on those who caught them unawares ... yet Cupid, rightly painted as blind, made him forget all this. Creeping round the house, he found the door, burst in, and caught her whose beauty had caught him: at once all the rest set about him and a fierce struggle followed, but at last he and his page managed to extricate themselves – though not quite scot-free, for their feet and legs had suffered all the damage the teeth and nails of the women could inflict. He took his loved-one with him, and for three days and nights did with her as he wished: but all this while he could get no word from her, though she surrendered passively to his love-making. Then, on the fourth day, she spoke these words: 'Hail, my sweetest one, and hale shall you be, healthy in body and prosperous in your doings, just so long as you do not taunt me either about my sisters from whom you have seized me, or with the place or sacred grove whence I came, or anything to do with it. But on the day you do so you will lose all happiness, and when I am gone you will ceaselessly mourn the loss, until you hasten your own end by your impatience.'

Vowing with every possible assurance to be always firm and faithful in his love, Edric summoned the nobles from far and near, and in this great company he solemnly married her. There reigned in those days William the Bastard [not an insult, but the usual title of the Conqueror] then newly King of England. Hearing of this wonder, and wishing to prove for himself that it was true, he sent for the pair to come to London, where they journeyed with many witnesses ... The lady's beauty, the like of which had never been seen or heard of before, was a convincing proof of her fairy origin, and amid the amazement of all they were sent home again.

Now it happened many turning years later, when Edric returned from hunting at about the third hour of the night, that he sought his wife and could not find her. He called her and had her summoned, and because she was slow to come he said with an angry look 'I suppose it was your sisters that kept you so long?' The rest of his sarcasm was spoken to empty air, for as soon as she heard the word 'sisters' she vanished. Then the young man bitterly regretted his ill-considered and foolish outburst, and at once sought out the place where he had found her, but neither tears nor appeals would bring her back. Day and night he cried out for her, but all in vain, and soon he pined away there for continual sorrow.

He left, however, an heir, his son by her for whom he had died: Aelnoth, a man of great piety and wisdom. When this Aelnoth was somewhat advanced in age, he fell into a palsy and shaking of the head and limbs, which all the doctors pronounced incurable. Certain knowledgeable persons nevertheless told him that he would undoubtedly recover his health if he could somehow get to Rome, where the bodies of the Apostles Peter and Paul were buried. But he replied that he could go nowhere without first presenting himself to St Ethelbert king and martyr, whose parishioner he was. He therefore had himself taken to [St Ethelbert's shrine at] Hereford [cathedral], where during the first night he spent before the martyr's altar he was restored to perfect health, and thereupon in thanksgiving he presented to God and St Ethelbert his whole manor of Lydbury North ... which belongs to this day to the bishopric of Hereford.

We have often heard of demons, incubi and succubi, and of the dangers of mating with them, but rarely or never do we read that the offspring of such unions ended their lives happily, as did this Aelnoth . . .

Set in the midst of Edric's home territory, Map's tale demonstrates the classic propensity of folk heroes for attracting stories that originally had nothing to do with them. For the theme of the disappearing elfin wife is common throughout European folklore, and by recounting it Map was probably indulging in a sly dig at his master Henry II, himself allegedly a descendant of a certain devilish Melusine who vanished through a chapel window when sprinkled with holy water. The 'authenticating' detail about the gift of Lydbury to Hereford (which actually occurred long before the Conquest) was attributed in a well-known local tradition recorded by Gerald of Wales to one Egwin Shaking-head, cured of his palsy in the days of the 8th-century King Offa.

Despite the suggestion that his martial success was due to diabolical aid – perhaps first put about by his baffled Norman opponents – Edric appears here as a normal human being, famous 'for his merry words and deeds'. But by the mid-Victorian era, when the pioneer folklore-collectors Jackson and Burne found tales about him still widespread in Shropshire, Edric had become a supernatural being. A magical fish that lurked in Bomere Pool near Shrewsbury was believed to guard his sword, which it would only give up when his true heir appeared, and his ghost was said to haunt the hills about Church Stretton in the form of a monstrous hound with fiery eyes.

Others held, and perhaps still hold, that Edric never really died, but was condemned to perpetual imprisonment in the lead-mines around the Stiperstones in southwest Shropshire as a punishment for surrendering to the Conqueror.

So there he dwells, with his wife and his whole train. The miners call them the 'Old Men' and sometimes hear them knocking, and wherever they knock the best seams are to be found. Now and then they are permitted to show themselves. Whenever war is going to break out, they ride over the hills in the direction of the enemy's country, and if they appear, it is a sign that the war will be serious.

In confirmation, a miner's daughter maintained that she and her father had seen them riding northwards at Minsterley shortly before the beginning of the Crimean War: her father, who had seen them heading south in Napoleon's time, 'bade her cover her face, all but her eyes, and on no account speak, lest she should go mad'. The whole band was dressed in green and white, the fairy colours, and dark-haired Edric rode a white horse and carried a hunting-horn while his wife – by now named as 'Lady Godda' – had golden locks flowing to her waist. Sightings continue to be reported, if always at one remove: a writer of 1938 had heard of none heralding the First World War, but a book published in 1969 claims apparitions before the Boer War and in 1914, though none in 1939.

The versatile Edric, then, has become a mine-spirit – similar 'Knockers' feature in the lore of Cornish tin-miners – as well as the master of the Wild Hunt, an aerial rout of demons or lost souls frequently heard of in Germanic mythology, where its leader is sometimes Woden and sometimes a female version of him named Gauden or Lady Gode, the guise now assumed by Edric's wife. Elsewhere in England the hunters, who bring death or madness if they are addressed, are headed by King Arthur, 'King Herla' or even, in the southwest, by Sir Francis Drake. Like Arthur and Drake, Edric has also taken on some of the trappings of an undying national hero who returns at times of trouble; but unlike those much-loved leaders his immortality is a punishment for crime, and his wickedness is further implied by his appearance as a black dog, notoriously the shape preferred by Satan or the spirits of evil men. The anthropological significance of these developments is no concern of this book, but Edric's 'perpetual imprisonment' is perhaps an echo of the Mortimer chronicle, while his evil reputation could be due to his being unfairly but understandably blamed for the misdeeds of his uncle and namesake, the deplorable Edric the Grasping. Finally, Edric's recruitment into the realms of Fairy may well owe something to the proximity of his haunts to the Welsh border, for no such transformation has ever been reported of his better-known counterpart in eastern England, Hereward 'the Wake'.

CHAPTER FIVE

'The English Resistance'

Hereward and the Fenland Revolt against William the Conqueror

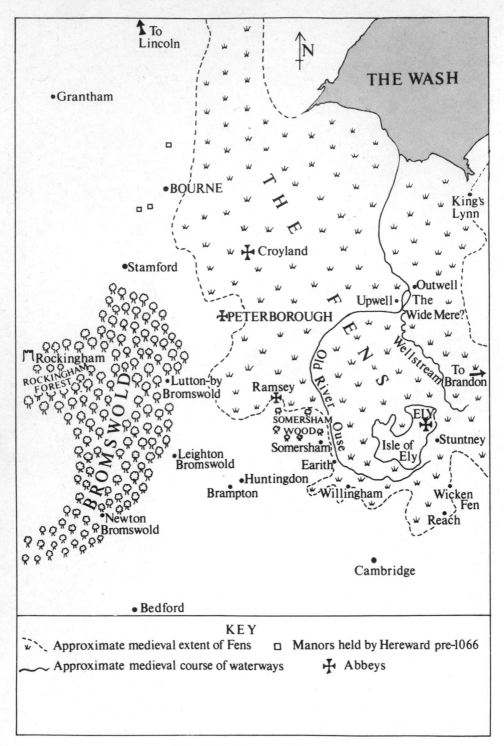

Map 7 *The adventures of Hereward*

THIS HEREWARD – who was originally called 'the Exile', and whose familiar surname of 'the Wake' must await explanation later – appears but briefly in strictly contemporary sources. The Peterborough version of the *Anglo-Saxon Chronicle* reports that the Danish fleet, which we left in the Humber, was joined in the early summer of 1070 by King Sweyn himself. Thereupon a strong detachment from it, commanded by Jarl Asbiorn and Bishop Christian 'and the Danish housecarles with them' sailed down the coast and up the Norfolk Ouse until they reached the marsh-girt Isle of Ely in the Cambridgeshire fens: 'and the English folk of all the fenland came in to join them, for they expected them to conquer the whole land.' Among those English were a certain 'Hereward and his gang', who led the Danes to the sack of the immensely rich monastery of Peterborough on 2 June 1070. Shortly afterwards, however, King William and King Sweyn came to an agreement, and at about midsummer the Danes left Ely to sail home with their loot. But Hereward and the native rebels remained defiant, and for the time being William was too preoccupied with a threat to Normandy to move against them: at some time between the summers of 1070 and 1071, moreover, they were reinforced by Earl Morcar of Northumbria and 'many hundred' other disaffected Englishmen. Then, in the summer or autumn of 1071, the Conqueror surrounded Ely by land and water and attacked it via a causeway built over the fens. At this, Morcar and the majority of the rebels surrendered – 'save Hereward alone and all that would follow him, and these he bravely led to safety.'

Thus Hereward is introduced without any explanation – perhaps the Peterborough chronicler assumed that his readers would already know all about him – while his career is left hanging in mid-air. Within the next century or so, however, an almost embarrassingly copious amount of information (albeit varying somewhat as to reliability or even credibility) appeared concerning his life and exploits. The earliest, written down during the 1120s, comes from Hyde Abbey at Winchester, a place so distant from Ely that its annalist did not apparently know even the name or whereabouts of the 'certain swamp in the middle of England' whence Hereward operated. With grudging respect he tells how 'this low-born man, though very strong in will and body', once took 'a certain castle' by pretending to be dead: his coffin was carried into the castle chapel, whereupon he leapt out fully armed and slaughtered the garrison with the aid of his 'funeral party' – a story told about many other folk heroes.

Nearer home, the Norman Geoffrey Gaimar, writing in Lincolnshire between 1135 and 1147, is both fuller and more complimentary, but the fullest account of all is the *Gesta Herwardi*, 'The Deeds of the Famous Hereward, Exile and Warrior'. This was apparently compiled around the middle of the 12th century by an Ely monk named Richard who claims (in a preface which surely proves him the earliest known English collector of folklore) to have based it on sources contemporary with Hereward himself.

Many of his fellow-monks, he tells us, had wanted to know about Hereward's famous exploits, and had asked whether any writings about him still survived at Ely. 'Wishing to satisfy their curiosity, I sought everywhere, but found only a few scattered pages, some rotted and defaced by damp and others cut up into pieces.' He had despaired of making anything of these until he discovered – 'in the very house whither Hereward returned to find his brother slain' – an English book about him composed by Leofric the Deacon, the hero's own priest. This, however, was incomplete, written in an obscure and antiquated style, and full of tales about 'giants and warriors out of old fables'. 'Therefore, I strove to dig out more, ever hoping for great discoveries and finding next to nothing . . . people were always telling me how a huge book of Hereward's deeds was kept in this or that place, but whenever I went there I found no trace of it.' Discouraged, he abandoned his work, but his brethren eventually persuaded him to try again, and he decided to augment his scanty findings with the reminiscences of the surviving members of Hereward's band, notably Leofric the Black and Siward, now a monk of Bury. It would indeed have been perfectly possible for Richard, as a youngish man, to have talked with the aged followers of his hero.

Our third principal source, the *Liber Eliensis* or 'Ely Book', was compiled before 1189 by a quite different monk also called Richard. He gives a somewhat confused account of the siege of the isle, centred round an abbreviated version of the *Gesta Herwardi*, but also incorporates other local traditions and a section telling the story from the Norman viewpoint. Finally, there is the *Chronicle of Croyland Abbey* in Lincolnshire, which purports to have been written by Hereward's contemporary Abbot Ingulf: though it is now known to be substantially a forgery of the 14th or 15th century, it may well contain genuine traditions of the monastery where the hero was allegedly buried.

According to both the Ely and Croyland chronicles, Hereward's father was an English thegn (a minor nobleman) called Leofric, Lord of Bourne on the fringes of the fenland in south Lincolnshire; while his mother was Aedina or Ediva, a descendant of Earl Oslac of Northumbria. Neither made their mark on history, and it is scarcely surprising that a 15th-century writer (who was followed by the Victorian novelist Charles Kingsley) confused them with the better known Earl Leofric of Mercia and his still more famous wife Lady Godiva, whose naked ride caused such a stir in Coventry. *Domesday Book* shows neither Leofric the thegn nor Hereward as Lord of Bourne before the Conquest – when it was owned by Earl Morcar of Northumbria – but it does record that Hereward was then a minor landowner in south Lincolnshire, holding three small estates around Bourne as a tenant of the abbeys of Peterborough and Croyland. It also proves that, at some unspecified date after 1062, he fled the country.

The most obvious explanation is that he was driven out by the Normans, but the legend insists otherwise. Hereward, says the *Gesta*, was a good-looking fair-haired boy, though he was either cross-eyed or had eyes of different colours (the Latin is not clear) and habitually wore a stern expression: short and stocky, he was agile for his stature, and excelled at wrestling and swordplay. Yet he had his faults: his manners were rough, he was inclined to be over-generous with his father's money, and above all he loved to stir up and pursue feuds both among his youthful companions and his elders in town and village. Wherever he went a riot soon followed, and time and again the exasperated neighbours complained to his father. Time and again, too, his parents rebuked and warned him, but to no avail, and eventually Leofric was forced to beg Edward the Confessor to send the boy abroad. 'And so it befell. Thus it was that Hereward got the nickname of "the Exile", for at the age of eighteen he was banished from his family and his fatherland.'

This unidealized account of Hereward's appearance and graceless youth sound authentic enough, but while his adventures in exile – presumably Leofric the Deacon's 'tales of giants and warriors' – may have some basis of truth, they read like pure romantic fiction, and need be recounted only briefly here.

First, we are told, he journeyed with his faithful servant Martin Lightfoot to the country 'beyond Northumberland' ruled by his godfather Gilbert, who kept captive there 'a monstrous bear, a son of the renowned Bear of Norway [and perhaps a relation of Earl Siward's]. As Danish fables confirm, this had (like its father) a human mind, understanding both the speech of men and their manner of fighting: for its father had once raped a maiden in the woods and got on her King Beorn of Norway.' One day the dangerous pet broke loose, and was about to devour Gilbert's wife and children when Hereward split its skull to the chin, earning undying fame among the peasantry but bitter hatred from the jealous local knights, who ambushed and tried to kill him. He therefore moved on to Cornwall, where he slew a Pictish bully, rescued a princess, and obtained a famous sword; and to Ireland, where he fought a triumphant campaign and learnt of his father's death. Shipwrecked and cast ashore in Flanders, he gained still more martial renown there, winning the mare Swallow, the ugliest yet the swiftest of steeds, and a wife named Torfrida, who was not only rich, beautiful and wise, but also 'most expert in the arts mechanical' – the contemporary term for sorcery.

Meanwhile, the Normans had conquered England, and Hereward, hearing that his fatherland was 'subjected to foreigners and nearly ruined by their exactions', decided it was high time to revisit his home: at this point the *Gesta* becomes both more circumstantial and more credible. Accompanied only by Martin Lightfoot, he reached Bourne at nightfall to find the village in mourning. Concealing his identity, he was told that on the previous day a party of Normans sent by the king had come to seize and plunder his inheritance: his young brother, striving to protect his widowed mother and the family goods, had killed two of them, but the rest cut off the boy's head and mockingly impaled it above the manor gate. And now there was none to avenge him, save only the long-exiled and faraway Hereward. Sighing, the hero retired to bed in a thegn's house, but soon afterwards he heard the sound of harps and viols and of voices singing and laughing – the Normans were celebrating their easy victory in his father's hall.

So Hereward called his servant and dressed, hiding his mailshirt under his tunic and his helmet beneath a black cloak . . . On his way to the feast, which had by now become a drunken revel, he found above the manor gate his brother's head, which he took down, kissed, and wrapped in his mantle. Then he peered in at the hall door, and saw that everyone within was hopelessly drunk, and the soldiers were lying around wrapped in the arms of women. In their midst a minstrel was singing insulting songs against the English, dancing about the plundered house imitating the manners of an Englishman [Anglo-Saxon attitudes?]. When the Norman chief threw him a reward, he began to mock the family of the boy they had killed the previous day. At this, one of the whores cried out: 'Don't forget that the lad you murdered still has a brother, the famous Hereward who's now in Flanders: if he were here, I tell you, not one of you would see tomorrow's sunrise.' To which the Norman leader angrily replied: 'We've heard about that fellow, and what a rogue he is. If he comes here we'll string him up on the gallows, but if he knows what's good for him he won't show his face this side of the Alps.' So the minstrel started up his rude song again, but as he did so Hereward, unable to stand any more, sprang forward and ran him through with his sword. Thus the feast turned into a fight. Some of the Normans were too drunk to stand up, while others couldn't reach their armour, and Hereward slew their chief and thirteen more: he had stationed his servant at the door, who cut down any that escaped his master. That same night Hereward set their heads above the gateway, where his brother's had stood . . .

In the morning this bloody proof of the returned hero's triumph struck the villagers with wonder, and though some warned him of the Conqueror's

'Thus the feast turned into a fight'.
The Victorian conception of Hereward, here shown slaughtering the Normans
in his father's hall at Bourne.

inevitable vengeance, fifty of his father's most able-bodied tenants and friends immediately presented themselves fully armed at his service. Not content with regaining his inheritance, Hereward had started a full-scale rising: the 'Frenchmen' fled in terror as revolt spread from manor to manor, and every day more 'fugitives and men disinherited or unjustly condemned' came in to join the rebel band.

Among these were many famous warriors of noble kin, and Hereward felt that to command them he himself needed a knighthood: he therefore went to request that honour from Abbot Brand of Peterborough, who was his overlord and whom the unreliable Croyland chronicler also makes his uncle. Certainly the historical Brand was an Englishman, and the ceremony was performed 'after the manner of the English', whereby the candidate laid his naked sword on the altar, to be blessed during Mass and laid on his neck by the officiating priest in token that true knighthood came from God alone. Norman knights, accustomed to receiving their rank from the king or a great lord, nevertheless sneered at their priest-made English counterparts as no more than worthless fakes *(quasi adulteratus et abortivus).*

Returning to Bourne, Hereward heard that one such Norman knight, Frederick, brother of the Conqueror's trusted friend William of Warenne, was hunting him high and low: he had sworn either to deliver him to the king in chains or set up his head at a crossroads as a warning to all rebels. But the tables were turned, for Hereward's band at once sought out Frederick's castle in Norfolk (where he did indeed own lands), surrounded it at dusk, and slew him. This exploit clearly caused a considerable stir: it is one of the few incidents in the *Gesta* also recorded by the far-off Hyde Abbey annalist, who added that the killing was 'done by a trick' and that it began a personal feud between Hereward and William of Warenne 'which nothing in the world could assuage'.

It was perhaps to avoid the immediate repercussions that the hero now decided to visit his wife in Flanders, promising to come back within the year. And so he did, bringing with him Torfrida and his own nephews Siward the White and Siward the Red, as well as a priest called Hugh the Breton – also called Hugh the Norman – and his brother Wiard, expert fighters all. Finding that no 'Frenchmen' had dared reoccupy Bourne during his absence, he began to reassemble his scattered band, burning three nearby upland villages – it is to be hoped they were Norman-held – as a pre-arranged signal that he was back in business.

The author of the *Gesta*, allegedly drawing partly on Leofric's book and partly on his own knowledge, here gives us a list of the best-known outlaws who flocked to Hereward's woodland rendezvous, the men who were to be his standard-bearers and troop-leaders. Minor folk heroes in their own right – some of their names are confirmed by Gaimar, and others may once have had separate tales told about them – these proto-types of Robin Hood's Merry Men came from all over eastern England. There were Tostig and Godric of Rothwell in Northamptonshire, said to be relatives of a mythical 'Earl Tostig of Warwick'; Azer the Hardy, son of a burgess of Lincoln; Ranald the steward of the fenland Ramsey Abbey, and a man called simply 'the Robber of Drayton', a village name in Leicestershire, Cambridgeshire and Norfolk. There was Wulric the Black – so called because he once covered his face with coal-dust to pass unrecognized among his enemies, spearing ten of them – and his friend Wulric the Heron: taunted with his nickname by 'the Norman butchers' who were hanging four innocent brothers on Wroxham bridge near Norwich, he slew them all and freed the prisoners. With them came Leofwine the Scythe, who had dispatched twenty brigands with that weapon; Leofwine the Cunning, whom no prison could hold; Duti and Outi, identical twins; Godwin Gille and Aluric Grugan, Liveret and Alfwine, Horkill and Osbern. Finally there were Hereward's immediate associates: his friend Winter, dwarfish but immensely strong; his nephews the two Siwards; Hogor his cousin; Leofric his chaplain and biographer; and Utlac his cook.

At about the same time, another band of English rebels – of whom more later – were gathering in the fenland Isle of Ely: hearing of Hereward's doings, they invited him and his band to join them. He gladly agreed, and decided for safety's sake to travel by water, taking ship at Bardney on the Lincolnshire Witham and sailing across the Wash and up the Nene and Ouse. Meanwhile, however, his enemy William of Warenne had got wind of his journey, and set a strong guard to ambush his vessels where the waterway narrowed at 'Herhethe' (Earith, Cambridgeshire). But Hereward landed on the opposite bank, and after an exchange of choice insults – 'worthless gannet' being matched by 'son of Belial' – shot an arrow across the river, striking Warenne on the mailed shoulder and toppling him unconscious from his horse. Amid the resultant confusion the outlaws got clear away, coming safely to Ely that same evening.

Until now the chronology of Hereward's adventures has been vague, though one late-medieval annalist places his recapture of Bourne in 1068, and he must have been knighted by November 1069, when Abbot Brand died. But with his arrival in the isle, almost certainly in the spring of 1070, Hereward enters recorded history, and at the same time the Ely *Gesta*'s tale is taken up by Geoffrey Gaimar and the *Ely Book*. Anxious to show their hero and their monastery in the best possible light, however, neither of the Ely sources mentions the Danish fleet which was probably Hereward's real reason for journeying to the isle, and both they and Gaimar gloss over and misplace his most controversial exploit, the ravaging of Peterborough Abbey. For this we must look to the vivid reports of the victims, recorded in the local version of the *Anglo-Saxon Chronicle* and more fully in the 12th-century writings of Hugh Candidus.

On 1 June 1070 the monks of Peterborough found themselves in an unenviable position. Known from its immense wealth as 'the Golden Borough', and famed for its collection of holy relics (headed by the right arm of Oswald, king and martyr, and including a piece of one of the loaves used to feed the five thousand) their monastery was a mere twenty-five miles from the nest of rebels and Danes at Ely. Nearer still, at Stamford, was their approaching new abbot, the Norman whom the king (following his usual policy of replacing Englishmen with his own compatriots) had foisted on them to succeed the dead Brand. This Thorold of Fécamp, moreover, was already notorious for bullying the native monks of Malmesbury with his bodyguard of Norman soldiers. 'Therefore,' records William of Malmesbury, 'the king transferred him to Peterborough, an opulent abbey but then much plagued by the robbers led by one Hereward, because it was situated in the fenlands. "By the Splendour of God," swore the Conqueror, "since this Thorold acts more like a knight than an abbot . . . I will find him someone to fight."'

'Then', reports the *Anglo-Saxon Chronicle*, 'the monks heard tell that their own men, namely Hereward [an abbey tenant] and his gang, wanted to plunder their monastery, for they had heard that the king had given the abbacy to Thorold . . . a very stern man, and that he had reached Stamford with all his Frenchmen.' 'Accordingly,' says Hugh Candidus, 'Hereward incited and invited the Danes to hurry to Peterborough as fast as they might, and to take whatever they could find there of gold, silver and other precious things.'

Now in the monastery there was a sacristan [in charge of plate and vestments] named Yware. That night he collected all the gospel books, chasubles, copes, albs and other small things he could carry, and immediately before dawn he went to Abbot Thorold at Stamford, telling him how Hereward and the Danes meant to sack the church. This he did on the advice of the monks.

That same day in the morning the aforesaid evil-doers came to Peterborough in many boats, but the monks and their servants closed the gates and defended them manfully, and there was a hard fight at the Bullhithe Gate. When Hereward and his accomplices saw that they could not overcome them, they set fire to the houses by this gate, and so forced an entrance by fire, burning all the monks' dwellings and all the town save the church and one house. The monks tried to dissuade them from these evil deeds, but they refused to listen: instead they rushed fully armed into the church and tried to carry off the great cross, but they could not. So they stole the jewelled golden crown from the head of the crucified Christ, and the pure gold rest beneath His feet; they also took two gold and nine silver reliquaries . . . and twelve precious crosses . . . Not content with this, they climbed the tower and carried away the great altar-frontal, all of gold, silver and jewels . . . which the monks had hidden there. No one can say or imagine how much they stole . . .

All this, they said, they did out of loyalty to the abbey, for the Danes would guard the treasures of the church better than ever the Normans would: and because Hereward was an abbey tenant, some men believed him. He himself afterwards swore many times that he had acted with the best of intentions, believing they would conquer King William and recover the land. So they carried all they could to their boats and sailed quickly away, for they feared the coming of the Normans: and when they got to Ely, they handed everything over to the Danes. Then these Danes, thinking they would soon overcome the French, drove away all the monks, save only one, called Leofwine the Long, who lay sick in the infirmary . . . All this was done on the second of June, and later that day Abbot Thorold came to Peterborough with a hundred and sixty well-armed Normans . . . he found everything both inside and out destroyed by fire, and only the church standing. Thus the place once called the Golden Borough was made the poorest of towns.

Prior Aethelwold, carried off to Ely with the treasures, managed while the Danes were feasting to take St Oswald's arm quietly from its container: concealing the precious relic in his bedstraw, he obtained the password from Hereward by pretending that he needed to send his servants to Peterborough for something he had forgotten, and so got it safe to

Ramsey. But the remaining spoil of the Golden Borough was scattered throughout Scandinavia, never to be recovered, when the faithless Danes soon afterwards made the private agreement with the Conqueror which allowed them to sail home unmolested with their loot.

Hereward emerges from these probably firsthand accounts as a basically well-meaning man (he clearly believed that he really was acting out of patriotism, and apparently kept none of the plunder for himself) if in some ways not a very astute one. Fooled by Prior Aethelwold, he was cruelly deceived by his Danish 'allies', who turned out to be much more interested in gain than in helping the English, and whose desertion almost nullified his chances of 'conquering King William and recovering the land'. In the end his ravaging of Peterborough succeeded only in outraging ecclesiastical opinion, and the English Bishop Aethelric, deposed and imprisoned by the Normans though he was, excommunicated him and all his band.

But Hereward was not to be discouraged. He still had the backing of Abbot Thurstan of Ely – a friend and nominee of King Harold's, whose fears that the Normans would take over his monastery far outweighed his disapproval of the sacking of Peterborough – and of his numerous and surprisingly warlike monks. Yet more to his advantage was the geographical situation of their great abbey: built round the shrine of its foundress Etheldreda or Audrey, most feared and revered of all English female saints, it stood in the midst of an island raised above the fenland, 'seven miles long, four miles wide, and containing within it twelve villages'. 'The soil of the isle', says the *Ely Book*, 'abounds in fertility, and it is most favoured with pleasant woods, famous for its wild game, no less rich in pasture and fodder for cattle, and surrounded on all sides by rivers teeming with fish . . . they call it Ely, that is in English "eel island", from the vast numbers of eel you can catch in the marshes there' – in the 13th century the monks received an annual rent of 172,900 eels from one manor alone.

Quite apart from adding their fish and equally numerous wildfowl to the already abundant food supply, and providing (says Hugh Candidus) 'wood and reeds for fuel, hay for animals and thatch for houses, and much else that is useful and necessary', the 'trackless swamps' round Ely also acted as a most effective defence. In Hereward's day they were as yet uncrossed by any causeway, and 'if you wished to traverse them you had to make a difficult and dangerous journey by boat', through shallow reed-choked channels and shifting mudbanks. 'These marshes', remembered a Norman veteran of the subsequent siege,

would hardly bear a man or even an animal, and you might easily be struck by arrows fired from afar off, or stray from firm ground and stumble into a pit full of spikes. Heavy rain, too, would make rivers and streams rise and join together in an instant, perilously forming great pools where only reedy fen had stood a moment before and sweeping you into the depths, as if you had been cast into an abyss. Elsewhere, just as you were thinking all was well, great deep fissures would suddenly appear in the ground.

The fens have now long since been drained to produce unending and perfectly flat expanses of fertile black farmland, and to gain some impression of their appearance in Hereward's time it is necessary to visit the one remaining sizeable area of unreclaimed fen, the National Trust reserve at Wicken near Soham. There, especially in the midwinter off-season, one can begin to appreciate what the Normans were up against – the impenetrable scrubby undergrowth, the absence of all landmarks, the eerie silence broken only by the derisively laughing calls of unseen water-birds and the ominous bubbling and gurgling of the waterlogged soil. Worst of all, as this author discovered, is the feeling of total insecurity engendered, while walking along what seems like a firm grassy path, by suddenly and heart-stoppingly sinking waist-deep into the mud – 'as if you had been cast into an abyss'.

The Isle of Ely itself, moreover, was strongly fortified by man as well as nature, and earlier in the century its defences had foiled even the great

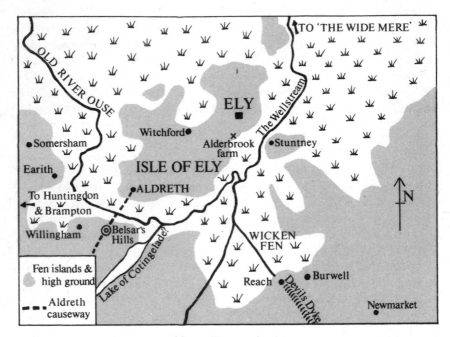

Map 8 The siege of Ely

Cnut. In short, it was almost the perfect outlaw refuge, and there Hereward seems to have been left undisturbed for almost a year after the harrying of Peterborough. So long as he remained merely an isolated robber, whose raids affected only his immediate surroundings, he presented no great challenge to the Normans, and the Conqueror was content to put off the difficult task of rooting him out until he was less preoccupied with more dangerous threats from Scotland and Flanders. With the surrender of Wild Edric, however, Hereward's Ely became the last enclave of freedom in England, and Hereward's example drew to it like a magnet those Englishmen who could not reconcile themselves to the new order and who believed that it might even now be overthrown. Thither, perhaps in May 1071, fled Earl Morcar of Northumbria, fearing that his stay as guest or hostage at William's court would soon change into downright imprisonment. There, from their exile in Scotland, sailed the outlawed Bishop Aethelwine of Durham and the nobleman Siward Barn, probably the 'Siward of Maldon, Hereward's ally' who before 1066 held wide lands in Essex and Suffolk. There too, if the *Ely Book* is to be believed, came the deposed Archbishop Stigand of Canterbury with his treasure, and the Abbot of St Albans with the relics of the first British martyr. Hundreds of lesser men followed their example: we hear of Ordgar and Thurkill, thegns perhaps from Cambridgeshire and Northamptonshire, and of a party from distant Berkshire intercepted on their way to join the rebels. What had once seemed only a localized nuisance was rapidly turning into the potential centre of a full-scale national rising, and by the summer of 1071 the Conqueror had no choice but to march against Ely.

There are many accounts of what followed, most of them – including those of Gaimar and the Croyland annalist – based on the contemporary record of the *Anglo-Saxon Chronicle*. 'When King William heard of this [the rebel gathering at Ely], he summoned ship-levies and land-levies and surrounded the place: he built a causeway and advanced into the fens, while the naval patrols remained to seaward. Then all the rebels surrendered, namely Bishop Aethelwine and Earl Morcar and all their followers: except Hereward alone and all who wished to go with him, and these he bravely led out to safety.' Florence of Worcester adds that the ships blockaded the eastern exits from the isle; that the causeway, which was two miles long, was on its western side; and that most of the rebels gave in as soon as they found themselves thus surrounded: while others report that the Normans built a castle or fortified camp in the course of the siege. All imply that the campaign was soon over, and one of the accounts in the *Ely Book* declares that William was in the isle by 27 October, presumably in 1071: certainly Bishop Aethelwine died in prison during 'the winter' of that year.

The Ely writers, however, tell a somewhat different and much more detailed story – if not necessarily a more historically correct one. The *Ely*

Book, treating what are clearly several separate accounts of the same events as if they each described different actions, strings them together into a rambling and confused narrative of a campaign allegedly lasting from 1069 until 1076, with no less than four successful sieges and Hereward flying in and out of the isle like a yo-yo. It nevertheless preserves lost sources and forgotten local traditions invaluable for augmenting the *Gesta*, whose more credible and unified description of the siege will provide the basis of our account of Hereward's finest hour.

It begins with the king already on the edge of the fens, determined to destroy Ely and all within it.

He therefore mustered all his army near 'Alrehethe', where the marshes and waters surrounding the isle were narrowest, though even here they were four stades [probably about half a mile] wide. In order to make a causeway over the great river that flowed there, he had brought in tools, wood, stone and all kinds of timber piles. Then they placed in the fen whole tree-trunks and beams, fixing them together and laying beneath them complete sheepskins and tanned hides filled with air [or sand, according to the *Ely Book*], so that they would better be able to sustain the load they would have to bear. But afterwards the causeway proved too narrow, and indeed utterly useless.

For, as soon as it was finished, so great a multitude rushed over it all together, thirsting after the great treasure of gold and silver which they believed to be hidden in the isle, that both the causeway and those who had hurried into the lead sank together into the water. Those in the middle of the column were also sucked down by the deep and liquid swamp, and only a few of those who brought up the rear, by retiring quickly and throwing away their weapons, barely managed to escape the waves that rolled through the mud. Thus countless attackers were drowned in the fen without even coming to blows with the defenders, so that even today many bodies in rotting armour are still dragged out of the depths. In fact I myself have seen not a few of them.

Weapons of the kind Richard saw still come to light in the marshes around Ely: recent discoveries include a horseman's lance-head which hints that the Normans were characteristically, but in this case mis-guidedly, using mounted knights among the fens. Such finds indicate fighting around Alderbrook and Braham farms, two miles due south of the cathedral and near a place known in medieval times as 'Hereward's Beach': this has led to speculation that 'Alrehethe' is Alderbrook farm, and that William's causeway was aimed there from Stuntney, to the southeast of the isle.

But Florence of Worcester insists that the causeway was on the isle's western side, and the goal of the attack was all but certainly Aldreth, six miles southwest of Ely town. Since we are told elsewhere that the Normans had to cross the 'lake of Cotingelade' – now represented by the Cottenham Lode, near the village of that name – before beginning their construction work, it is probable that the Conqueror's advance followed the line of a prehistoric fen trackway which began near Willingham, and that his causeway crossed the Ouse ('the great river that flowed there') in the area of the modern Aldreth High Bridge. Straddling this trackway, a mile east of Willingham church, is the enigmatic circular earthwork called Belsar's Hills; whose name is derived by legend from 'Belasius, general of the king's army' and in fact from the Norman-French 'Belassise' – 'beautiful foundation'. This, no doubt, was the 'castle by the torrent of Ouse' used by the Normans during the siege, though whether it was a new work or a re-utilized prehistoric fortress is unknown: it looks more like the former, and is certainly large enough to protect a sizeable force.

Wherever exactly this first assault took place, the Ely writers leave us in no doubt of its outcome. Not one of the defenders, who had built turf ramparts along their bank of the river, was killed or even wounded, while only a single Norman reached the isle alive – Deda, a famous and valiant knight and a personal friend of the Conqueror, who had led the charge over the causeway in an attempt to gain the reward promised to the first man into Ely. Far from having him killed, Hereward praised his bravery and made much of him for several days, demonstrating to him the strength of the English stronghold and its numerous and experienced garrison: then, after swearing to report truly only what he had seen and heard, he was sent back to the king.

William, meanwhile, had posted guards round Ely and retired in despair from the fens to bewail his losses at 'Brandune' – either the Suffolk Brandon, or, since it was apparently near Somersham, the royal manor of Brampton by Huntingdon – and there Deda told his story to the council which was deciding whether to renew the assault or make peace with the rebels. Hereward the Exile, he declared, was the most formidable warrior he had ever met, and his followers were more valiant than any soldiers he had seen in France, Rome, or even Constantinople. Their stronghold, moreover, was impregnably fortified not only by man and nature, but also by the power of St Etheldreda and the wisdom of Abbot Thurstan and his monks, who had called in the outlaws because they scorned to see a Norman set over their abbey. Asked if the English were short of food, Deda replied that the island was replete with corn and cattle, 'and our siege has kept neither the ploughman from his plough, the hunter from his hunting, nor the fowler from his nets, for their soldiers keep everything safe.' The woods and fens were full of deer and hare, and there were enough otters, weasels, stoats and polecats to furnish fur coats against the coldest winter. The meres teemed with fish – 'eels innumerable, great pike and pickerel, perch, roach, burbots, lampreys, salmon and sturgeon, the fish royal' – and Deda himself had seen nearly a thousand birds – 'geese, teal, ducks, cormorants, sea-gulls and herons' – netted in foggy weather from a single pool.

In the refectory monks and soldiers sat side by side 'after the English custom', while the abbot shared the high table with Hereward and the rebel leaders: behind each man, monk and outlaw alike, hung his armour and weapons, for all were ready for action at any time, and the monks were as fierce and expert as the soldiers. 'And this I tell you, lord king . . . it would be best to make peace with these men, for you will never overcome them, however long you go on fighting.'

Hereward's old enemy Warenne, boiling with rage, cried out that Deda must have been bribed to tell the Conqueror such a pack of lies and fables: but a knight just come from the outpost at Reach near Burwell, where the Dark Age Devil's Ditch meets the fen, cut in to back up Deda's testimony. The previous day, he reported, he had seen a party of only seven rebels, five of them monks, come out of the isle and burn Burwell, 'right under our very noses'. Then they had strolled calmly and slowly towards the outpost – 'I've never seen such brave men in all France, for they seemed to have no fear of our lances' – and slaughtered nine of the ten knights who charged down to take them. The survivor fought single handed against Wulfnoth the Monk, and Hereward – for he himself led them – would not allow the rest to join in, saying it was shameful for two or three to attack one. Even when the main body of Normans arrived, they only managed to kill one Englishman and take another before the raiders escaped in their boats – probably rowing down the Roman-cut drainage ditch which links Reach to Ely.

Hearing this, the king was much inclined to make terms, for he saw that he could not even contain the islanders, let alone conquer them, and it would be perilous indeed to leave them at large while he campaigned elsewhere. But the Norman lords, afraid of losing the estates they had usurped from the rebel leaders, argued vehemently that no Englishman would ever again fear William's government unless the outlaws were slaughtered. Then the wicked Ivo Taillebois – who is reviled by the Croyland chronicler for 'torturing and harassing, incarcerating and tormenting' his English tenants, and whose inveterate hatred of Hereward was doubtless due to the fact that his principal lands lay in south Lincolnshire – produced a new plan. He knew, he said, of an old witch, who by her magic alone could drain away the courage of the rebels and make them so shake with fear that the Normans could enter Ely unopposed. The Conqueror shook his head in doubt, but eventually the lords persuaded him to send secretly for the witch and muster his army for a new assault, meanwhile strengthening the guards on the island approaches, lest the English should learn his intentions and start casting counter-spells of their own.

Thus, though the rebels guessed that 'something evil' was being cooked up against them, they could tell neither what it was nor how to oppose it:

so, holding a council of their own, they decided to send out a spy, and when no one suitable could be found Hereward insisted on going himself. Heedless of the dissuasions of his followers, he saddled his swift but scruffy looking horse Swallow, hacked short his aristocratically long hair and beard, and put on filthy old clothes: when he had travelled a little way, moreover, he acquired the wares of a travelling potter, and so disguised rode into 'Brandune'.

Potter impersonations, as M. H. Keen remarks in his *Outlaws of Medieval Legend*, subsequently figured in the repertoires of the heroes Eustace the Monk, William Wallace and Robin Hood, and it was with typical hero's luck that Hereward,

coming into the town at dusk, put up by chance at a certain widow's house, the very one where the old witch who had come to destroy the rebels was also staying. That evening he heard the two women discussing in French how they were going to overcome the islanders by their magic arts: for they, thinking him a yokel who could not understand their lingo, took no notice of him. Later on, in the silent middle of the night, he noticed them slipping out to the springs which rose on the eastern side of the garden. Hoping to interfere with their enchantments, he followed them at once: but though he heard them addressing strange questions to the Guardian of the Springs and then standing as if they were listening attentively to it, he himself could hear nothing of its answers . . .

The next morning Hereward gathered up his pots and left, to go wandering about near the palace and calling out, as potters do:

> 'Pots, pots, good pots and crocks
> All earthenware vessels of the best.'

Eventually the king's servants took him into the kitchen to show off his wares. The bailiff of a nearby village happened to be standing there, and as soon as he noticed the potter he exclaimed that he had never seen anyone who looked so like Hereward . . . This news spread quickly, and all the grooms and pages came running to look at the man who so resembled the renowned outlaw: then they took him into the great hall, so that the knights and squires could see him too. Everyone stared hard at him, and many argued that such a stunted little peasant couldn't possibly be anything like the famous warrior they had heard so much about. Meanwhile [says the *Ely Book*] Hereward stood gaping like an idiot, pretending not to understand when they questioned him in French, though really he understood them perfectly. At last someone asked him whether he had ever seen the wicked outlaw, and he answered in English: 'I wish that son of Belial were here now, so that I could get even with him. He took my only cow and my four sheep and turned me out to beg, leaving me only my pots and my old nag to maintain my wife and two boys.' Just then orders came to hurry with the king's dinner, so for the time being they let him alone, and he went back to the kitchen.

When the meal was over, however, the cooks and scullions began eating and drinking themselves, and soon they got very tipsy. Peering at Hereward, they decided he must be a half-wit, so they poured wine and cider down his throat, thinking they would get him drunk and have some sport with him. First they blindfolded him, pushing him around so that he smashed his own pots to smithereens: they then started poking him and knocking him about, pulling out tufts from his beard and trying to shave his head. When he refused to submit to their horseplay, one of them grabbed him and hit him hard, but he quickly recovered from the blow, punched the man under the heart, and laid him out cold. Then the rest of the cooks all set upon Hereward with their tridents and meat-forks, but he snatched up an iron spit from the hearth and fought them all off, killing one and wounding many others.

The noise of the struggle soon brought Norman reinforcements from the palace, and at last Hereward was taken. They decided to lock him up until the king returned from hunting, and a soldier marched him off, carrying fetters to chain him in one hand and a drawn sword in the other. But Hereward suddenly seized the weapon, ran his captor through with it, and killed others who tried to stop him: thus liberated, he crept unseen through the outbuildings, found his horse, and rode quickly away. [A page managed to raise the alarm before Hereward slew him, and] many chased after him, but Hereward outrode them one and all, and disappeared into Somersham wood [seven miles northeast of Huntingdon]: then, travelling by hidden paths throughout the evening, the moonlit night and the early hours of the morning, he made his way back to Ely. His pursuers could get neither word nor sign of him, except for one who strayed into the woods, where his horse promptly collapsed exhausted: he himself was too tired to stand, and as he lay panting on the ground Hereward chanced upon him and asked who he might be. 'I', said he, 'am one of the king's courtiers, and I'm chasing a peasant who today killed a page and escaped from the palace. If you've seen or heard anything of him, in God's name tell me.' 'Since you ask in God's name,' replied Hereward, 'I must tell you that I'm the one you seek, and also who I really am. And so that you can report this to the king, I'll take your sword and lance as souvenirs and let you go alive.' When William heard what had happened, he marvelled at Hereward's spirit, giving special orders that he was to be kept unharmed if by any chance he was captured again.

Though his plans were now known to the islanders, William pushed on his preparations for a second assault on Aldreth: he set about constructing a new causeway, fortifying his camp (at Belsar's Hills?) and building timber rafts to support his siege engines. But when he summoned the local fishermen to ferry materials across the Cottenham Lode, Hereward slipped in among them, once again disguised and travelling in a fast sailing-boat (*lembo*): the new recruit seemed the keenest of them all to speed on the work, but as soon as dusk fell he set fire to the half-finished constructions and burnt the lot. Not to be deterred, the king set strong guards on the operations by night and day, and after a week of continual skirmishing everything was ready.

Thus on the eighth day the Normans set out with all their power to conquer the island: in their midst was the sorceress ['Pythonissa'] raised on a high place ['a kind of wooden tower', says the Croyland chronicle] so that she would be well protected and better able to employ her magic arts. From thence she began fulminating against Ely and all its inhabitants, calling down ruin and destruction on them and shrieking out insults and lies: then, with arms outstretched, she started her spells and incantations. But meanwhile Hereward's men had crept through the swamp and hidden themselves in the reeds and bushes all around: and as the witch repeated her vile ritual for the third time, they set fire to the under-growth on the side whence the wind was blowing, so that clouds of smoke and flame began to rush towards the Norman position. The noise of the fire roaring and crackling through the thickets and willow trees was horrible, and the English, rising suddenly out of the fen only a few yards away and charging upon them, appeared through the flames like ghastly spectres. Then the Normans, appalled and overcome with terror, fled in all directions through the marsh, but they did not know how to find firm ground, and in their flight not a few plunged into the water. Thus many were immediately sucked under and drowned, and others were shot full of arrows as they swam in the pools; while those who escaped both the fen and the pursuers were swallowed up by the conflagration. One of the first to die was the evil witch-woman: now terrified for her own safety, she fell from her tower and broke her neck.

Among the few who escaped from the slaughter was the king, knocked almost senseless when an arrow thudded into his shield and carried to his tent by his bodyguards. Those that saw this gave up hope, for they thought him mortally wounded and their cause utterly lost. To dispel their fears, William shouted: 'It's not a wound that makes me cry out, but the fact that I wouldn't listen to good advice – that's what has caused all our troubles, and made us lose nearly all our comrades. I was a fool to trust in that wretched old woman and her detestable arts, and now her spells have rebounded on us : we deserve all that we've suffered.'

One of the *Ely Book*'s accounts adds that he retired, cursing, all the way to Cambridge. But another version in the same volume, written from the Norman viewpoint, tells a quite different story. It admits that an initial attack over the causeway – presumably the one before Hereward's spying trip – was abandoned after heavy casualties, but when the assault was renewed:

The king, in order to encourage the faint-hearted, himself led them across the river, though he was submerged almost to the point of his helmet. Then, coming at last close to the isle, they reached a horrible and apparently bottomless lake, filled to the brim by streams from every side: on the further bank stood the enemy, heaping together a turf rampart and preparing to oppose their crossing with stones and other missiles. The Normans were at first thrown into disorder and doubt by this obstacle, but the king ordered forward the small boats he had caused to be dragged through the swamps; and with great ingenuity and much labour these were fixed together to make a kind of engine of war [a pontoon-bridge?] which they now thrust towards the defenders. On our side were a thousand mailed and helmeted knights, and on the other three thousand pirates [Danes?] and many English warriors from the Midland shires, not to mention the common folk of the isle. When the Normans shot a cloud of crossbow-bolts at them, all these retired in confusion and took to flight, and the king, hastening to cut them off, at once led his army across the hazardous and trembling bridge of boats, beams and hurdles. It was hard indeed to struggle over the lake . . . and reach dry land at last, yet in the end the sound of victory's voice rang out, and the rebels fled from the isle as fast as they could run.

Was the second Norman assault, then, really repulsed by Hereward's masterfully timed stroke of psychological warfare, or did it actually end with a hard-fought victory for the Conqueror? The latter conclusion certainly accords with the bald account of the *Anglo-Saxon Chronicle*, but the author of the *Gesta* (backed by passages in the *Ely Book*) records a different ending to the siege, one which preserves the invincibility of his hero, but reflects little credit on his monkish predecessors: for, he declares, it was they who finally betrayed the isle to the enemy.

Despairing of taking Ely by main force, the king had turned to creating a fifth column among its defenders. The means were at hand, for he already occupied the estates which the monks owned in half a dozen counties outside the isle: now he threatened to make these over permanently to his followers, thus impoverishing the great abbey forever. 'Considering', says the *Ely Book*, 'their sacred duty to maintain their magnificent temple of God and St Etheldreda', the monks reacted just as William had expected, and Abbot Thurstan came hurrying with the terms he wanted to hear. In return for the restoration and confirmation of their lands, the monks would guide the Normans secretly into the rebel stronghold.

'They decided this', of course, 'without telling Hereward'; but it is clear that the other great men in Ely – Morcar 'the dissembling earl', Siward Barn and the rest – were privy to the monks' plot, and were as ready to capitulate as they. The *Anglo-Saxon Chronicle*, indeed, implies that these aristocratic rebels had lost heart as soon as William began the siege, and Ordericus reports that Morcar 'was induced to surrender by the false promises of wily go-betweens'. Perhaps, in the hard light of reality, they were not so very wrong: their fellow-countrymen had not risen *en masse* to support them; the Scots, Welsh and Danes could or would send no aid; and the indefinite defence of one small and unimportant corner of England – even assuming that their supplies did not give out – could in itself achieve nothing.

The only flies in the peace-party's ointment were Hereward and his band of diehards, and it was agreed that, 'in order to avoid bloodshed or serious fighting', the king was to delay his coming until the gang were out on a raid. And so it befell. Aelfwine Orgarsson, one of the outlaws' special friends among the monks, set out to warn them of the plot: but they had already got wind of it, and he met them storming back to Ely in a fury, bearing bundles of brushwood to burn the town and abbey, as they had burnt Peterborough, rather than let it fall into enemy hands. With much difficulty he persuaded them that they were too late – William and his whole army were already in the isle, marching as hard as they could through Witchford, only two miles away: the Normans would reach Ely before they did.

So, leaping into the boats they kept well stocked with arms and provisions against just such an emergency, the outlaws pulled swiftly for 'the Wide Mere by Well' – probably the great pool once formed around Upwell and Outwell by the confluence of the Nene and Wellstream – 'where the waters lay open and spacious, and whence they could most easily get away'. Yet they did not escape scot-free: attacked on the Wide Mere by both Norman outposts and English locals – doubtless the vengeful victims of earlier raids – Hereward was at one time so hard pressed that he slew his beloved Swallow with his own hands, 'so that no lesser man should boast of taking Hereward's horse'.

Geoffrey Gaimar provides us with another version of the escape, or perhaps another incident from it.

Hereward got away with few folk/Geri with him, his kinsman/With them were five comrades
A man who sold fish/To the guards among the fens
Acted like a brave and courteous fellow/Into his boat he took them/With reeds and rushes covered them
Towards the guards he rowed/As dusk was falling . . .
The Frenchmen were in a tent/Guy the Sheriff was their leader
Well they knew the fisherman/They expected his coming/Of him they took no heed
When night came, they went in to dine/Then Hereward leapt from the boat/His comrades after him
The knights were surprised at their meal/The English burst in, axes in hand
They did not hesitate to strike hard/Twenty-six Normans they slew . . .
These helped their escape/For they left their horses saddled up
The outlaws mounted at leisure/Not one was left to stop them/Each chose a good steed
A wood was near, they rode into it/They did not go astray/For well they knew that country.

Thus, by one means or another, Hereward eventually won clear of his pursuers. Back in Ely, where the Conqueror was working his will, many must by now have been wondering whether surrender had been such a good idea after all. 'The king caused all the defenders to be brought before him, first the leaders and then anyone else of rank or fame. Some he sent to perpetual imprisonment' – among them the deluded Morcar, Siward and Bishop Aethelwine – 'others he condemned to lose their eyes, their hands or their feet' – William rarely hanged men, preferring to give them time for repentance – 'while most of the lesser folk he released unpunished'. Then, to ensure that Ely would not trouble him again, he ordered that a castle be built in the monastic precinct (where its mound still stands) and that both it and his fort on the Aldreth causeway, the key to the isle, should be garrisoned with faithful Normans. Next, going into the abbey, 'he stood as far as possible from the tomb of the holy Etheldreda and threw a gold piece on to her altar: he dared not go any closer, because he feared the judgement of God on the wrong he was doing to her shrine.' And well he might, for though the monks kept their estates and their English abbot, King William soon found an excuse to levy an immense fine on them, so that they were forced to sell almost all the adornments of their church: when their payment proved a few coins short, moreover, he increased his demands still further, and they lost the few treasures that remained. 'But even after all this', mourns the *Ely Book*, 'no one believed they would be left in peace' – and nor were they.

We, however, must now follow Hereward out of the fens and into the forest – that other favourite outlaw refuge – and, at the same time, out of history and into legend: for after the fall of Ely on 27 October 1071 our hero disappears altogether from the contemporary sources, leaving us with only Gaimar, the *Gesta* and the Croyland chronicle to guide us.

All these agree that Hereward – joined by members of his scattered band as he went – 'now crossed over to *Bruneswald*, and also lurked in the great woods of Northamptonshire, devastating the country with fire and sword.' Some modern writers, connecting 'Bruneswald' with 'Brunne', the old spelling of Bourne, have therefore declared that the outlaw 'returned to the woods round his old home': which, considering that it was the one area most likely to be heavily guarded by his enemies, is surely the last thing he would have done. In fact 'Bruneswald' – 'Brun's weald' or 'Brun's wood', now Bromswold – lay much nearer Ely, about twenty-five miles west of the isle and along the boundaries of modern Cambridgeshire and Northamptonshire. Though this great tract of woodland has now vanished, we know from place-names that it once stretched from around Lutton (formerly 'Lutton-by-Bromswold') near Peterborough, via Leighton Bromswold near Huntingdon, at least as far south as Newton Bromswold near Rushden in Northamptonshire. It formed, indeed, a connecting link between the other two 'great woods' of the county, between the immense Forest of Rockingham round Corby in the north and Whittlewood and Saucey Forest in the southeast: thus, in Hereward's time, the proverbial squirrel could perhaps have leapt from tree to tree all the way from the outskirts of Peterborough and Stamford to the Buckinghamshire border and beyond.

Small wonder, then, that though William called out the levies of all the east Midland shires to hunt Hereward down, they could find no trace of him – one wonders how hard they actually tried, most of them being Englishmen themselves: for, while they 'sought him everywhere among the woods by Peterborough, where he was then operating', he had already 'retired into the remoter parts of the Northamptonshire forests, there to await the friends he had summoned to his aid'. 'At this time', continues the *Gesta*, 'he caused his horses' shoes to be put on crosswise (*ex transverso*), so that they would know from his tracks whither he was heading and where he was' – a trick which, apart from being virtually impossible in practice, was surely as likely to attract the attention of the enemy as of the outlaw's supporters. Perhaps brother Richard really meant that the horses were shod backwards to confuse pursuit, a scarcely more practicable ruse attributed to later heroes like Dick Turpin and the fugitive Charles II.

However they found him, recruits came in 'one after another, by any means they could', and soon his band had swollen once again to 'a hundred chosen warriors and two hundred other strong men, besides a few crossbowmen and archers'. Among the familiar faces were strangers who, 'hearing of Hereward's fame, had come to be trained in the arts of war', and even deserters from the king's court, whom he forced to take oaths of fidelity.

Before long Hereward had less welcome visitors, a Norman army headed by his old enemies Ivo Taillebois and Abbot Thorold, and including, no doubt, the band of knights whom (the Peterborough annalists complain) the latter employed to guard him, misappropriating two-thirds of the abbey lands for their support. But such mailed horsemen were as handicapped by the overhanging trees as they had been by the fens, and the outlaws led them a merry dance: dividing themselves into three companies, they kept appearing and disappearing among the glades, pretending to flee towards their hidden camp and luring detachments of pursuers into ambushes of concealed bowmen. Then, when the enemy at last turned for home, 'exasperated beyond measure' by a long day of this frustrating and deadly hide-and-seek, the English suddenly fell on their rearguard and captured five of their leaders, among them the abbot himself. The Croyland chronicler, ever ready to abuse the foremost persecutor of his house, blames the disaster on Taillebois: for while he led all the knights in a wild-goose chase to the right, Hereward rushed out from the woods to the left and snatched the unguarded Thorold.

The abbot, at any rate, was 'kept confined in secret places' until he paid a huge ransom – though it is hard to believe the Croyland assertion that it amounted to 3000 marks (about £800,000 by today's reckoning) still less the *Gesta*'s report of ten times that sum. In return for courteous treatment among the outlaws he also promised to leave them alone in future, but on his return to Peterborough he not surprisingly began planning a new attack. Hearing of this, the outraged Hereward struck first, burning the town and carrying away the treasures of the church while Thorold cowered in hiding.

Whether this second harrying of Peterborough actually took place, or whether (as is far more probable) it is really a confused memory of the attack of 1070, the *Gesta* uses it to introduce a tale of supernatural intervention, the only one in the whole Hereward story. On the night after the raid, it seems, the hero dreamed that 'a being of wondrous form stood before him, an old man of terrible visage, all clad in shining robes. Threatening him with the great key it held in its hands, it ordered him sternly – as he wished to save his soul and avoid an immediate and miserable death – to restore at once the church's goods he had just stolen.' Saint Peter himself had come to reclaim the treasures of his own borough, and Hereward, 'shaking with holy fear', obeyed him at once. Thorold, presumably, was not in the saint's confidence, for the outlaws replaced their spoil unnoticed: but on their way home they got lost.

Then a wonder and a miracle occurred, if we can truly say that such a thing might be granted to these men of blood. For while they were wandering in the dark and stormy night, not knowing which path to take among the winding woodland tracks, a huge wolf appeared before them, greeting them like a friendly dog and running ahead as if to show the right way. In the gloom its grey coat made it seem like a white hound, and they told each other they should follow it closely, thinking it was a dog from their village. Even as they did so, burning candles suddenly appeared on the tips of their lances, so that they could better see their way in the silent midnight. (These did not shine very brightly, but looked rather like the lights countrymen call nymphs' candles or St Elmo's fire: and if anyone tried to pull them off or extinguish them, they flew away from his hand.) Thus, struck dumb with astonishment, they followed always where the wolf led; until, with the coming of daylight, they at last saw to their even greater amazement the true nature of their guide. And while they were disputing among themselves about all this, behold!, the candles vanished and the wolf appeared no more, but the outlaws found themselves beyond Stamford, and on a path well known to them. So they gave thanks to God, wondering greatly at the things that had come to pass.

Whatever brother Richard's readers may have thought about the 'candles' – and his circumstantial details sound almost like an eyewitness report – they will have been in no doubt about the significance of the white wolf. It was the symbol of St Edmund of East Anglia, special protector of the English, sent to guide the repentant patriots and reward them for their swift obedience to Peter, prince of the Apostles.

Gaimar and the *Gesta* relate other tales of Hereward's adventures in Bruneswald, tales very like those afterwards told of that more famous greenwood hero, Robin Hood. There is the comic episode where he chases a spy 'from house to house and garden to garden' and through the midst of a bemused wedding-party, finding him at last 'with his head stuck through the hole in the privy seat, roaring loudly for mercy' – which Hereward grants; and the incident where he single-handedly defeats a certain Gier and six others: 'Four he slew, three fled/Wounded, bleeding, they fled.' But Hereward is not always shown as effortlessly successful, especially when he comes up against men of his own race. He only just manages to beat the English champion Letold the Saxon, using a sword thrown to him after his own had snapped; while his attempted raid on Stamford is a downright failure – 'He was able to do no wrong there/For the townsmen defended themselves/So that Hereward was chased away.'

If the *Gesta* is to be believed, the manner in which Hereward at last ended his long resistance to the Conqueror was still less heroic. How long he had held out is not clear, for while brother Richard implies that he was still at large after the revolt of Earl Roger in 1075, Gaimar seems to suggest that he surrendered early in 1073. Both agree, however, that his peace was made through a woman, whom Gaimar calls Alftrued (Aelfthryth?) and the *Gesta* simply 'the widow of Earl Dolfin': history records no such nobleman, but we know of several lesser men named Dolfin in Northumbria, and Charles Kingsley makes the lady an old flame from the hero's bear-slaying days there. This 'very powerful woman' had often written to Hereward while he was still in Bruneswald: she had long loved him from afar, and if he would consent to marry her she would engineer his honourable reconciliation with King William, over whom she had great influence. Perhaps because he was tiring of the struggle, but more because he was besotted with 'the most beautiful and desirable woman in the land, famed for her riches', Hereward eventually agreed. He already had a wife, of course, the faithful Torfrida of Flanders: but now he did not hesitate to cast her aside – 'whereupon, choosing a more holy life, she retired to Croyland Abbey and took the veil of a nun'.

This sordid little tale may, of course, be a clumsy attempt to reconcile two independent traditions about Hereward's marriage; for Gaimar mentions only Alftrued and not Torfrida, while the Croyland annalist (who claims that Torfrida, 'weary of the changes of this transitory world, took the veil with the permission of her husband') fails to mention any interloper. Yet its very sordidness gives it a ring of truth, and brother Richard goes on to point the moral, revealing incidentally the hitherto unsung part that Torfrida had played in her husband's career: 'for this reason many troubles later came upon Hereward, because Torfrida was the wisest of women, and her good advice had been invaluable in times of crisis. But after he had turned her away – as he himself often lamented – his affairs did not go half so prosperously.'

Hereward's troubles were indeed far from over. For though the Conqueror received him in friendship, praising to the skies the forty chosen outlaws he brought to court as his escort, the Norman household knights were furious that 'these strangers, whom they had never managed to defeat, should now so quickly come to grace and favour with the king'. While Hereward waited alone to swear homage to William and receive back his father's lands, therefore, the courtiers persuaded a certain Ogger, the strongest and most quarrelsome of their number, to pick a fight with him: if Hereward was slain, so much the better; if not, he could be blamed for starting the trouble. Half aware of their designs, the outlaw long refused to be provoked and then fought only half-heartedly; but finally he lost his temper and ('as was always his custom in any fight, pressing his enemy hardest at the last') wounded Ogger severely in the right arm.

Then the conspirators rushed clamouring against 'the traitor Englishman' to the Conqueror who, though loath to believe them, sent Hereward 'for the time being' in chains to Bedford castle. There he languished for nearly a year, his release delayed by the lies of William of Warenne, Ivo Taillebois and a new enemy, Robert Malet (whose father is believed to have died fighting in the fens). But his jailor, 'the worthy man Robert of Horepol', treated him fairly, and soon he was visited by his old friends Leofric the Deacon – 'who pretended to be a half-wit when gathering intelligence' – and Utlac the Cook – 'who knew how to please foreigners with his jokes'. They came disguised, but Horepol was well aware of their true identity, and made sure that they overheard when he lamented: 'Woe is me, for I must soon take Hereward to Rockingham castle and hand him over to that proud and hateful Taillebois. If only some of his old followers could follow in our tracks: they might even ambush us along the way and free their lord and master.'

No further hint was needed. Though the garrisons of three Norman castles turned out to escort Hereward to Rockingham, his swiftly re-formed band surrounded and slaughtered them in the Northamptonshire woods, Robert of Horepol being preserved almost alone to receive the hero's thanks and ride to William with the true story behind his wrongful imprisonment. Meanwhile Hereward insisted on wearing his fetters as a token of his continued obedience to the Conqueror's commands, and soon he was not only taken back into favour but at last granted his father's estates. 'And these he enjoyed for many years after, serving King William faithfully and also devotedly pleasing his friends and fellow-countrymen, until in the end he died in peace. On whose soul may God have mercy, Amen.'

So ends the *Gesta*, while the Croyland chronicle – written, it must be remembered, in the 14th or 15th century – reaches much the same conclusion, adding that Hereward, 'by his special choice', was buried by Torfrida's side in Croyland Abbey church, and that his lands at Bourne then passed to his unnamed daughter 'who married the illustrious knight Hugh of Evermue, Lord of Deeping [in Lincolnshire]'.

How much truth is there in this story? The worthy Robert of Horepol cannot be identified from contemporary records, and it is uncertain whether Bedford castle was even begun in Hereward's time. But the knight 'Ogger' – perhaps the same as the 'Gier' whom the hero pur-portedly defeated in Bruneswald – is probably the historical Oger or Ogier, a Breton follower of the Conqueror. That Hereward really fought him somewhere is not unlikely, for in 1086 *Domesday Book* records Ogier as owning both the outlaw's alleged home at Bourne and two of the nearby manors which undoubtedly did once belong to Hereward – the third and largest of them, Witham-on-the-Hill, being now in the hands of Asfort, a retainer of none other than Abbot Thorold. Thus it seems doubtful that Hereward actually did die in peaceful possession of his lands, or that he passed them on to his daughter, if she ever existed.

What, then, do we know of the girl's supposed husband? Hugh of Evermue, or rather Envermeu, in Normandy, certainly did exist: he was indeed 'Lord of Deeping' in about 1100, and seems by then somehow to have gained possession of Bourne as well – though he cannot have done so by marrying Hereward's daughter, since Hereward had never owned Bourne in the first place. But the most significant thing about Hugh was that he was also an ancestor of the purely Norman family called Wake, and it is this relationship which at last explains two vexed questions – Hereward's traditional but demonstrably unhistorical ownership of Bourne and, more important, the origins of his now familiar byname, 'the Wake'.

For by the mid-12th century, when the *Gesta* was written, the Wakes owned not only Hugh's former lands at Bourne and Deeping – which had nothing to do with Hereward – but also, via Asfort, Hereward's old manor of Witham-on-the-Hill. Their combined estates were known as the 'honour of Bourne' and, by confusion of the part with the whole, it thus came to be believed that Hereward must have owned Bourne itself. From here it was a simple step to adopt the famous hero into the Wake family by 'marrying' his 'daughter' to their ancestor Hugh. Later still – for it is not until the 1360s, three hundred years after his lifetime, that Hereward is first recorded as 'the Wake' – the outlaw was actually given the surname of a Norman family who had no connection with him other than their owner-ship of a manor once stolen from him. The English patriot may well have revolved in his grave, for this shameless piece of ancestor-poaching has certainly deceived and confused generations of writers: some, for instance, have declared that 'Wake' is an Anglo-Saxon nickname meaning 'watch-ful' (whereas *wac* really conveys 'weak' or 'timid') and others that Hereward bore as his arms the 'Wake Knot', the badge used by his proud 'descendants' in the 15th century.

Having rejected the notion that Hereward died a peaceful landowner, we must now consider the sources which give his career a more violent conclusion. The late and unreliable 'Excerpts about Hereward's Family', for what it is worth, reports that his son-in-law Hugh, 'inspired by a malign urge', picked a quarrel with Hereward and murdered him at Huntingdon. But the *Chronicle of Hyde Abbey*, probably the earliest of our sources, asserts that 'after many pacts made with the king and boldly broken, he and all his accomplices were one day surrounded by enemies and miserably slain.' This, moreover, broadly agrees with Geoffrey Gaimar's account, certainly the most dramatic and perhaps the most authentic description of Hereward's death.

After the truce arranged for him by Alftrued, says Gaimar, Hereward was ordered within the month to join the Conqueror's expedition against the rebels of Maine on the borders of Normandy. William did indeed use English levies for this campaign, which took place early in 1073, and may well have thought it safer to keep the newly surrendered outlaw under his eye. But Hereward apparently never left England, for when a party of Norman knights heard of his surrender:

They broke the peace, they assailed him/At his meat they set on him
If Hereward had been prepared/The hardiest would have seemed a coward
But Ailward kept bad watch/His chaplain, who should have guarded him/Yet fell asleep on a rock
In short, he was taken unawares/Yet nobly he bore himself/He and Winter his comrade
Though he had no time to fetch his mailshirt/Nor to leap on his charger
Yet he grabbed a shield lying near/A lance and a sword . . .
And proudly he cried to the Frenchmen
'The king has granted me his peace/But you come in anger
Steal my goods and kill my folk/Sneak on me at my dinner
Foul traitors, I will sell myself dear . . .'
A knight was going about/Through all the field he was seeking/Calling everywhere for Hereward
Up rushed the hero/And let fly a javelin
Straight through the knight's shield it flew/It pierced his mail, nothing could stop it
It split his heart . . . and killed him/He had no time for confession
Then the Normans set on Hereward/Shot at him and hurled their lances
On all sides they surrounded him/Wounded him in many places
But he fought them like a savage boar/As long as his lance lasted
And when his lance failed him/With his steel brand he dealt great blows
With his sword he slew four Normans/His strokes made the woods resound
And when his sword shattered/On the helm of a knight
He took his shield in both hands/And with it slew two Frenchmen
But four more came at his back/They ran him through the body/With four lances they pierced him
No wonder that he sank down/On his knees he sank down
Yet threw his shield so hard/That one of those who struck him/It broke his neck in two
The man was named Raul of Dol (in Brittany)/From Tutbury he had come
So both fell together/Hereward and this Breton
Then Halselin smote Hereward/And struck off his head.

A Geoffrey 'Halselin' is recorded by *Domesday Book* as holding lands in south Lincolnshire, so Hereward's murder may have been a paying-off of old local scores.

Through all the varying accounts of the outlaw's last days, then, runs the same thread of tradition: King William could forgive him, but the Norman rank and file would not, and it was through their treachery (in which a Breton named Ogier, or Raul of Dol, was somehow implicated) that he was imprisoned or slain. We shall probably never know more, and, unless some new source comes to light, the end of Hereward's career must remain as obscure as its beginnings.

Yet two things are certain – that Hereward was the last Englishman to carry on organized resistance to the invaders, and that he was long honoured for it. A hundred and fifty years after his death, says Roger of Wendover, men still journeyed to see ' a wooden fortress in the fens, which the locals call Hereward's Castle', and as late as the 15th century songs about his deeds could still be heard in the streets of Croyland.

He was remembered, first of all, because his doings made good tales, tales which spanned the gap between the old and new fashions in folk heroes: for if his fabulous youthful adventures in distant lands enrol him among the saga heroes of the Germanic past, his tricks and disguises among the fens and his ransoming of wicked abbots in the greenwood make him the father of the medieval outlaws who upheld the rights of the common man against wrong and oppression. On a deeper level, no doubt, the memory of this Lincolnshire thegn was cherished because, by holding out while his noble betters surrendered or temporized, he had gone some way towards salvaging the national honour of the beaten and demoralized English. Yet the conquerors also remembered him with respect: the Norman Wakes were only too anxious to be believed his descendants, and perhaps his most telling epitaph is that put into the mouth of Hereward's Norman murderer by the Norman chronicler Gaimar:

> Halselin swore by God and his honour,
> And so swore the spectators too,
> Many times they swore hard,
> That such a brave man as Hereward had never been known,
> And if there had been but three more like him,
> The Normans would have rued the day they came to England.

CHAPTER SIX

'The Outlaw General'
William Wallace and the Scottish War of Independence 1296–1305

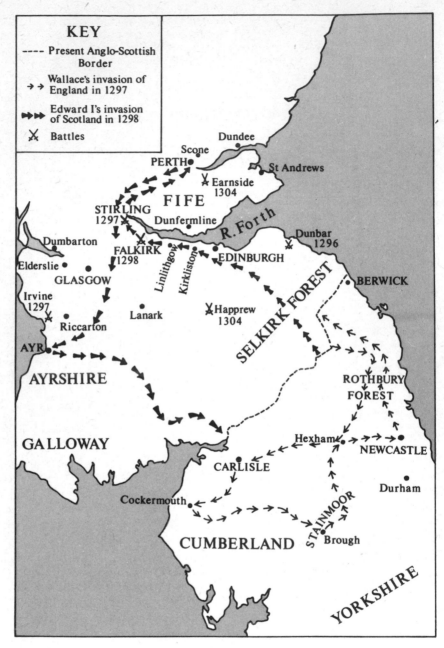

KEY

- - - - Present Anglo-Scottish
Border

→ → Wallace's invasion of
England in 1297

▶▶▶ Edward I's invasion
of Scotland in 1298

✕ Battles

Dundee

Scone

PERTH

St Andrews

✕ Earnside
1304

FIFE

STIRLING
1297

Dunfermline

R. Forth

Dunbar
1296

Dumbarton

Elderslie

FALKIRK
1298

Linlithgow

Kirkliston

EDINBURGH

SELKIRK FOREST

BERWICK

GLASGOW

Irvine
1297

Lanark

✕ Happrew
1304

Riccarton

AYR

ROTHBURY
FOREST

AYRSHIRE

Hexham

NEWCASTLE

GALLOWAY

CARLISLE

Durham

Cockermouth

STAINMOOR

Brough

CUMBERLAND

YORKSHIRE

Map 9 Campaigns of William Wallace and Edward I

HEREWARD CAME TO BE honoured as a hero by Saxon and Norman alike, but medieval Englishmen and Scots could never be brought to agree about William Wallace: to English annalists Wallace was one of the great villains of all time: 'vicious, false, forsworn, a sacrilegious thief and incendiary, a murderer more hard-hearted than Herod, more crazed than Nero', he was a war criminal who richly deserved his terrible death; while to the Scots he was an incomparable paragon, a wise governor and invincible warrior, a heaven-blessed avenger of his nation's wrongs, and a holy martyr welcomed into Paradise amid the miraculous ringing of earthly bells.

It is easy to see why this should be so. For while Norman devotees of Hereward, secure in their firmly established conquest of England, could well afford the romantic indulgence of making their long-vanquished opponent into a hero, the men who wrote of Wallace did so against a backcloth of the Anglo-Scottish enmity – if not open war – which continued almost uninterruptedly for two and a half centuries after his death in 1305. It is far less easy to arrive at a balanced view of Wallace, a picture painted not in English black or Scottish white, but in the shades and half-tones of historical truth.

The task is made still more difficult by the fact that all the strictly contemporary accounts of Wallace are English, and therefore hostile, while none of the Scottish – and therefore laudatory – accounts of him are contemporary, having been compiled between sixty and a hundred and seventy years after his death. The only sources which are both contemporary and relatively unbiased are some chance-preserved items in the archives of the English government. Never meant for public circulation, and therefore free from propaganda, such private letters and bald records of payments throw invaluable though fitful light on his career.

Of the contemporary English chronicles, the most important are those produced in the north, nearest to the scene of the action. By far the most detailed is that of Guisborough Abbey in north Yorkshire, a house which had a special interest in Scottish affairs, since its founder was an ancestor of Robert Bruce and a sizeable proportion of its lands lay north of the border. This certainly includes eyewitness accounts of many of the events it describes, as do the chronicles of Lanercost Abbey in Cumbria; the *Scalacronica* of Sir Thomas Gray (compiled by the son of a man who had narrowly escaped death at Wallace's hands); and perhaps the violently anti-Scottish rhyming annals of Langtoft of Bridlington. The most abusive of all the English attacks on Wallace, however, appears in a chronicle written far from the borders, possibly by William Rishanger and certainly at St Albans Abbey in Hertfordshire. Other valuable southern annalists include the Oxford academic Nicholas Trivet and the Norwich monk Bartholomew Cotton, and to these must be added a long and scurrilous Latin poem 'On the Scottish Wars' and the propagandist official lists of accusations published against Wallace and his supporters.

No Scots annals written in Wallace's lifetime are now extant, but some were almost certainly known to the Aberdeen priest John of Fordun, who 'wandered about like an inquisitive bee' gathering material for the Latin chronicle he produced between 1363 and 1384. His comparatively brief but highly commendatory chapters on Wallace, the basis of all subsequent Scottish accounts, were heavily drawn on by the still more eulogistic Andrew of Wyntoun, whose *Orygenale Cronykil* of about 1420 adds material derived from the romances or 'gestis' then circulating about the hero:

> Of his good deeds and his manliness
> Great Gestis, I heard say, are made . . .
> Whoever his deeds would all endite
> Would need a mighty book to write
> And all of them to write in here
> I want both wit and good leisure.

More reliable and informative, though equally adulatory, is Abbot Bower's *Scotichronicon*, an amplification of Fordun's work, written around 1440 and surviving in several versions, one of which ends with the belligerent and revealing statement:

> *Non Scotus est, Christe/ Cui liber non placuit iste*
> He is no Scot, by Christ, that finds this book displeasing.

Avowedly propagandist though they are, all these are far outdone both in nationalism and hero-worship by Blind Hary's *Wallace*. Written in about 1468, this immensely lengthy and tedious poem – it runs to nearly 12,000 lines of Scots-English verse – was tacitly accepted as a major 'authority' on Wallace until at least Victorian times. Only very recently, indeed, has the work of Mr M. McDiarmid fully revealed it for what it is: a kind of historical-political novel, written partly to compliment the poet's friends and patrons by giving their (real or imaginary) ancestors starring roles in the hero's adventures, and partly to condemn the pro-English policies currently being pursued by the unpopular King James III of Scotland, and to stir up hatred for:

> Our old enemies come of Saxon's blood.
> That never yet to Scotland would do good

Except by force and clean against their will
Though great kindness has been shown them-till
It is well known on many divers sides
How they have wrought through all their mighty pride
To hold Scotland under evermore.
Yet God above has oft their plans impaired.

Wallace, the most ruthless and unswerving of all the Scots enemies of England, was therefore an ideal subject, and Hary is quite as ruthless in promoting his hero's cult. Shamelessly distorting facts and manipulating chronology, he borrows for Wallace exploits actually performed by many other Scots heroes, plagiarizing a wide variety of literary sources, including perhaps the *Gesta Herwardi*. The end-product is a somewhat two-dimensional figure, endlessly outnumbered but inevitably victorious in all encounters with the English, and insatiable for 'Southron' blood from his youth:

To cut their throats or stick them suddenly
He waited not, if he could do so safely;

until the eve of his execution when:

'I grant', he said, 'some Englishmen I slew
But in my quarell I thought not half enew.'

His slaughters, massacres and burnings are, however, always justified by English treachery and by his sacred mission to liberate Scotland.

It would be both unfair and unwise, therefore, to treat Hary's novel as history, but not all his statements can be totally disregarded. For he enjoyed the patronage of his hero's namesake and descendant Sir William Wallace of Craigie, and thus had access to Wallace family traditions which, like the Wallace folktales he also used extensively, are now quite lost to us.

To Hary, as to most late-medieval Scots and English, the mutual hatred and suspicion between their two nations seemed as ancient and immemorial as the border hills. Yet the two kingdoms had not always been at enmity, and for all but the last of the 80 years before Wallace's first recorded appearance in 1297 there had been peace between them, if not exactly friendship. To see how and why this peace gave way to 250 years of bitter war, we must look briefly at the previous history of Scotland and of its relations with its southern neighbour.

Scotland attained roughly its medieval form during the early decades of the 11th century, when the kingdom of the Picts and Scots north of the Forth and Clyde finally annexed Anglian Lothian, the rich English-speaking land between the Forth and the present border. Later in the century the creeping anglicization of what had previously been a purely Celtic state was considerably increased by English refugees flying from

William the Conqueror, and perhaps most of all by the saintly Margaret, sister of Edgar Atheling, who married the great Scottish King Malcolm Canmore and did much to encourage his acceptance of English courtiers, traders and churchmen.

But it was the sons of Malcolm and Margaret, and especially King David I (1124–53), who introduced what was to become the dominant racial element into medieval Scotland. Themselves more Anglo-French than Celtic in culture and sympathy, they invited to their kingdom a stream of Anglo-Normans, men like Robert Bruce and Bernard de Balliol, both from Yorkshire, and the Anglo-Breton Walter Fitz Alan, whose father's principal estates lay on the Welsh border and whose progeny, taking his title of hereditary Stewart ('Steward') as a surname, were eventually to become monarchs of all Britain. Given lands all over south-eastern, eastern and central Scotland in return for military service to the Scottish crown, these castle-building incomers and their descendants turned the lowlands into a state almost as feudal as Norman England. By the time of Wallace's birth in the later 13th century, then, Scotland was effectively two nations within a single kingdom. In the highlands and the north, Celtic custom and the Gaelic language still held sway, but in the far richer lowlands a largely Norman-descended aristocracy ruled a generally English-speaking people.

Yet if much of Scotland now bore a superficial resemblance to the land south of the border, the Scots – whatever their descent – were far from regarding it as a mere province of England. Since the days of Alfred's son Edward, nevertheless, the kings of Wessex and later of England had from time to time included Scotland in their claim to the overlordship of all Britain, and Scottish monarchs had sometimes been forced to swear fealty to them. But in 1189 Richard I had sold them release from all such reluctant oaths, and when in 1278 Alexander III of Scotland had indignantly refused his allegiance, Edward I of England had not pressed the point, though he reserved the right to reopen the question at a later date.

His opportunity arose within a dozen years. In 1286 Alexander, last of Canmore's line, fell from his horse and broke his neck while galloping through a stormy night to the arms of his young second wife, leaving as his only direct heir a sickly granddaughter. Four years afterwards she too died, facing the Scots nobility with a succession disputed between several of Alexander's distant cousins and the threat of imminent civil war between the two leading 'Competitors', Robert Bruce the Eldest and John Balliol. Their 'good neighbour' King Edward, to whom they now turned for help and mediation, insisted in return that they recognize him as 'Lord Superior of Scotland', and both they and all the claimants eventually agreed to do so, though what was meant by this rather vague title was at first far from clear. To the more optimistic Scots, no doubt, it was scarcely more than a form of words, a regrettable concession necessary for the maintenance of peace during the interregnum: but to King Edward – who, to give him his due, really believed in the justice of his claim – it meant that Scotland and its inhabitants would henceforth be effectively as subject to the English crown as Kent or Norfolk.

His meaning became apparent, to the increasing dismay of the Scots, soon after John Balliol was selected by a predominantly Scots panel of jurors and enthroned as king of Scotland in 1292. Not content with repeatedly ordering King John to answer the complaints of his own Scots subjects in English courts, in 1294 Edward peremptorily demanded the service of Scotsmen for an impending English expedition against France. Instead, goaded beyond endurance and impatient of Balliol's vacillations, the Scots nobility forced their king into an offensive and defensive alliance with Edward's French enemies, and with this act of open defiance the great War of Independence began.

It was the Scots who struck the first blow, foraying over the border on 26 March 1296 and unsuccessfully attacking Carlisle: four days afterwards, by contrast, Edward's army took Berwick-on-Tweed at the first assault, massacring its inhabitants – who had unwisely jeered at the English across their inadequate palisade – almost to a man. A savage Scots reprisal raid against Northumberland achieved little, and a greater reverse was to follow. For when the main Scots array, splendidly accoutred but almost totally inexperienced in warfare, encountered a smaller force of English veterans near Dunbar castle on 27 April, it was at once driven into ignominious flight. Thereafter Scots resistance collapsed as suddenly as had that of the English after Hastings, and Edward's subsequent campaign through Scotland was more like a triumphal progress. Edinburgh castle held out for a mere eight days; Stirling, the strongest fortress in the land, was left abandoned; and in July the miserable King John, deserted by all but a handful of his subjects, surrendered. Publicly humiliated and stripped of the trappings of royalty, he was sent a prisoner to England along with the captives of Dunbar, the holiest relics of the Scottish saints, and the ancient Stone of Scone on which Scottish kings were crowned.

For Edward had determined on the effective abolition of the Scottish state. By August 1296 he was back at Berwick, receiving the surrender and allegiance of virtually all those Scots notables who had not already capitulated: the thirty-five great parchment rolls of their submissions still survive, so hung about with their seals that they were mockingly nicknamed 'the Ragman's Rolls'. Henceforth Edward would refer to 'the land', never 'the kingdom' of Scotland. He had, he believed, solved the 'Scottish problem' once and for all, and as he handed over the conquered country to the care of Earl Warenne, the victor of Dunbar, with Hugh of Cressingham as his treasurer and William of Ormsby as his chief justice, he washed his hands of it with a contemptuous joke. *Bon bosoigne fait qy de merde se deliver*, the *Scalacronica* reports him as saying – 'It does a man good to rid himself of shit'.

Earl Warenne, too, took care not to soil himself; and, claiming that the 'corrupt air' of Scotland was injurious to his sixty-five-year old health, he stayed on his Yorkshire estates, leaving his charge to Treasurer Cressingham. An illegitimate priest who had clawed his way to the top of Edward's civil service, Cressingham was described by the Guisborough chronicler as a fat, bombastic man, smooth and oily but full of pride and totally devoted to avarice – precisely the character that emerges from his self-seeking letters to the king. But though he was suspected of skimping on Edward's works to line his own pockets, he was undoubtedly efficient, and this made him doubly hateful to the Scots, who called him not Treasurer but 'Treacherer'. While he confiscated the wool of all the merchants in Scotland, Chief Justice Ormsby carried out the king's order to extract an oath of allegiance from each and every Scots adult: his clerks added insult to injury by extorting a penny from all who took the oath, and those who refused it were outlawed 'without distinction of person'.

What little information we have suggests that Scotland gave Ormsby and Cressingham little trouble during the winter and early spring of 1296–7. The Scots, indeed, appeared incapable of resistance, for their king was disgraced, their natural leaders were imprisoned, exiled or sworn to Edward, and their castles and towns 'stuffed all with Englishmen'. The sudden outbreak of revolt in May 1297, then, seems to have taken the occupation government completely by surprise, and it is probable that the first inkling Cressingham had of it was the news that a certain William Wallace had slain the English sheriff of Lanark.

Who was this Wallace, and whence had he sprung? The contemporary English chronicles provide tantalizing hints, declaring that he was 'a common thief' (Guisborough), 'a bloody man . . . who had formerly been a leader of brigands' (Lanercost); and that 'he had many times been outlawed', either 'by his own people for his crimes' or – as Guisborough seems to imply and Wallace's subsequent actions suggest – by Ormsby: certainly neither his name nor those of any of his family appear on the Ragman's Rolls. Finally, Rishanger states that he was 'a young man', 'an expert archer who made his living by bow and quiver' – perhaps laying the foundation of his later reputation as 'the Scottish Robin Hood'.

These are clearly hostile reports, yet further reliable evidence about Wallace's previous career is lacking. It is tempting to identify him with 'William le Waleys, thief', who in June 1296 assisted a renegade priest to steal three shillings worth of beer (about 36 gallons of the best brew at contemporary prices) from one Christiana of Perth. Perth, moreover, is the scene of several of the youthful adventures of Wallace which occupy no less than six of Blind Hary's twelve books: it is there, for instance, that William goes disguised as a priest to visit the mistress who nearly succeeds in betraying him to the English; and near there, during a probably mythical battle at Shortwood Shaw by Cargill, that he is made to demonstrate his skill as an archer:

> The bow he bore was big and well beseen
> His arrows too both long and sharp with-all
> There was none other that Wallace's bow could draw.

Many of Hary's tales about this period can be dismissed as either plagiarized – like Wallace's victory at Loudoun Hill or his pursuit by bloodhounds, which really belong to the Robert Bruce saga – or as merely fabulous, like his encounter with a head-throwing ghost in a deserted hall. But others, derived from romantic 'gestis' or family traditions, may perhaps contain elements of history. Such are the stories of how he slew three of Sir Henry Percy's soldiers, who snatched the fish he had caught in the River Irvine by Riccarton in Ayrshire; or how he was afterwards imprisoned in Percy's castle at Ayr, where he was fed on stinking herrings until he caught dysentery and was thrown for dead onto a dunghill, to be found by his old nurse and revived with milk from her daughter's breast. Henry Percy was indeed Edward's warden of Ayr in 1296–7, and Ayrshire was Wallace's home territory, Riccarton, in fact, being one of the estates held by his family.

For the English annalists were certainly wrong when they declared that he was 'sprung from the lowest-born of parents', 'a peasant rascal [*ribaud*] from nowhere'. Rather, as the Scots chroniclers rightly insist, he was of gentle, if not exactly noble stock, being the second or third son of a Sir William or Sir Malcolm Wallace who held lands in Kyle in Ayrshire, where 16th-century Scots authors say William was born, and perhaps also at Elderslie in Clydesdale, now in the outer suburbs of Paisley by Glasgow and the more usually accepted birthplace of the hero. The family's name (which William himself spelt 'Walays' and Latinized as 'Wallensis', and which contemporaries sometimes rendered as 'le Waleys') means 'the Welshman': and the fact that their estates lay in the former British kingdom of Strathclyde has led some writers to suggest that they were of Strathclyde-Welsh origin. But in reality they were descended from a Normanized Welshman of Wales, Richard le Waleys, a man-at-arms who served the Fitz Alan family in Shropshire. Coming to Scotland in the mid-12th century with Walter Fitz Alan 'the Stewart', he had been given an Ayrshire manor which took his name of 'Richard's Town' or Riccarton, and in the hero's time the Wallaces recognized as their overlord Walter's descendant James the Stewart.

Fordun implies that William's father was dead by 1297, and states that his elder brother, who was already a knight, had inherited the family estates: so it is as a landless younger son, and perhaps the black sheep, of a respectable family that we may picture the hero at the time when 'he raised his head from concealment and slew the sheriff of Lanark'. Other than that he was 'a young man', we have no certain knowledge of his age at this time, though the totally unhistorical time-scheme of Hary's novel makes him about twenty. Nor have we any reliable information about his appearance. No medieval painting of him survives, and Bower's 15th-century pen-portrait is misleading: 'He was tall of stature [Hary says six feet nine inches] and massive of frame, with a clear countenance and a cheerful manner, broad shoulders, large bones and a slim belly . . . with a pleasing aspect but a fierce expression. He had large loins, and strong arms and legs: his fists were hard, and all his joints firm and compact.' For this panegyric is taken almost word for word from a stock description of the Emperor Charlemagne, while Hary's description is based partly on Bower and partly on the appearance of Alexander Duke of Albany, the hero of the anti-English party in the poet's own period.

There are better clues, however, as to why Wallace struck when and where he did. Bower states at first that he was moved to revolt simply 'because he saw the misery of his countrymen, and how the possessions of Scots were given into the hands of the enemy': but he later adds that his elder brother Sir Andrew was 'fraudulently slain by the English', thus presumably leaving the family inheritance to William. Now, according to the record of Wallace's indictment, William Hazlerig, sheriff of Lanark and Clydesdale, was holding a local assize at the time of his murder. Since his jurisdiction probably included some of the Wallace lands, and his court would deal with matters of inheritance, he would surely be more likely to confiscate the estates than to award them to a man who was apparently already an outlaw. It may even be that Hazlerig had arranged the death of Sir Andrew precisely in order to grab his lands, and it is certainly possible that Wallace's attack was a direct reaction to seeing his own 'possessions . . . given into the hands of the enemy' at the sheriff's assize.

A more romantic – and therefore now most generally accepted – explanation is provided by Wyntoun (doubtless drawing on a 'geste') and elaborated by Hary. One day, it seems, as Wallace went swaggering through Lanark market dressed in May-time green, with his favourite long sword over his shoulder and his fancy dagger at his belt, a gang of English soldiers began to jeer at him. He undoubtedly came off best in the exchange of insults:

> ENGLISHMAN: With your long sword you make great boast
> WALLACE: Your wife likes a long weapon most
> ENGLISHMAN: What cause have you to dress in green

WALLACE: No cause, but to make you teen [vex you]
ENGLISHMAN: You should not bear so fair a knife
WALLACE: So said the priest that screwed your wife,
                     So long he called that lady fair
                     That now his bastard's made your heir
ENGLISHMAN: I think you're putting me to scorn
WALLACE: Your wife was a whore before you were born.

He also quitted himself well in the fight that inevitably ensued:

> There he gave them dint for dint
> There was no armour his strength might stint . . .
> As he was in that brawl fightand
> From one he struck off the right hand . . .
> But from the stump, as he were wood [mad]
> He thrust right suddenly the blood
> Straight into William Wallace's face . . .

Until eventually, half-blinded by blood and heavily outnumbered, William had to flee to the house of his lover, with the pursuers close behind. Hary maintains that the lady was his lawful wife, and calls her Marion Braidfute: but this, suspiciously, was the family name of some of the poet's neighbours.

> She got him quickly within her door,
> But soon they burst it to the floor
> Yet she had led him privily
> Out of another door thereby
> And with her wiles she delayed then
> His foes, while to the woods he won.

So she herself was taken, and at the assize Hazlerig had her executed while Wallace watched from concealment. That very night, therefore, he gathered thirty companions and broke into the Englishman's lodgings:

> With that the sheriff was all aghast,
> 'Who is there' he shouted fast
> Said William Wallace, 'Here am I . . .
> The woman's death of yesterday
> I'll now requite it, if I may . . .
> And just as quickly after that
> The sheriff by the throat he gat
> All the high stair he hauled him down
> And slew him there in Lanark town.

It is, of course, just as likely that the attack was not spontaneous or personally motivated at all, but was instead a carefully planned operation, designed to catch the sheriff in a town which had neither defensive walls nor a castle. What is certain, from the *Scalacronica*'s eyewitness testimony, is that William surprised Hazlerig during the hours of darkness, and with a force strong enough to overwhelm his bodyguard: for the chronicler's father, 'who was at that time in the said sheriff's retinue', was stripped naked and left for dead all night, 'laying between two houses which the Scots had fired, whereof the heat kept life in him until daybreak'. Thereafter, 'having insulted wounded and slain Hazlerig', says the indictment, 'Wallace chopped his body into little pieces, in contempt of the king'.

In the light of a subsequent practice of Wallace's, it seems probable that he then sent portions of the sheriff's flesh through all the surrounding countryside, a macabre 'fiery cross' to prove that a Scot had at last dared to rise against his nation's oppressors.

However that may be, chroniclers from both sides of the border agree that the local Scots now came flocking to join Wallace 'like bees to a hive'. Their descriptions of the men who 'acclaimed him as their leader' are, however, rather different. To Guisborough, they appeared as 'vagrants, fugitives and outlaws', but to Fordun they were 'all those who were bitter in heart, and heavily oppressed by the intolerable servitude of English domination'. With this ever-growing force, says a version of Bower, William 'made various assaults on strong bodies of English who gathered in arms against him . . . and so drove them out of his home area'. It is likely that it was he who captured a number of castles in nearby Galloway which temporarily fell to the Scots during May 1297, and it is perhaps to this period – if indeed the incident was not merely invented by Hary for his own sadistic relish – that we should date Wallace's burning alive of 300 sleeping English soldiers quartered in 'the Barns of Ayr':

> Some naked burnt and blazed full merrily
> Some never rose but smothered where they lay
> Some rushed out fast, to fresh air they would win
> Blinded in fire, their ending was fall dim
> The reek mixed with stench of carrion
> Among the flames, right foul offension . . .
> If any broke by luck out of that stead
> With swords they soon were beaten all to death.

But it was not only Wallace's military success, or the bloody evidence from Lanark, that drew men to his banner. For a disturbing rumour had begun to circulate in the southwest, where people were 'told for a certainty that King Edward meant to seize all the middle folk of Scotland' – the small farmers, merchants and burgesses – 'and send them beyond the seas in his service, to their great damage and destruction'. Better, then, to resist the oppressor at home than to die in his wars in some foreign land. Whatever the truth behind this rumour, its circulation was almost certainly the work of two secret supporters of Wallace who were neither 'vagrants' nor 'middle folk', but among the greatest men in Scotland.

These were James the Stewart, Wallace's overlord, and Bishop Robert Wishart of Glasgow, his ecclesiastical superior and the acting head of the Church of Scotland. Both had done homage to Edward in 1296, but now, according to the Lanercost and other English chroniclers, 'though not yet daring openly to break their pledged faith . . . they conspired together to cause a certain bloody man, William Wallace . . . to revolt against the king and assemble the people in his support'. Whether their support for him began before or after his attack on Lanark is uncertain, as are the Stewart's reasons for revolt: but Wishart's motives are clear enough. For Edward had made it plain that he meant to subject not only the Scottish people but also the Scottish Church to English rule, and had already ordered that only English priests might fill vacant parishes in Galloway: before long, as Wishart obviously feared, he would extend the order to the whole country. If the Scottish Church was not to become merely an arm of Edward's government, Bishop Robert must defend both it and his nation in any way possible. And the means lay ready to hand, for his office gave him control of the only 'medium of mass communication' available in the 13th century: through his parish priests Wishart could spread rumours of conscription and the call to revolt from every pulpit in the southwest, if not in all Scotland. As King Edward later complained to the Pope, 'it was by abettment and counsel of the prelates and clerks of their land that the Scots rose with William Wallace'.

And not just with Wallace. For a hundred and fifty miles to the north of Clydesdale, in the region round Inverness, the Scots also rose in arms during May 1297. To what extent their revolt was influenced by Wishart's 'abettments' or Wallace's example is impossible to say: for, since we do not know the exact date of the Lanark affair, we cannot tell whether news of it had reached these highland rebels by the time they began on 26 May to besiege the English-held castle of Urquhart by Loch Ness. At their head, commanding a mixed force of his father's tenants and the burgesses of Inverness, was an esquire named Andrew Moray. A young man of a very different class from Wallace – the eldest son of a baron and the sole heir to great estates – he had been taken at Dunbar, but had somehow managed to escape from his prison at Chester and make his way back to his family lands in the north. There we must leave him and his followers for the time being, and return to the southwest; where, though Wishart's and the Stewart's support for him apparently still remained covert, Wallace had now been openly joined by another nobleman, Sir William Douglas 'the Hardy'.

It was from this rough, unruly, and reckless old soldier, no doubt, that William obtained the additional forces, the horses, and perhaps even the idea for his next exploit – an eighty-mile cross-country dash to attack Chief Justice Ormsby at Scone in Perthshire. Certainly it was a masterly plan: to catch one of Edward's most hated agents as he arrogantly held his court at the ancient crowning-place of the Scottish kings would carry the war into the heart of Scotland with a tremendous stroke of propaganda. And though Ormsby was warned just in time and narrowly managed to make his escape, the sudden appearance of Wallace and Douglas did indeed spark off a general rising in the rich lands between Forth and Tay. Backed by Macduff, son of the Earl of Fife, the rebels there 'now proceeded not secretly, as before, but openly, slaying with the sword all the English they could find': and according to the eyewitness account used by the Guisborough chronicler, the wave of racial hatred engulfed not only English soldiers but also the 'carpet-baggers' of the occupation, the intruded English clerics and burgesses.

They even dragged English monks violently from monasteries . . . and made a sport and a spectacle of them. . . . For they took old men, priests and women of the English nation (whom they had specially kept alive for the purpose) to bridges over rivers: and when they had tied their hands or feet together so that they could not swim, they threw them or pushed them into the water, laughing and jeering as they struggled and went under. Among their victims were two [English] canons of St Andrews, who were carried to the bridge at Perth: but as they stood there, being subjected to a kind of mock-trial before that bandit Wallace and expecting death at any moment, God suddenly saved them in this way. For a messenger arrived hot-foot from certain Scots lords, and at his coming the robber-chief ordered them to be fettered and put in safe custody, and . . . later, having paid a ransom and promised they would leave Scotland at once and never return, they were released. One of them afterwards stayed for a while at Guisborough, and told us of his adventures with his own mouth. He also told us about three Englishmen who had been given a house at St Andrews, who fled from Wallace and his men and ran to the sacred stone called St Andrew's Needle, believing that there they would be protected by the sanctuary of Holy Church: but the Scots pursued them, and cut them down at that very stone.

The messenger from whom Wallace seems to have been so anxious to conceal his 'sport' was almost certainly sent by Wishart and the Stewart, and bore the news that they had at last abandoned caution and openly risen against the English. Yet though they now had with them young Robert Bruce of Carrick, the future King of Scotland; and though Douglas (if not certainly Wallace) returned from Perth to join them, the revolt of the southwestern lords rapidly turned into a fiasco. For as soon as their army encountered a fast-marching English expeditionary force under Henry Percy and Robert Clifford near Irvine in Ayrshire at the beginning of July 1297, they begged for peace terms without striking a blow – an action which so disgusted one of their followers, Sir Richard Lundy, that he promptly changed sides. Wallace, if he was present, was not among those who signed the capitulation, and it was perhaps he who led the raid on Percy's baggage train which constituted the only real Scots resistance during the whole 'campaign'.

Far away in London, and secure in his conviction that only aristocratic rebels were worthy of his concern, King Edward gave thanks for the news from Irvine with extra-large offerings at Mass, declaring that his troubles in Scotland were now as good as over. But this was very far from the case, as the worried Cressingham – who alone seems to have grasped the full gravity of the situation – made clear in a series of letters.

The general revolt, he wrote on 10 July, had now gained such a hold that 'not one of the king's officials . . . can raise a penny of revenue . . . because of the multitude of perils which daily threaten them': and, a fortnight later, 'some have abandoned their posts, and others will not or dare not return . . . and in some places the Scots have set up officers of their own', so that only the two counties nearest Berwick 'are in proper order, and that only lately'. Yet the English commanders were displaying quite extraordinary overconfidence, sloth and gullibility. Percy and Clifford, insisting that their bloodless victory had subdued all effective rebellion south of Forth, refused to allow Cressingham to mount an expedition against Wallace, who in the middle of July was reported 'lurking with a large force in Selkirk Forest, like one who holds himself against the peace'. 'Whereupon', lamented the treasurer, 'it was determined that no action at all should be taken until the Earl of Warenne's arrival, and thus matters have gone to sleep.'

But the king's lieutenant for Scotland slept just as soundly in Yorkshire, and it was not until 1 August that he finally appeared at Berwick, where he gave every indication of putting down roots. By now, however, even he realized that things were going from bad to worse. Save that the English sheriff of Aberdeen had (for reasons we can only guess at) thrown in his lot with the enemy, there was an ominous lack of news from the north, where Andrew Moray had in fact now overrun the country as far south as Perth. More urgently, it was gradually becoming apparent that Bruce, Wishart and the Stewart were still dragging out the negotiations about the exact terms of their capitulation merely to buy time for Wallace. 'And thus', reports Guisborough, 'day after day slipped by in time-wasting bickerings and arguments, while that bandit Wallace gathered the people to him . . . By now, indeed, he had raised an immense army, for all the common folk of the land followed him as their general and prince. All the retainers and tenants of the noblemen also came in to him: and though the nobles themselves were with our king in body, yet their hearts had long been with their own people.'

Having 'raided' – no doubt by agreement – Wishart's manor at Ancrum and carried off the bishop's arms and horses (as well as his sons, 'whom they call his "nephews"') to equip his men, Wallace now moved northwards from Selkirk Forest. Probably near Perth and around the middle of August he joined forces with Andrew Moray's southward-advancing columns, and the united 'army of the realm of Scotland' sat down to besiege the English-held castle of Dundee. They had not yet taken it when the news came in that, after the failure of a despairing last-ditch attempt to resign his command, Warenne had at last lumbered into action.

By the first week in September his army had reached the south bank of the Forth at Stirling, whose castle, which guarded the vital river-crossing linking the northern and southern parts of the country, was still in English hands. Here, reports the Guisborough chronicler, almost certainly drawing on the painfully honest eyewitness account of his Yorkshire neighbour Sir Marmaduke de Thweng:

> The Stewart, the Earl of Lennox and some other Scots noblemen came in to ask us whether we would delay a little while, to see if they could pacify their retainers and the other Scots folk in any way. So we gave them until 10 September, when they returned saying that they could not do as they had hoped, but that they would nevertheless come to join us the next day with 40 knights . . . Yet as they were leaving our camp that evening, they met a band of our returning foragers and began abusing them, and Lennox wounded a foot-soldier in the neck with his sword. When this was known to our army, everyone hurried to arm themselves, and they brought the wounded and bleeding man before the Earl of Warenne, crying out that vengeance should be taken that very night . . . But the earl replied, 'Let us wait tonight, and see whether they will keep their promise in the morning: then we shall better be able to demand satisfaction for this insult'.
>
> Thus it was ordered that everyone should be ready to pass over the bridge of Stirling the next morning, and more than 5000 of our infantry, with many Welshmen, did in fact then cross it: but they were called back again, because the earl had not yet awoken from his sleep. When he did eventually arise, he found everyone ready armed, and made several new knights, of whom many were to fall that day. Meanwhile our infantry were crossing the bridge a second time, but they were ordered back yet again, for the Stewart and Lennox were seen riding in with only a small retinue, and not with the 40 knights they had promised. We thought, therefore, that they must be the bearers of good tidings . . . but they only made excuses, saying they could neither persuade their followers to submit nor even obtain horses or weapons from them.

The noblemen had either been cannily hedging their bets or – as is more probable and as the Lanercost chronicler unequivocally declared – deliberately and courageously delaying the English from making the all-important river crossing until Wallace and Moray could march the fifty miles from Dundee. By the morning of 11 September, at any rate, the 'army of the realm of Scotland' had appeared across the Forth on the slopes of the Abbey Crag, where the Wallace Monument now stands, 'so we sent across two Dominician friars . . . to that robber Wallace, to see if by any chance he wished to put forward any peace terms. But the bandit replied: "Go back and tell your people that we have not come here for peace: we are ready, rather, to fight to avenge ourselves and to free our country. Let them come up to us as soon as they like, and they will find us prepared to prove the same in their beards." The Scots had, it is said, 180 horsemen and some 40,000 foot.'

These numbers are probably exaggerated, for Wallace's army is unlikely to have numbered more than 15,000: but the disproportion of cavalry to infantry is notable, and the important fact is that they were considerably outnumbered by the English.

When this message was returned, our rasher men cried 'Let us go up to them at once: their numbers are but small'. But the wiser ones declared: 'We ought not to advance until we have carefully considered how it would be best to attack them'. Then said the noble knight Richard Lundy, who had come over to us at Irvine: 'My lords, if we cross that bridge now, we are all dead men. For we can only go over two abreast, and the enemy are already formed up: they can charge down on us all together whenever they wish. There is, however, a ford not far from here, where 60 men can cross at a time. Give me 500 cavalrymen, then, and a small body of infantry, and we will outflank the enemy and attack them from behind: while we're doing that, the earl and the rest of the army will be able to cross the bridge in perfect safety.' But our leaders refused to accept this sound advice, declaring that it would be unsafe so to divide our army. We had nearly 1000 knights and 50,000 footmen in all [probably another exaggeration, though the English must certainly have numbered more than the 300 knights and 10,000 infantry mustered from Northumberland alone] quite apart from the 300 cavalry and 80,000 chosen infantry which Henry Percy had brought from Cumbria and Lancashire. But while these last were approaching Stirling, Cressingham had ordered them home, saying that our army was already quite large enough, and that there was no point either in putting themselves to needless trouble or in spending more of the king's treasure than they could help. And so it was done, though the soldiery were so furious when they heard of it that they were ready to stone Cressingham.

And now, as we argued among ourselves about whether to cross the bridge or not . . . that same pompous Treasurer cried out. 'It will do us no good, my lord earl, either to go on bickering like this or to waste the king's money by vain manoeuvres. So let us cross over right away, and do our duty as we are bound to do' . . . Thus (amazing though it is to relate, and terrible as was to be its outcome) all these experienced men, though they knew the enemy was ready at hand, began to pass over a bridge so narrow that even two horsemen could scarcely and with much difficulty ride side by side . . . and so they did all the morning, without let or hindrance, until the vanguard was on one side of the river and the remainder of the army on the other. There was, indeed, no better place in all the land to deliver the English into the hands of the Scots, and so many into the power of so few.

For, having got across, the English vanguard found themselves on a tongue of land scarcely half a mile wide, surrounded on three sides by a horseshoe-loop of the Forth and closed to the north by the Scots on the Abbey Crag. The terrain, moreover, was low-lying and probably swampy, traversible by the infantry spearmen who formed the vast majority of the Scots army but, save for a narrow causeway running from the bridge to the Crag, highly unsuitable for the heavy knightly cavalry which constituted the main English striking-force. Wallace and the Stewart, in fact, had lured their enemies into a trap, and now that trap was sprung. 'When the Scots saw that as many of us had crossed as they thought they could easily overcome, they at once began to move down from their hill, sending meanwhile a large body of spearmen to block the [northern] end of the bridge, so that no English could either come across or retire over it.'

According to the *Scalacronica*, Wallace actually caused the bridge to be broken down at this point, and Hary tells an elaborate story of how he employed 'a subtle wright' to saw almost through its main beam in advance, so that it was supported only by a wooden pin. This carpenter was then slung in a concealed cradle, and at William's horn-signal he knocked out the pin, whereupon the bridge and its load of Englishmen – but not the wright himself – plunged into the Forth. Yet Sir Marmaduke de Thweng, Guisborough's informant, makes it clear that the structure remained standing for the time being.

One of the foremost of the vanguard, at the outset of the battle Thweng characteristically ignored the real danger from the lowborn Scots spearmen to charge and disperse the tiny force of enemy horse. But as his company then reined in and looked over their shoulders, they saw that Wallace had cut off their retreat to the bridge, and one of them cried: '"Let's see if we can swim back across the river: it'll be better to take our chance in the water than to charge into the enemy ranks and get ourselves killed for certain. . . . We'll never get through all those Scotsmen!" To which Sir Marmaduke retorted, "My dear fellow, don't tell me to drown myself on purpose. Forget all that nonsense and follow me, and we'll hack a path through the midst of them." So they set spurs to their chargers and rode into the Scots, cutting down men right and left . . . until they reached and crossed the bridge almost unscathed.'

Apart from a few English footmen and a solitary knight who managed to swim the river, they were the only members of all the vanguard to survive. A hundred knights (says Guisborough) including the standard-bearers of the king and of Earl Warenne, and some five thousand infantry were either drowned in the Forth or borne down and impaled by Scottish spears, and among these last was Treasurer Cressingham. 'Clad not in the spiritual arms and priestly vestments of his calling, but in helmet and mailcoat', he had led the advance: 'but of all the many who were deceived that day, he was deceived most of all, and . . . the Scots afterwards flayed his fat body, and divided strips of his skin amongst them, not as holy relics, but in mockery of him'. The *Scalacronica* says they made saddle-girths from his hide, while Lanercost declares that Wallace himself 'caused a broad strip of it to be taken from the head to the heel, and had made therefrom a shoulder-belt for his own sword'.

Among the uncommitted remnant of the English army on the south bank, meanwhile, all was confusion. Warenne, who had prudently hung back from crossing the bridge, had just enough presence of mind left to order it now be broken down, thus avoiding an immediate Scots follow-through. But then he took to his heels and, 'forgetful of his advanced years', spurred the hundred miles and more to Berwick 'so quickly, they say . . . that his charger never once tasted food during the whole journey'. The rest of his force followed as best they could, and as they began to run the Stewart's men issued from their hiding places in the woods round the camp, to slaughter the fugitives and carry off the rich English baggage train.

The 'army of the realm of Scotland', then, had won a great victory: one made all the more glorious by their minimal casualties, and marred only by the wounding (mortally, as it later turned out) of Andrew Moray. The English, conversely – whose almost unbelievably crass stupidity had led them to fight on ground carefully chosen by the enemy – had suffered both great losses and a terrible blow to their morale. Not only was Warenne's the first English army to be defeated by the Scots since before the Norman Conquest; worse still, it had been defeated by a numerically much inferior force: and, worst of all, by an inferior force of unarmoured infantry spearmen, led by a mere esquire and a 'bandit chief'. Nor could the disaster have come at a much more inopportune moment. For King Edward had sailed to Flanders about the time that Warenne began his campaign, leaving the government in the weak hands of his adolescent son, and a powerful faction of English magnates on the verge of open rebellion.

Small wonder, therefore, that Wallace encountered scant resistance as he swept triumphantly southward from Stirling. 'With none to lead or to protect them', the newly planted English burgesses of Berwick town – which Warenne made only a token effort to defend and which Cressingham's penny-pinching had left unwalled – abandoned it to Scots reoccupation, while all the inhabitants of Northumberland 'fled in terror to Newcastle with their families, beasts and goods'. On this occasion, nevertheless, Wallace halted at the border: he had work enough to clear Scotland of enemy garrisons.

But apart from these troublesome enclaves, Moray and Wallace (for so their names were invariably ordered in their pronouncements) were now effectively the rulers of Scotland. And though as yet they entitled themselves only 'commanders of the army of the kingdom and of the community of the realm', they could write in early October 1297 to the mayors of Hamburg and Lubeck – as they doubtless wrote to the other German Hanseatic towns whom Edward had hitherto barred from his ports – that 'since the kingdom of Scotland . . . has now been recovered by battle from the power of the English', their trading ships would henceforth be welcome in Scottish harbours. The election on 3 November, at Wallace's command, of the staunchly patriotic William Lamberton as the new Bishop of

St Andrews and *de facto* primate of Scotland is perhaps still more telling evidence of the power he now wielded, even in his absence. For by then Wallace had invaded England.

The English and Scots chroniclers differ, as usual, about his reasons for crossing the border. Langtoft of Bridlington insists that he only dared do so because he had been falsely assured that King Edward was dead and buried in Flanders, while other English annalists attribute the invasion to pure greed and malice, and Wallace must indeed have been tempted to exploit the obviously defenceless state of northern England. The Scotsman Bower, however, provides a more creditable (and in some ways more credible) motive. When autumn came, he relates, Scotland was afflicted by a great dearth of corn, the result of bad weather – and, we might infer, of the fact that many Scots must have been away campaigning at harvest-time. Rather than allow his soldiers to consume the scanty provisions needed by less able-bodied folk, Wallace decided to lead them into England 'to get their winter living from the enemy'.

On or about 18 October 1297, Guisborough relates, the Scots:

splitting up into separate troops, and sending out scouts before them, came suddenly and secretly into Northumberland . . . whose inhabitants, thinking that the enemy would not now come, had foolishly returned to their homes. Quickly spreading all over the county, they slew many and carried off much spoil: they set up a camp in Rothbury Forest [not far from the border] and came and went just as they liked, for there was no one to scare them off. At that time the service of God totally ceased in all the monasteries and churches between Newcastle and Carlisle, for all the monks, canons and priests fled before the face of the Scots, as did nearly all the people. And thus the enemy went on plundering and burning . . . with no opposition save from our men in Alnwick castle and a few other strong places . . . until about 11 November, when they gathered themselves together and moved off, harrying as they went.

Burning their way into northern Cumbria, they soon came to Carlisle, whose strong walls – recently repaired and equipped with giant mechanically operated crossbows – were stoutly held by its warlike bishop. Lacking siege-engines himself, Wallace had little hope of taking the place, but that did not prevent him from

sending in some shameless priest, who said, 'William the Conqueror, whom I serve, commands you to give up this town and castle without bloodshed: then you may leave unharmed with all your goods. But if you do not instantly obey him, he will attack and kill you all'. To which the defenders retorted, 'Who is this Conqueror you're talking about,' and he said, 'William, surnamed Wallace'. Then cried the English, 'Our king has given us the custody of this place . . . and we don't think he'd be best pleased if we handed it over to your William. So go and tell him that if he wants it, he can try his hand at taking it by force, like a real Conqueror . . .' And with that they went off to make ready their engines.

Seeing this, the Scots drew off from Carlisle, devastating everything through the midst of Inglewood Forest . . . as far as Cockermouth [near the Cumbrian coast].

But when they thought to advance into the Bishopric of Durham [presumably at a point near Bowes on Stainmoor] they were halted by God and St Cuthbert, the glorious patron of that county. For during the week after Martinmas [11 November] such a great storm of snow and ice rose up that many of them died of cold or hunger. Besides, their scouts reported that an immense number of Durham folk were ready to meet them in arms, while they themselves had not 100 knights and scarcely 3000 foot. (Many English had indeed assembled earlier to oppose them, but by now most had run away.) Yet if men were lacking, St Cuthbert's power was in no way diminished . . . and the enemy's plan to enter his land was foiled.

The Scots, therefore, headed for home, turning eastwards on their way to ravage the lower Tyne valley almost to the gates of Newcastle. Then, having divided the spoil with the wild men of Galloway who had accompanied them, they returned to Scotland (according to the Lanercost chronicle) on 22 November 1297, 'without, however, having been able to capture a single English castle'.

In purely military terms, then, Wallace's invasion of England achieved little. But we can well believe the Scots tradition that King Edward, still in Flanders, 'was roused to a rabid fury' by the news of William's temerity, and that he wrote the hero 'an abusive letter, saying amongst other things that if the king had been at home, Wallace would never have dared attempt such a thing: but if he had the audacity to invade England again, his presumption would immediately receive the punishment it so richly deserved, and that from the king's own hand.' Wallace is said to have replied that he would return to England before the next Easter, and contemporary Englishmen apparently believed that he also boasted that he would come to London in triumph, to wear Edward's own crown in Westminster Hall. By the 15th century, moreover, many Scots had – quite wrongly – come to think he had actually carried out part of his threat. Bower, deliberately or inadvertently misunderstanding the events of November 1297, makes Wallace invade England a second time in the spring of 1298, putting to flight at Stainmoor a huge English army under Edward himself: while Hary, not content with this, takes him as far south as St Albans before he chivalrously succumbs to the tearful pleas of Edward's queen and returns home.

English chroniclers naturally tend to dwell more on the horrors of the invasion. But while Guisborough and his fellow-northerners recount no specific atrocities, the southern annalists provide – in almost mathematical proportion to their distance from the front – more and more sensational details, like the following from Rishanger of St Albans: 'Driving together English men and women, the vile Scots torturers tied them back to back and made them dance naked, lashing them with whips and scorpions until they dropped. They even snatched up babes from the cradle or their mothers' breasts and cut them open, and they burned alive many children in schools or churches.' Their credibility, however, is considerably diminished by the fact that almost the selfsame words had been used to describe a Scots incursion of 1174 by earlier chroniclers, who had in turn borrowed them from an account of a still earlier attack in 1138. One Scots invasion, the southerners evidently assumed, must be very like another.

Much more enlightening, both as to Wallace's character and the nature of his soldiery, is Guisborough's relation of what happened when, on their homeward march through Northumberland:

The Scots came to Hexham Priory, whither three canons, having no fear of death, had shortly before returned. When these men saw the enemy approaching, they fled into the church they had newly repaired . . . thinking to end their lives in a holy place. Soon afterwards some Scots spearmen broke in there, shaking their weapons and shouting, 'Bring out the treasures of your church, or we'll kill you at once'. To which one of the priests replied, 'You and your countrymen have only just carried off almost all that we owned . . . Now we have only what you see here`. At that moment William Wallace himself entered, and abusively ordered his men to get out: then he requested the canons to celebrate a Mass, and straightway they began to do so. After the elevation of the Host, Wallace left the church to remove his armour, while the priest made ready to distribute the bread and wine, with the Scots soldiers crowding round him in hopes of stealing the chalice. Indeed, when he returned from washing his hands in the sacristy, he found that not only the chalice but all the ornaments of the altar had been pilfered . . . so that he could not finish the Mass he had begun, because everything had been stolen. And while he stood wondering what to do, Wallace returned, saw what had happened, and told his followers to pursue the men who had done that sacrilege and hang them: but of course they were never found, for the soldiers only pretended to seek them. Then said Wallace to the canons, 'Don't go away: stay with me, and I will protect you. These are indeed evil men, but it is impossible to bring them to justice or punish them'. So they stayed with him for two days, while the enemy raided all the surrounding area . . . and before he left Wallace gave them his letters of protection in the following form: 'We, Andrew Moray and William Wallace, commanders of the army of the realm of Scotland in the name of the famous prince John [Balliol] by the grace of God king of Scotland, and by the consent of the community of the realm . . . inform all men that we have received the prior and convent of Hexham into the firm peace of the said king . . . Therefore we forbid anyone to inflict damage on their persons, lands or goods . . . on pain of forfeiting all they possess: or to kill them . . . on pain of losing their own lives. Also we grant safe-conduct for one canon . . . to come to us, wherever we may be, whenever it is expedient for the convent . . . in such manner that none may molest him in any way . . . This to remain in force as long as we so desire.'

We see here, then, a Wallace who is neither a black ogre nor a snow-white paragon, but simply a commander doing his best in the face of considerable difficulties. He respects the Church, and clearly admires the courage of the canons, but he cannot control his followers when they scent plunder, or even persuade them to obey a direct order to leave the priory. For though he may issue high-sounding proclamations in the name of an exiled king and a fellow-commander who probably lay dying in Scotland,

*Egfrid, King of Northumberland, and an Ecclesiastical
Synod offering the Bishopric of Hexham to St Cuthbert,
from a 13th-century manuscript.*

his only real authority is the undefined 'consent of the community'. Like a
lion-tamer, or like the robber-chief the English named him, he must in fact
command only by the sheer force of his personality.

Yet despite all this, Wallace had proved that he could not only beat the
English in the field, but also invade their land with impunity, and when he
returned to Scotland in November 1297 his reputation stood at its highest.
During the next few months, moreover, many of the difficulties he had
faced at Hexham would be removed, for the death of Moray gave him
undivided command of the army, and his position as *de facto* ruler of
Scotland was at last regularized. After being knighted by 'one of the
leading Scots earls' – perhaps Lennox or Robert Bruce – he was officially
'elected' sole guardian or regent of Scotland by a council of nobles and
churchmen: and by the end of March 1298 he could write himself 'Sir
William Wallace, Guardian of the Kingdom of Scotland and commander
of its forces, in the name of King John and by consent of the community . . .'

'Sir William Wallace, General and Governor of Scotland',
in 17th-century guise.

Nor was this change of title a mere form of words. For though English chroniclers might sneer that 'you could no more turn a brigand into a knight than a crow into a swan', by the letter of the law of chivalry Wallace was now a theoretical equal of any other 'noble man', and even Edward subsequently referred to him as 'Sir William': he was, in fact, now qualified to lead by rank as well as personality. And though the English government circulated the captive King John's statement disowning all acts done in his name – 'for he had found in the Scots such malice, deceit, treason and trickery . . . that he wanted nothing more whatever to do with them' – its form gave it little weight in Scotland, and Sir William the Guardian now had the official backing he needed to tackle the problems of his country.

Or, rather the single problem: for the overriding preoccupation of Wallace's Guardianship was the defence of Scotland's newly won liberty against the inevitable English counterblow. Immediate English reactions to the invasion had, admittedly, been pitifully ineffectual. A large force assembled by Warenne at the beginning of 1298 succeeded only in

reoccupying deserted Berwick and temporarily relieving Roxburgh castle
before its operations ground to a halt: either (as Lanercost states) because
it ran out of supplies or (as Guisborough believed) because King Edward,
who had good reason to doubt Warenne's capabilities and no wish to risk
another Stirling Bridge, had ordered it to stand on the defensive until he
himself returned from France to lead it.

But Wallace well knew that Edward's return could not much longer be
delayed, and that Scotland would then have to face the onslaught of the
foremost general in Europe, with an almost unbroken record of martial
success reaching from the day he had crushed Simon de Montfort's rebel
army at Evesham in 1265. He knew, too, that despite his sixty years,
Edward retained all the vigour that had carried him triumphantly through
the gruelling mountain warfare of his conquest of Wales, and that he
would stop at nothing to avenge the insult of the Scots invasion. And,
perhaps most daunting of all, he knew that the conclusion of Edward's
continental entanglements meant that he could now direct against Scotland
all the military resources of a realm whose population and wealth was
perhaps ten times greater than hers. With these behind him, he could and
would field the formidable new kind of semi-professional army which he
had developed during twenty years of campaigning: English lords and
their mounted retainers, backed by 'selected infantry' carefully chosen
from the best men the shire-levies could produce, would be reinforced by
Welsh archers, mercenary Irish kerns and experienced troops from English
Gascony. Nor would they be serving, like the old-fashioned feudal array,
as unpaid and probably unwilling volunteers for a strictly limited amount
of time: but as paid and disciplined professionals, for as long as the king
should need them.

How was Wallace to counter such a leader, and such an army? Assuredly
not with the unruly band of plunderers who followed him to Hexham.
Neither could he hope to raise a semi-professional force on the English
model: for Scotland – never rich, and now ravaged by war and occupation
– could afford to pay no troops and hire no mercenaries, and its small
population (probably no more than 400,000 all told) would allow no
picking and choosing of 'selected infantry'.

Could he, then, rely on support from the nobles of Scotland, the
'natural leaders' and defenders of the realm, who with their armoured and
mounted followers made up the traditional feudal array? Subsequent
events show clearly that he could not, but the reasons for their virtual
absence from Wallace's army, and indeed the whole nature of his relations
with the Scots nobility, remains a vexed question. Some modern historians argue forcibly that the magnates were willing enough to assist the
Guardian, but that circumstances frustrated their effectiveness. It is
indeed true that their pride and confidence must have been severely

shaken by the humiliations of 1296 and the ignominy of Irvine, and it may even be that these events had so discredited the lords that their retainers would no longer follow them. It is true, too, that many of the nobles who might have helped Wallace were actual prisoners in England or virtual prisoners with Edward's army in Flanders.

Yet against all this must be set the unanimous statements of the Scots chroniclers, that a sizeable proportion of the nobility were at best indifferent to Wallace, and at worst actively hostile to him. 'Many of the magnates and great men of the realm, eaten up by envy, secretly conspired against the Guardian, speaking fair words to his face but murmuring sedition behind his back. Even those to whom he restored their towns and estates, after driving out the English, remained proud of heart and bitter in spirit, whispering among themselves and saying, "We will not have this fellow to rule over us".' Bower implies that hurt aristocratic pride and outraged class-prejudice were the roots of the trouble: but the faults may not all have been on one side, for Fordun indicates that Wallace had little patience with the sensibilities of his 'betters'. 'He swiftly made all the great nobles obey him, whether they would or no. And as for those who would not willingly serve him, he arrested and imprisoned them, keeping them locked up until they submitted to his good pleasure.' Finally, it is by no means impossible that some among the Scots aristocracy disapproved as much of Wallace's methods of total warfare as of his origins or lack of tact. To these, war was still a chivalric game for gentlemen, a matter of ransoms, jousts and noble gestures: but to the Guardian it was a deadly serious fight for survival, to be waged by any means available, massacres and mutilations not excepted.

Lacking effective aristocratic support, and failing the expeditionary force of veterans which English chroniclers believed he had requested from his nominal French allies, Wallace raised against Edward a kind of army which long pre-dated both professionalism and feudalism. Known to King Alfred as the 'fyrd', to the French, aptly, as the 'levée-en-masse', and to Wallace's contemporaries, significantly, as 'the common army of Scotland', its recruitment was based on the immemorial obligation and privilege of every free man to defend his hearth and home in person. In short, he raised the whole nation in arms, using his new powers as Guardian to the full to do so. Bower describes how,

In every sheriffdom and shire, barony and lordship, and in each town, village, city, and burgh, as well as in the depths of the countryside, he caused detailed lists of all able-bodied men between sixteen and sixty to be made, so that not a single one of them was overlooked. And in order to give force to his commands, he had gallows erected in every barony and principal town, from which were to be hanged all those who without reasonable cause attempted to evade their summons to arms . . . and when certain burgesses of Aberdeen and elsewhere refused to join him . . . he went thither with great speed and hanged all those who had dared to stay behind . . .

As he had begun, so he meant to go on: there would be no more of the indiscipline of Hexham.

In all his enterprises he exhorted his fellow-soldiers to fight for the liberty of their nation, and to keep that cause always before them. And he strictly ordained, on pain of death, that every man should submit to his superiors . . . Out of each five men, he set the one that seemed strongest and worthiest over the other four; they were to obey him in everything, or be slain out of hand. Similarly he set a stronger and more worthy man still over nine others, calling him a Decurion, and likewise a twentieth over nineteen others, and so on up to the Chiliarch whom he set over a thousand . . . But the Guardian himself ruled over them all both in battle and in camp, and every man of the army was bound to follow him to the death.

It is hard to believe that Wallace actually gave his officers Latin and Greek titles, and difficult to know whether the decidedly Biblical flavour of his rank-structure ('And Moses chose able men out of all Israel, and made them heads over the people, rulers of thousands, rulers of hundreds, rulers of fifties and rulers of tens': *Exodus* XVIII) is a chronicler's flight of fancy, or whether, encouraged perhaps by his clerical supporters, the Guardian really did organize his army on Old Testament lines. But it is certainly probable that, as a man who had himself risen by his own abilities, Wallace took the then revolutionary step of appointing his officers from the most capable rather than the best-born men: another reason, possibly, why the aristocracy held aloof.

By and large, then, the 'common army' was indeed a people's militia, composed of the lesser and 'middle folk' of Scotland, fighting unarmoured on foot and equipped for the most part with the twelve-foot-long spear, the traditional weapon of the lowland Scot. How many men it mustered is uncertain, but it was probably assembled and in training by April 1298 when, according to the Lanercost chronicle, Wallace began the second stage of his preparations for Edward's coming: the destruction of Roxburgh, Haddington 'and nearly all the other towns south of the Forth, so that the English should find no place of refuge in Scotland'. By sacrificing part of his own country's prosperity to the dictates of total war, he was initiating the ruthless 'scorched-earth' policy which subsequently became such an effective part of Scots strategy during the War of Independence.

South of the border, meanwhile, King Edward's own preparations for the showdown were almost complete. On the grounds that 'the land of Scotland was and is his property and possession' he brushed aside attempts by the Pope and the King of France to arrange a last-minute truce, and summoned his troops to muster on the border on Midsummer Day 1298. He occupied himself meanwhile in a round of pilgrimages to the shrines of the injured northern saints, borrowing the sacred banners of St John of Beverley and St Cuthbert of Durham to head his army.

That army, as contemporary documents prove, was a task force designed specifically to defeat the spearmen whom Edward knew he would have to fight, and whose Welsh counterparts he had defeated a few years before: it was therefore composed almost exclusively of the types of troops Wallace conspicuously lacked – heavy cavalry and bowmen. Nearly 2500 armoured horsemen, more than half in the king's own pay and the rest from the feudal followings of the English earls and of the warlike Bishop Anthony Bek of Durham, were accompanied by about 13,000 archers – 10,500 longbowmen from Wales, 2000 more from Lancashire and Cheshire, and around 500 English and Gascon crossbows, all paid men. 'As for ordinary infantry', says Guisborough, 'the king took little care to get any': refusing to encumber himself with a ragtag and bobtail of English volunteers, he relied instead on mercenary Irish, whose principal duty was probably foraging for supplies.

Such foraging soon became as vital as it was difficult, for when Edward's force crossed the border in early July it found itself in a countryside swept bare of both population and provisions. According to Guisborough (whose eyewitness-derived account will henceforth be followed), 'they could not discover a single soul to tell them the whereabouts of the Scottish army' and a contingent sent to besiege Dirleton castle were too weak to fight 'because they had to subsist on nothing but a few peas and beans dug out of the fields'. Wallace's scorched-earth policy was beginning to bite, and to bite all the harder because the supply ships Edward had ordered to attend his advance were turned back by adverse winds.

By the time the invaders reached Kirkliston, a few miles west of Edinburgh, some of the Welsh bowmen were actually dying of hunger, and the solitary ship which now appeared only made matters worse. For its cargo was not corn but wine, and the barrels sent to revive the Welshmen's morale got them fighting drunk. All their hatred of the 'allies' who had completed the conquest of their homeland not three years earlier now boiled over, and 18 English footmen were slain before the knights charged in and drove the Welsh to spend the night in sulky isolation, muttering threats to change sides if once they saw the Scots gain the upper hand. 'Let them go where they like', blustered Edward when he heard, 'Who cares if all our enemies join together? With God's help we shall then defeat the whole lot of them in one go!' Yet all this bluster could not hide the condition of his starving, disintegrating army, and on 21 July he prepared to order a retreat on Edinburgh, 'there to await supply ships before going against the Scots by another way' – or, more probably, to begin a general withdrawal.

But before Edward could give the order, a young man – a spy employed by the pro-English Earl of Dunbar – was brought before him, with a report that changed everything.

'My lord king', said the boy, 'the Scots army and all your enemies are no more than 18 miles away from here, just outside Falkirk. . . . They have heard that you intend to retreat to Edinburgh, and they mean to follow you and attack your camp tomorrow night, or at least to fall on your rearguard and plunder your baggage.' Then the king cried: 'May God be praised, for He has solved all my problems. The Scots will have no need to follow me, for I will march to meet them at once.' Then he immediately ordered everyone to arm themselves, though he did not announce where he meant to go . . . and at about nine o'clock in the morning he himself led them out of Kirkliston towards Falkirk, proceeding slowly and without any kind of hurry, while everyone speculated about his change of plan. And when they came to the moor on the eastern side of Linlithgow, they made camp there for the night, lying on the bare ground with only shields for food and weapons to drink: even their horses had only their iron bits to chew, for each was tethered ready hard by its master . . . Thus it happened that, at about midnight, the king's own charger (carelessly secured by its groom) suddenly lashed out backwards and kicked him as he slept: whereupon the soldiers, hearing that the king was wounded, at once began to shout that they were betrayed and that the enemy was upon them . . . but the king, crying out that his injury was but slight, managed to calm them down. [Other chroniclers report that two of Edward's ribs were broken, but that he nevertheless insisted on mounting his horse and riding about to show himself.] When at last dawn came, the English rose up and marched through the town of Linlithgow. Then, raising their eyes to a neighbouring hill, they saw on its summit many spearmen, whom they thought must be the whole Scots army: so they put themselves in battle order and advanced quickly upon them, but when they reached the top of the hill, not a soul was to be seen. So they paused and set up pavilions, and therein the king and Bishop Bek heard the mass of St Mary Magdalene, for it was her feast day [i.e. 22 July 1298]. And when the service was over and men could recognize each other in full daylight, they saw in the distance the Scots preparing their position for battle.

Wallace, then, had decided to stand and fight: and modern critics, with the benefit of hindsight, have almost unanimously condemned him for doing so. It might indeed have been better to continue retiring and wasting the land before Edward's army, which must surely have soon abandoned the pursuit through lack of food: but, given the character of the king, it would have retreated only temporarily, to return again next month or next year. Nor had the Scots yet learned, as they were to learn under Robert Bruce, that wars could be won by shunning pitched battles and relying entirely on scorched-earth and guerrilla tactics:

> In strong places keep all store/ And burn the plain land them before
> Then shall they pass away in haste/ When that they find no-thing but waste
> This is the purpose and intent/ Of Good King Robert's Testament.

To avoid a confrontation now might well have destroyed not only Wallace's slender credit with the nobility, but also his more valuable prestige among the lesser and middle folk.

Neither was the moment Wallace chose for the battle a bad one, at least in theory. For Edward's force was, to all appearances, at the very end of its tether: the loyalty of most of his infantry was highly suspect, and all his men were weakened and starving, while the night's false alarm – exacerbated no doubt by horror tales of Stirling Bridge and of the Guardian's cunning and ferocity – demonstrates that their nerves were at breaking point. Had the spy's revelation not frustrated Wallace's original plan of a surprise night attack on the retreating English, indeed, he might have won the war at a single victorious stroke. Nor is it impossible that he persisted with such plans even after Edward turned to march against him, and that the mysterious spearmen at Linlithgow were in fact a Scots attacking force, arriving just too late for a pre-dawn assault.

So Wallace now made ready for a defensive battle – the only kind he could fight with an army of footmen against one strong in cavalry – 'on the slope of a little hill by Falkirk', with a stream, widening at one point into a marshy pool, between him and the English. The site cannot be precisely identified, but it is probable that the 'common army' blocked the old Roman road from Linlithgow (now the A 803) at a point to the south and east of Falkirk College, with its rear protected by Callendar Wood and its front by the shallow valley of the Westquarter Burn. His position, however, was nothing like so strong as the one he had occupied at Stirling: and since its natural defences would impede rather than halt the approach of the dreaded English cavalry, he arranged his men into a series of human fortresses. Langtoft's rhyming chronicle reports:

Back to back stood their ranks/ With spears point over point
Their schiltrons were so thick and solid/ That like castles on a plain they seemed.

Guisborough is more specific: 'The Scots drew up all their infantry in four great bodies, each of them circular in shape ... which they called "scheltrouns" ... Each was made up entirely of spearmen, standing shoulder to shoulder in deep ranks and facing towards the circumference of the circle, with their spears slanting outwards at an oblique angle.' These schiltrons – bristling hedgehogs of spearmen which were to be the usual Scots battle-formations until the 16th century – are here mentioned for the first time in the annals of Anglo-Scottish warfare: and though their name (derived from the Anglo-Saxon *scyld-truma*, a 'shield-wall' or 'testudo') indicates an ancient origin, it has been suggested that they were of Wallace's own devising. Certainly they were the best possible way of confronting cavalry with half-trained spearmen who could not be relied on to execute complex manoeuvres and who would gain support from the near proximity of large numbers of their fellows: for horses are extremely and understandably reluctant to charge a body of men which they can see neither over nor through, and even those trained animals which could be brought to charge must be impaled on the hedge of spear-points.

According to Rishanger and others, moreover, Wallace reinforced his human fortresses with 'a kind of stockade, fixing a great number of long stakes into the ground and tying them together with cords and ropes like a fence, so that they would obstruct the passage of the English.' This obstacle may have stretched along the whole Scottish front, but it is more probable that each of the schiltrons had its own stockade, and that the roped enclosures reminded the Guardian and his men of the 'rings' which, in happier times, men set up on village greens for wrestling matches or dancing competitions. For Wallace's single recorded speech before the battle was a dour and homely joke: 'I have browghte you to the ringe, hoppe yif ye kunnet', he said, 'I have brought you to the ring, now dance if you can'.

In the gaps between the great circles of spearmen stood bodies of Scots archers from Wallace's old haunts in Selkirk Forest, commanded by Sir John Stewart of Jedburgh, brother of the Stewart: and at the rear of the whole army waited the Guardian's aristocratic supporters with a small squadron of cavalry.

Against this array, at some time between six and nine in the morning, rode the English army in its three or four glittering and banner-bedecked divisions, the first two composed entirely of cavalry. Guisborough continues:

Then at once, the earls who commanded the vanguard led their men forward in line, for they did not realize at first that a peaty bog lay between them and the enemy: but when they saw this, they directed their men round the western side of it, and so were a little delayed. Meanwhile the second division, under Bishop Bek of Durham and 36 chosen knights, swung round the bog to the east, making as much speed as possible so as to be the first into battle. And when the bishop urged them to slow down, so as to allow the king and the main body [of infantry] to catch up, Ralph Basset of Drayton cried out to him, 'It's not your business, bishop, to tell us knights how to fight . . . Go then and say your Masses, and leave us to do the job we know about'. Thus they pressed on and attacked the first Scottish schiltron, while the earls charged with the vanguard on the other side of the field. The Scots cavalry fled without striking a blow the moment our men appeared, though a few of their lords remained to command the spearmen [among these was Macduff of Fife, while Sir John Stewart] . . . captain of the Selkirk Forest archers, dismounted from his horse and stood in the midst of his people until both he and they – men of noble form and great stature – were all cut down.

But though the Scots cavalry fled and their archers fell, the vital schiltrons 'stood their ground and fought manfully', says Lanercost. 'Their spears', adds Guisborough, 'were as impenetrable as the branches of a thick wood, so that when our knights charged them they could by no means break into the circles, and while trying to strike at the outermost ranks many of our men were pierced through and through.' Partially protected by mail though they were, the English horses – at which Wallace had doubtless trained his men to aim – probably suffered more than their fully armoured riders: according to the account of compensation paid for horses killed at Falkirk, the royal household knights alone lost 92, and among those which fell screaming from the spear-points were some (like Sir Eustace de la Hecche's 'bay charger with a white hind foot') worth more than a labourer could earn in a lifetime.

The native tenacity of the 'common army' spearmen, and the discipline instilled in them by Wallace, then, had brought the battle to a temporary impasse. But before the schiltrons could leave the hampering protection of the stake-rings to counter-attack, King Edward arrived with the main body of his infantry, the knights were called off, and the real slaughter of Falkirk began. If, as some English chroniclers believed, the Welsh at first hung back, they did not hang back for long, and soon the Scots were subjected to a devastating hail of yard-long arrows – 13,000 average bowmen could fire around 100,000 of them a minute – crossbow-bolts, and showers of 'the round stones that abounded on the battlefield'. The effect on the closely packed schiltrons, powerless to retaliate and unable to break ranks and retire for fear of the lurking cavalry, must have been devastating. 'They fell', says Rishanger in a heartless metaphor, 'like blossom in an orchard when the fruit has ripened . . . and their bodies covered the ground as thickly as snow in winter.' Those who escaped death in the outer ranks, frantic to avoid the arrows, turned in panic and threw the men behind them into disorder, and as the schiltrons dissolved into chaos 'our knights charged in again and destroyed them all'.

How many of the 'poor common folk of Scotland' died during the battle, or drowned in rivers and bogs during the rout that followed, is uncertain: English estimates of 100,000 – far more than the number engaged on both sides – can be dismissed, but Sir Thomas Gray's figure of 10,000 slain may not be too far out. And though we need not believe the chronicle statements that the English lost only thirty infantrymen and 'five or six esquires, who charged the schiltrons too hotly and rashly', it is certain that Edward's casualties were incomparably lighter, and probable that only two English-men of note were killed: Sir John de Sawtry, who fell among the spears, and Sir Brian le Jay, Master of the English Knights Templar, slain by fugitives when his horse sank belly-deep into a bog.

The Scottish chroniclers, firm in their proud belief that only Scots could beat Scots, 'that our nation is rarely or never defeated by the English save through the malice of our own aristocracy, or through the treason of Scotsmen who help the enemy', declare unanimously that the 'common army' was betrayed at Falkirk. And though their tale of Robert Bruce's clinching the victory by leading a force of English against Wallace's rear is pure fiction (because, if present at all, he was fighting on the Scots side), their contention that the disaster was due to the flight of the Scots nobles is not entirely without foundation. For – as was to be proved time and again – spearmen unsupported by horse were no match for a properly handled combination of knights and archers. Few and inexperienced as they were, the Scots cavalry would probably have made little impression on the English, even had they stayed: but their flight made the eventual destruction of the schiltrons certain.

It was this knowledge, no doubt, that caused Wallace to leave the field at a relatively early stage in the battle. Both English and Scots sources attest that he did so, though the former say he fled with the nobles, while the latter, making an important distinction, report that it was only after he realized that the cavalry had abandoned him that 'the Guardian escaped by another way . . . seeing nothing else for it as matters stood'. To sacrifice his life among the doomed spear-rings might perhaps have been more romantic and chivalrous: but Wallace was above all else a realist, who knew that his death could serve only to make the English victory more complete. His responsibility as Guardian, rather, was now to minimize its effects: to save Scotland from a repetition of the humiliations of 1296 by denying Edward the provisions he needed to continue the invasion. Thus when the king marched northwards from Falkirk to Stirling and Perth he found them both smoking ruins, burnt probably on Wallace's orders. And not much more than a month after the battle, lack of supplies forced him to break off the campaign altogether and return to England.

Although the Lanercost chronicler might declare that:

> Berwick, Dunbar and Falkirk too
> Show all that traitor Scots can do
> England exult, thy king is peerless
> Where he leadeth, follow fearless,

Edward's victory had in fact won him little, but Wallace's defeat meant the end of his Guardianship. 'Not long after the battle', says Fordun, 'he gave up his office at a place by the water of Forth, of his own free will: for he was disgusted by the open treachery and malice of the nobles, and chose rather to suffer among the people than to lead them again into so great disaster and ruin.' No doubt there were bitter accusations and counter-accusations, and it may well be that Sir William's 'resignation' was actually forced on him by pressure from the magnates: certainly he was now in no position to resist them, for his reputation for invincibility was shattered, and the 'common army' on which his power had rested was no more. Most of the lords, at any rate, will have been glad to be rid of the overbearing interloper and his unorthodox methods, and by the autumn of 1298 Robert Bruce and John Comyn of Badenoch had jointly assumed the Guardianship.

With Wallace's passing from the centre of the stage his movements become increasingly difficult to trace, but it is clear that he never abandoned for a moment his determination to liberate Scotland. No longer a ruler, but too proud and too formidable to be ruled, he would henceforth ask no man's leave to fight his own war against the English by his own methods: and if his fellow-countrymen could not or would not cooperate, he must seek help abroad. Thus in August 1299, reporting to his English masters on a meeting of the Scots nobility, a spy wrote gleefully that:

At the council Sir David Graham demanded the lands and goods of Sir William Wallace, because he was leaving the kingdom without the permission or approval of the Guardians. And Sir Malcolm, Sir William's brother, answered that neither his lands nor his goods ought to be forfeit, for they were protected by the peace which Wallace himself had established in Scotland, and because Sir William was now leaving to work for the good of the kingdom. Thereupon the two knights called each other liars, and pulled out their daggers . . . and when it was reported that a fight had broken out . . . John Comyn [Graham's overlord] leapt at Robert Bruce [Sir Malcolm's overlord] and seized him by the throat, and the Earl of Buchan turned on the Bishop of St Andrews . . .

The destination of Wallace's self-appointed foreign mission is not recorded, but it is possible that his search for military or diplomatic aid took him first to Norway, whose King Haakon V is known at some stage to have sent him a safe-conduct. So too did the much more powerful King Philip the Fair of France, whose realm Sir William certainly visited, though sources differ as to how he was received there. One English chronicler declares that the hero and his five knightly companions were arrested soon after their arrival, and narrowly escaped being shipped back in irons to King Edward, but a later version of Bower's chronicle reports that their mission was such a great success that 'many songs were afterwards sung about it, both in Scotland and in France'. According to these, apparently, Wallace not only overcame pirates during his journey, but also fought against the English invaders of France with such vigour that King Philip promised him honour, wealth and lands if only he would make his home there. Blind Hary, moreover, recounts Wallace's French adventures in considerable (and almost certainly fabulous) detail, the high points being his sea-fight with the piratical Red Rover – who afterwards becomes his inseparable companion – and a single combat with a demented French lion.

It is possible, of course, that King Philip imprisoned Wallace at first, but afterwards changed his mind and honoured him. The only really reliable evidence concerning the French mission, however, is Philip's letter of November 1300 to his agents in Rome, instructing them to solicit the Pope's favour 'for our beloved Sir William le Walloys of Scotland, in the matters which he wishes to forward with His Holiness'. It looks, therefore, as though the famous Scots hero did eventually find favour in France, and it may even have been his urgings that persuaded Philip, not long before the letter was written, to insist on Edward's granting the Scots a six-month truce. Neither is it unlikely that William himself put his case to Pope

Boniface, or that his visit played some part in the pontiff's decision to release John Balliol (whom Edward had reluctantly placed in papal custody) into the hands of the French, whence he could more easily return to his kingdom if occasion offered. The 'bandit chief', in fact, seems to have displayed a surprising talent for personal diplomacy, which his curiosity value alone cannot entirely explain, and which his probable ignorance of French, Latin or Italian makes all the more remarkable. By the middle of 1302, it is true, the European situation had caused both Philip and Boniface to withdraw effective support from the Scots cause: but by then Wallace was again in Scotland, and back in the thick of the fray.

He returned in time for the summer and autumn campaigns of 1301, when his old friend Bishop Wishart raised the tenants of his diocese of Glasgow and sent them under Wallace and Bruce to drive off the English invaders of Galloway. Nothing is known of his movements during the succeeding two years, but he probably served as an independent captain in his native southwest, with little say in the overall direction of the war: nor is he recorded as participating in the notable Scots victory at Roslin near Edinburgh in February 1303. Yet the mere fact that he was once more in the field convinced some panicky English chroniclers that he was still the principal agent of Scots resistance, and that the Scots had once again 'chosen William Wallace as their chief leader and commander'.

Many Scots must soon have wished they had actually done so. For in May 1303, after much careful preparation, King Edward once again crossed the border in full force. This time he was not delayed – as Wallace had delayed and hampered him five years before – by the necessity to seek supplies in a burnt countryside, and within less than a fortnight he had crossed the Forth on prefabricated wooden bridges shipped from Norfolk. By June he had occupied Perth; by September, marching inexorably northward and taking castle after castle and town after town, he had penetrated to the Moray Firth; and by the time he went into winter quarters at Dunfermline in November he was well on the way to subduing all Scotland.

Wallace, we may be sure, did what little he could to halt his progress. In June 1303 he was almost certainly among those Scots who raided Cumbria in the vain hope of drawing the king back to England, and it was probably not long afterwards that Bishop Lamberton of St Andrews, who owed his election to Wallace, wrote him a desperate letter from France, informing him that he had commanded all his clergy and servants to support him with supplies and 'begging him, for the love that he bore the said bishop, and with his blessing, to aid and counsel the community of the realm with all his power, as he had done in former times . . .'.

By the beginning of 1304 the 'former times' had indeed come again, and the wheel of Scotland's fortunes had turned full circle. Just as in 1296

Edward's show of strength had shocked and demoralized the Scots magnates into defeat; they now once again flocked to make the best terms they could with the invader. Bruce had long since defected, Comyn the Guardian was negotiating his capitulation and (if Langtoft's report can be believed) even Wallace himself was prepared to discuss peace: though he took care to do so only through intermediaries, making the condition that he should not have to surrender in person, and adding the insolent rider that Edward must buy his submission with a gift of hereditary estates. At this suggestion, says the chronicler, the king not unnaturally flew into a rage, consigning Wallace to Hell and promising the then vast sum of £200 to anyone who would bring in his head.

Though the Scots chroniclers are probably right in insisting that Wallace never offered or considered surrender, the last part of Langtoft's tale is completely credible. For it is clear that Edward was by now determined on nothing less than Wallace's death, which he henceforth sought to encompass by every means in his power. Nor should we be surprised if his relentlessness 'bore all the marks of a personal vendetta'. In the king's eyes – as in those of nearly all his English subjects – Wallace was first of all a brutal and dangerous war-criminal, a man in every sense outside the law. He was also the man whose revolt had plunged the king into seven years of costly and laborious war; who had shamed him by defeating his knights at Stirling with peasant spearmen; who had humiliated him by invading England with impunity; who had come near to humiliating him again in the days before Falkirk; and whose worst crime, perhaps, was that he was but the son of a petty backwoods knight. Finally, policy as well as personal animosity dictated that Wallace must not be left at large in a conquered Scotland: for, backed by the common folk, might he not do again what he had done in 1297?

In early February 1304, therefore, when Edward offered more or less lenient peace terms to various named Scots who were still holding out, he specifically declared that he would offer no such guarantees to Wallace: if he chose to surrender, he must throw himself on the king's 'mercy'. Later in that month elaborate plans were laid for his capture. Learning from a 'certain Scots groom' that Sir William and his ally Simon Fraser of Tweedale were lurking in Selkirk Forest, the king sent against them a strong force of cavalry under three of his most capable captains, accompanied by Robert Bruce and directed by a local guide. Nor did he underestimate his old enemy, for the hunters were ordered to check their ranks at intervals for 'strangers' – presumably Wallace-supporters who might warn him of their coming – while all the crossings of the Forth were carefully guarded lest he should slip through the net and strike northwards: the watchers, moreover, were strictly enjoined not to offer peace terms to Wallace or any of his band unless they 'surrendered absolutely and in all things to our will'. But, for all these precautions, and though the searchers found and 'discomfited' Wallace and Fraser at Happrew near Peebles on 6 March, both of them managed to escape unscathed, and Edward had to be content with pressuring the Scots 'parliament' he held soon afterwards into formally outlawing them – a move that was later to prove useful to him.

July brought the surrender of Fraser and the fall of Stirling, the last native-held fortress in Scotland: but it did not bring in Wallace, and Edward now hit on the unattractive notion of striking at him through his former friends. 'James the Stewart', he ordered, 'is in no wise to be admitted to peace until William Wallace is given up' and, still more vindictively, 'Sir Simon Fraser, Sir John Comyn, Sir Alexander Lindsay [who had supported the hero in 1297] and Sir David Graham are to exert themselves until twenty days after Christmas to capture William Wallace and hand him over to the king. And the king will take careful note of how each conducts himself, so that he may show most favour to the one who takes him . . . with regard to mitigation of his sentence of exile or fine.' At the same time Edward's competent general Aymer de Valence was combing Lothian for the fugitive with three hundred archers 'under the banner of St George', and it may have been this force, accompanied by the Constable of Dundee's men, that encountered him in September 1304, 'under Earnside' by Lindores in Fife: but though the pursuers (after the loss of several of their war-horses) once again 'put Wallace to flight', once again he eluded their grasp.

Despite all that Edward could do, and despite the fact that the price on his head would make his betrayer rich for life, Sir William remained at liberty for nearly another year, protected by the love and loyalty of the 'poor common folk'. But someone did at last betray him, and on the night of 3 August 1305 he was taken 'as he lay in bed with his whore' (sneers Langtoft) in his native southwest, probably at Glasgow and possibly in the suburb of Robroyston. The reasons for his presence there, apparently alone, are unknown. The papers found on him would doubtless have told us much, but only a brief description of them has survived: he may have come to plot a new blow against the English (as implied by 'divers letters of confederation between certain Scots magnates and the said William') or (as is suggested by the 'safe-conducts from the kings of France and Norway') he may finally have grown weary of life on the run, and have been preparing to take ship on the Clyde and sail abroad.

Nor are the circumstances of his capture clear. According to the unreliable English chronicler Robert Mannyng, he was betrayed by his body-servant 'Jak Short', who thus revenged Wallace's murder of his brother: while another English source says the informer was 'one of Wallace's esquires'. This was perhaps Ralph Haliburton, who was released from prison in February 1305 'to see what he could do against Wallace', and who may have insinuated himself into the hero's confidence on the strength of his family's good service in 1297. Certainly Edward later rewarded 'a certain esquire' who 'spied on William Wallace'.

The Scots chroniclers, however, unanimously throw all the blame on the man who actually made the arrest: Sir John Stewart of Menteith, the Scotsman whom Edward had appointed sheriff of Dumbarton in 1304. 'Most fraudulently and treasonably', they declare, 'he took Wallace un-awares, . . . from motives of pure malice and jealousy', while Blind Hary, who blackens his name still further by making him so close an old friend of Sir William that the hero had twice stood godfather to his children, reports that the spying esquire was Menteith's nephew. But though Sir John certainly received £100-worth of land for his share in the capture, he may in reality have been doing no more than his bare duty: for once informed that Edward's arch-enemy lurked within his jurisdiction, what could Edward's sheriff do but arrest him?

To Edward, at any rate, Wallace was now sent, doubtless under heavy guard: but the king – either creditably avoiding the temptation to crow over his old opponent or, more probably, out of contempt – refused to see him, sending him instead to London. The capital, however, made the most of him, as the detailed English report of his last days confirms: and on 22 August gaping crowds flocked to see the captive monster led through the streets to overnight imprisonment. They turned out again the next morning, when the Lord Mayor and a great concourse of notables conducted him, like the trophy of some Roman triumph, to Westminster Hall: where, in a mocking ceremony which came uncomfortably close to parodying Christ's passion, Wallace was seated on a bench and crowned with the victor's wreath of laurel 'because, as it was popularly said, he once declared he would wear a crown in that same hall'.

The mockery continued in more solemn form when the justiciar of England summoned Wallace, not to trial, but simply to judgement. For, since Edward had already caused him to be outlawed by the Scots parliament, his guilt could technically be taken as self-evident: the letter of the law thus required neither jury, defence or prosecution, but only that sentence be passed and executed. Before this was done, however, a list of charges against him, carefully devised by a legalistic king's legal advisers, was read out.

King Edward, it declared, had conquered Scotland in 1296, whereupon the king, nobles and people of that nation had submitted to him, so that the land was at peace. Yet William Wallace 'unmindful of his fealty and allegiance', had thereafter 'committed all the felonies and seditions he possibly could' against the king. He had 'gathered together an immense number of criminals', risen in rebellion, 'attacked Edward's lieutenants and ministers', and killed and mutilated the sheriff of Lanark. He had usurped the office of 'lord superior' of Scotland, sent out writs ordering parliaments, and counselled the prelates and magnates to ally themselves to France for the destruction of England. He had invaded the northern English counties, burnt churches and desecrated holy relics, and slain priests and nuns, old men, women and children. He had, moreover, committed manifest high treason by seeking the death of the king himself, and by displaying his banners against him in time of war. Finally, he had refused to submit to Edward's mercy in 1304, thus bringing on himself public sentence of outlawry and forfeiting the right to defend himself or even to reply to the charges.

Yet Wallace did manage to cry out 'that he had never been a traitor to the king of England', presumably because he had never been his subject or at any time sworn allegiance to him: 'but his other crimes he admitted', for to deny them would be to deny his greatest achievements. His condemnation was in any case a foregone conclusion, and he was at once led away to the multiple death which medieval law, with hideous attention to detail, decreed for his several 'offences'.

First, for the treason he had never committed save by Edward's decree, he was stripped, bound, laid down, and dragged behind horses from Westminster to the Tower and thence through the city streets to Aldgate. Doubtless he was first tied onto a hurdle, or, as was the custom, wrapped in a bull's hide, lest the stony roads should batter and rip him to death before he could suffer his punishment 'for homicide, robbery and felony' at Smithfield, where London's slaughterhouses now stand. There he was hanged briefly from the common gallows, cut down alive, and slashed open, his heart, liver and lungs being ripped from his body before he was beheaded as an outlaw. Nor did his punishment end even with his death. Because he had destroyed churches and holy relics, the 'entrails from which his perverse plans had arisen' were burned, and for his 'crimes against the people of England and Scotland' his corpse was hacked into quarters. Finally, 'as an example to others', his head was fixed on London Bridge, while his tarred quarters were sent to be displayed on the gibbets of Newcastle, Berwick, Stirling and Perth.

So died Sir William Wallace, and England's popular-song writers worked overtime to celebrate their nation's triumph; one of them wrote:

> Sir Edward our king, that is full of piety
> The Wallace's quarters sent, unto his own country
> In four towns for to hang, their mirror for to be
> Thereupon to think, that many might it see
> > And dread
> Why could they not beware
> Of the battle of Dunbar
> > So evil did they speed.

Another jingled, harping as usual on the hero's ignoble birth:

> Thus may men learn
> A peasant to spurn
>   And dwell in peace
> For it falls in his eye
> That aims over high
>   Learn from Wallace.

The Lanercost chronicler descanted on the same theme:

> Thou pillager of many a holy shrine
> Butcher of thousands, threefold death be thine
> So shall the English from thee gain relief
> Scotland be wise, and choose a nobler chief.

No contemporary Scots replies have survived, but in the 15th century Wyntoun wrote with dignity and truth:

> In all England there was not then
> As William Wallace so true a man
> Whatever he did against their nation
> They made him ample provocation
> Nor to them sworn never was he
> In fellowship, faith or loyalty.

By now Wallace was a Scots folk-hero of the first rank:

> There is no story that I hear
> Of Little John or Robin Hood
> Nor yet of Wallace wicht but weir [bold without doubt]
> That me thought half so good.

And he was well on the way to unofficial canonization as a martyr; both Bower and Hary declare that English monks saw visions of the hero's reception into Heaven within minutes of his 'martyrdom', and the medieval Scots view of Wallace is perhaps best summed up in an anonymous poem on the same subject:

> There was no force might make him hold
> Nor yet reward of worldly goods
> But Scotland aye defend he wold
> From subjection to Saxon blood
> Thus for his realm steadfast he stood
> And to his death was bought and sold
> Therefore in Heaven his soul was I hold
> Ere he was cold, thus I conclude.

If from this end of history Wallace appears as neither a saintly paragon nor a war criminal, there can be no doubt that he was a hero of heroes. Unswerving in his dedication to his cause, undaunted by difficulties and undismayed by defeat, he alone 'stood steadfast' while others all around him – Bruce, Lamberton, Wishart, Comyn, the Stewart, even Fraser – bent to the changing winds of circumstance. Brutal at times he certainly was, yet no more brutal than his opponents. Wallace mutilated dead enemies, but Edward tore apart their living bodies; Wallace distributed fragments of Cressingham, Edward distributed quarters of Wallace; Wallace killed civilians in Northumberland, Edward massacred them at Berwick; Wallace slew English without mercy at Stirling Bridge, Edward slaughtered Scots at Falkirk. It is apparent, moreover, that the loathing the English felt for Wallace sprang less from what he did than from who he was: actions which were excusable, even commendable, in a king and an army of nobles were beyond measure reprehensible when perpetrated by a knight's son at the head of a force of 'middle folk' and peasants.

The root of Wallace's tragedy, indeed, was that he was born too low in the hierarchy of a society founded on hereditary status. For though a conservative Scotland was at first prepared to let him do the work which her inadequate king and vacillating nobles could not or would not do, the nation was not yet ready to unite for long behind a man who was neither king nor noble. Wallace taught the commons to resist, but without the support of the lords they could not defend Scotland: neither could the lords do so without the commons, as was proved in 1296 and 1303. But his labour was not entirely in vain. For when, six months after Sir William's death, the aristocratic Robert Bruce seized the crown of Scotland and renewed the struggle for independence, 'the poor common folk' whom Wallace had first inspired were ready to take the field again, and king, nobles and commons together eventually won through to victory.

Bibliography

List of Maps

Sources of Illustrations

Index

Bibliography

CHAPTERS I AND II
Caratacus and Boadicea

D. F. Allen: 'Coins of the Iceni' in Britannia, I (1970)

R. Bromwich (ed.): Trioedd Ynys Prydain (Welsh Triads), Cardiff, 1961

A. H. Burne: More Battlefields of England, London, 1952

William Camden: Britannia (ed. R. Gough), London, 1806

K. Carroll: 'The date of Boudicca's Revolt' in Britannia, X (1979)

E. M. Clifford: Bagendon, a Belgic Oppidum, Cambridge, 1961

B. Cunliffe: Iron Age Communities in Britain, London, 1978

Dio Cassius: Roman History (ed. and trans. J. Jackson), London, 1924

D. R. Dudley and G. Webster: The Roman Conquest of Britain, London, 1965

D. R. Dudley and G. Webster: The Rebellion of Boudicca, London, 1962

S. S. Frere: Britannia (2nd edn), London, 1978

Geraldus Cambrensis: The Journey Through Wales (ed. and trans. L. Thorpe), Harmondsworth, London, 1978

R. Graves: The Greek Myths, Harmondsworth, London, 1975

Lady Gregory: Cuchulain of Murthemne (translation), Gerrards Cross, 1925

C. H. Hartshorne: Salopia Antiqua, London, 1841

I. Henderson: The Picts, London, 1967

Lucan: Pharsalia (ed. J. D. Duff), London, 1928

The Mabinogion (trans. G. Jones and T. Jones), London, 1974

R. Merrifield: The Roman City of London, London, 1965

Polydore Vergil: Anglia Historia (ed. H. Ellis), Camden Society, London, 1844

A. F. L. Rivet and C. Smith: Place-names of Roman Britain, London, 1979

A. Ross: Pagan Celtic Britain, London, 1967

J. K. St Joseph: 'Aerial Reconnaissance in Wales' (on Caratacus' last stand) in Antiquity, no. 140 (1961)

Silius Italicus: Punica (ed. J. D. Duff), London, 1927

Suetonius: The Twelve Caesars (ed. R. Graves), London, 1957

Tacitus: Agricola (ed. R. M. Ogilvie and I. Richmond), London, 1967 (English translation by H. Mattingly in Tacitus: On Britain and Germany, London, 1948)

Tacitus: Annals (ed. J. Jackson), London, 1937 (English translation by M. Grant in Tacitus: The Annals of Imperial Rome, London, 1977)

J. Wacher: The Towns of Roman Britain, London, 1974

G. Webster: Boudica, London, 1978

CHAPTER III
Old King Cole

The nursery rhyme

W. Chappell: English Songs and Ballad Music

W. King: Useful Transactions in Philosophy, London, 1709

I. and P. Opie: The Oxford Dictionary of Nursery Rhymes, Oxford, 1951

Thomas Cole of Reading

T. Deloney: Thomas of Reading, or the Six Worthy Yeomen of the West, London, 1929

Cole of Colchester and St Helena

GENERAL

Acta Sanctorum (Bollandist): August vol. iii, Paris, 1867

F. Arnold-Forster: *Studies in Church Dedications*, London, 1899

S. Baring-Gould and J. Fisher: *Lives of the British Saints*, London, 1911

F. Bond: *Dedications and Patron Saints of English Churches*, London, 1914

A. Butler: *Lives of the Saints*, London, 1959

S. S. Frere: *Britannia* (2nd edn), London, 1978

J. H. Round: *St Helen's Chapel, Colchester*, London, 1886

J. H. Smith: *Constantine the Great*, London, 1971

PRINCIPAL ROMAN AUTHORS ON HELENA

St Ambrose: *Funeral Panegyric on the Emperor Theodosius*

Eusebius: *De Vita Constantini*

St Jerome: *Interpretatio Chronicae Eusebii* (ed. Migne), Paris, 1848

J. Morris (ed.): *Prosopography of the Later Roman Empire* (on Helena), Cambridge, 1971

Orosius: *Historia Contra Paganos* (ed. Migne), Paris, 1849

PRINCIPAL MEDIEVAL VERSIONS OF THE LEGEND

The Brut (ed. F. W. D. Brie), Early English Text Society, London, 1906

John Capgrave: *The Newe Legende of England*, London, 1516

Geoffrey of Monmouth: *History of the Kings of Britain*, Harmondsworth, London, 1966

Henry of Huntingdon: *Historia Anglorum* (ed. T. Arnold), Rolls Series, London, 1879

Layamon's Brut (ed. G. L. Brook and R. F. Leslie), Early English Text Society, London, 1903

The Colchester Abbey Chronicle in Sir W. Dugdale: *Monasticon Anglicanum*, London, 1823

The Colchester Town Chronicle in *The Red Paper Book of Colchester* (ed. Benham), Colchester, 1902

THE LEGEND IN THE 16TH TO 19TH CENTURIES

M. Alford: *Britannia Illustrata sive . . . Helenae, Constantini Patria et Fides*, Antwerp, 1641

W. Camden: *Britannia* (ed. R. Gough), London, 1806

F. Drake: *Eboracum*, London, 1736

E. Gibbon: *Decline and Fall of the Roman Empire*, London, 1782

P. Morant: *History and Antiquities of Essex*, London, 1816

Polydore Vergil: *Anglia Historia* (ed. H. Ellis), Camden Society, London, 1844

J. Stowe: *Annals*, London, 1631

Coel Hen

EARLY SCOTTISH VERSIONS OF THE RHYME

D. Herd: *Scottish Songs and Ballads*, Edinburgh, 1776

J. Johnson: *The Scots Musical Museum*, Edinburgh, 1787–1803

Vocal Harmony, or No Song, No Supper (no imprint), 1806

AYRSHIRE LOCAL TRADITIONS

D. Wilson: *The Archaeology and Prehistoric Annals of Scotland*, Edinburgh, 1851

The Old Statistical Account, Edinburgh, 1798

Topographical Dictionary of Scotland (ed. Lewis), London, 1846

THE 16TH-CENTURY LEGEND

Anon: *The Mar Lodge Translation of Boece*, Scottish Text Society, Edinburgh, 1946

J. Bellenden: *Boece's Scottish History*, Scottish Text Society, Edinburgh, 1935

Hector Boece: *Scotorum Historiae*, Paris, 1574

W. Steward: *The Buik of the Croniclis of Scotland*, Rolls Series, London, 1858

THE HISTORICAL COEL HEN

R. Bromwich (ed.): *Trioedd Ynys Prydein* (Welsh Triads), Cardiff, 1961

H. M. Chadwick: *Early Scotland*, Cambridge, 1949
N. Chadwick: *The British Heroic Age*, Cardiff, 1976
Genealogies in *Y Cymmrodor* vols VIII and IX, London, 1887, 1888
A. A. M. Duncan: *Scotland: The Making of the Kingdom*, Edinburgh, 1975
P. Hunter Blair: 'The Origins of Northumbria' in *Archaeologia Aeliana*, Newcastle, 1947
K. Jackson: 'The Britons in Southern Scotland' in *Antiquity*, London, 1955
K. Jackson (ed.): *The Gododdin*, Edinburgh, 1969
L. Laing: *The Archaeology of Late Celtic Britain and Ireland*, London, 1975
J. Morris: *The Age of Arthur*, Chichester, 1977
Nennius: *Historia Brittonum* (ed. Morris), Chichester, 1980
St Patrick: *Libri Epistolarum* (ed. L. Bieler), Dublin, 1952
M. Rowling: *Folklore of the Lake District*, London, 1965
N. F. Skene: *The Four Ancient Books of Wales*, Edinburgh, 1868
N. F. Skene: *Chronicles of the Picts and Scots*, Edinburgh, 1867
Taliesin: *The Poems of Taliesin* (ed. Sir I. Williams, trans. J. E. C. Williams), Dublin, 1968
W. J. Watson: *History of the Celtic Place-names of Scotland*, Edinburgh, 1926

CHAPTER IV
Anglo-Saxon Heroes

General

The Anglo-Saxon Chronicle (ed. and trans. G. N. Garmonsway), London, 1972
F. M. Stenton: *Anglo-Saxon England* (3rd edition), Oxford, 1971
R. M. Wilson: *The Lost Literature of Medieval England*, London, 1970

Early English Heroes

Tacitus: *Germania* (ed. H. Mattingly as *On Britain and Germany*), Harmondsworth, 1948
J. Morris: *The Age of Arthur*, Chichester, 1977

Place-names

E. Ekwall: *The Concise Oxford Dictionary of English Place-Names*, Oxford, 1977
K. Cameron: *English Place-Names*, London, 1977

St Edmund of East Anglia

Memorials of St Edmund's Abbey (ed. T. Arnold), Rolls Series, London, 1890–92

Alfred

Asser's *Life of Alfred* and the *Annals of St Neots* (ed. W. H. Stevenson), Oxford, 1909
William of Malmesbury: *De Gestis Regum Anglorum* (ed. W. Stubbs), Rolls Series, London 1887–9
A. P. Smyth: *Scandinavian Kings in the British Isles*, Oxford, 1977

Heroes of the Danelaw

R. M. Wilson, op. cit.
Robert Mannyng: *Metrical Chronicle* (ed. F. J. Furnivall), Rolls Series, London, 1887 (on Skarthi)
E. Gillett: *History of Grimsby*, Oxford, 1970 (on Grim)
Vita et Passio Waldevi Comitis in J. A. Giles, *Lives of Anglo-Saxons*, London, 1854 (on Siward)
Henry of Huntingdon: *Historia Anglorum* (ed. T. Arnold), Rolls Series, London, 1879

The Norman Conquest

Stenton, op. cit.
For an extreme pro-Saxon view see E. A. Freeman: *History of the Norman Conquest of England*, Oxford, 1870–79; for a pro-Norman view see R. A. Brown: *The Normans and the Norman Conquest*, London, 1969

The Harold Legends

Freeman, op. cit.
De Inventione Sanctae Crucis Walthamensis
and *Vita Haroldi Regis*: both in J. A.
Giles, *Lives of Anglo-Saxons*, London,
1854
Brut y Tywyssogion (ed. T. Jones), Cardiff,
1941

Wild Edric

HISTORY
The Anglo-Saxon Chronicle, op. cit.
Domesday Book for Herefordshire and
Shropshire, in the *Victoria County
Histories* of those counties.
Florence of Worcester's Chronicle (ed. and
trans. T. Forester), London, 1854
Ordericus Vitalis: *Ecclesiastical History of
England and Normandy* (ed. and trans.
T. Forester), London, 1853
William of Malmesbury, op. cit.
The Wigmore Chronicle in Sir W. Dug-
dale: *Monasticon Anglicanum*, vol. IV,
London, 1817–30

LEGEND
C. S. Burne and G. F. Jackson: *Shropshire
Folk-lore*, London, 1883–6
Giraldus Cambrensis: 'Vita Sancti
Ethelberti' in *Opera* (ed. J. S. Brewer),
Rolls Series, London, 1863
Walter Map: *De Nugis Curialium* (ed. T.
Wright), Camden Society, London,
1850
J. Simpson: *Folklore of the Welsh Border*,
London, 1976

CHAPTER V
Hereward

Original sources

PRINCIPAL SOURCES
The Anglo-Saxon Chronicle (ed. and trans.
G. N. Garmonsway), London, 1972
Ingulph's Chronicle of Croyland Abbey (ed.
and trans. H. T. Riley), London, 1908
Chronicle of Hugh Candidus (ed. W. T.
Mellows), London, 1949 (trans.

W. T. and C. Mellows, Peterborough,
1966)
Chronicle of Hyde Abbey (ed. E. Edwards),
Rolls Series, London, 1866
(*Domesday Book*) *The Lincolnshire Domes-
day and the Lindsey Survey* (ed. C. W.
Foster and T. Longley), Lincoln
Record Society XIX, Horncastle,
1924
(*Ely Book*) *Liber Eliensis* (ed. E. O.
Blake), Camden Society, London,
1962
Geoffrey Gaimar: *Lestorie des Engles* (ed.
Sir T. D. Hardy and C. T. Morton),
Rolls Series, London, 1889
Gesta Herwardi Incliti Exulis et Militis in
Lestorie des Engles, above

MEDIEVAL SOURCES OF LESSER IMPORT-
ANCE
Chronicon Angliae Petriburgense (ed. J. A.
Giles), London, 1845
'Excerpts about Hereward's Family' in
Vita Quorundum Anglo-Saxonum (ed.
J. A. Giles), London, 1854
Florence of Worcester's Chronicle (ed. and
trans. T. Forester), London, 1854
Ordericus Vitalis: *Ecclesiastical History of
England and Normandy* (ed. and trans.
T. Forester), London, 1853
Roger of Wendover: *Flores Historiarum*
(ed. H. G. Hewlett), Rolls Series,
London, 1886–9
William of Malmesbury: *Gesta Pontificum*
(ed. N. Hamilton), Rolls Series,
London, 1870

Secondary works

H. C. Darby: *The Medieval Fenland*,
Cambridge, 1940
H. C. Darby and I. B. Terrett: *The
Domesday Geography of Midland England*,
Cambridge, 1954
D. C. Douglas: *William the Conqueror*,
London, 1969
English Place Name Society (volume for
Northamptonshire), Cambridge,
1933
E. A. Freeman: *The Norman Conquest of
England*, London, 1876

M. H. Keen: *The Outlaws of Medieval Legend* (revised edition), London, 1977
Charles Kingsley: *Hereward the Wake* (novel, in various editions)
E. Porter: *The Folklore of East Anglia*, London, 1974
Proceedings of the Cambridgeshire Antiquarian Society: articles by T. C. Lethbridge, vols XXXI, XXXIV; J. Beckett, vol. XLIV; C. Hart, vol. LXV
J. H. Round: *Feudal England*, London, 1909
J. Steane: *The Northamptonshire Landscape*, London, 1974
F. M. Stenton: *Anglo-Saxon England* (3rd edition), Oxford, 1971
Victoria County Histories, volumes for Cambridgeshire, Huntingdonshire, Lincolnshire and Northamptonshire
R. M. Wilson: *The Lost Literature of Medieval England*, London, 1970

CHAPTER VI
William Wallace

Chronicles

ENGLISH CHRONICLES
Bartholomew Cotton: *Historia Anglicana* (ed. H. R. Luard), Rolls Series, London, 1859
——: *Eulogium Historiarum* (ed. F. S. Haydon), Rolls Series, London, 1858
Sir Thomas Gray: *Scalacronica* (trans. H. Maxwell), Glasgow, 1907
Walter of Guisborough: *Chronicles* (ed. H. Rothwell), Camden Society, London, 1957
Ranulph Higden: *Polychronicon* (ed. J. R. Lumby), Rolls Series, London, 1865–86
The Chronicle of Lanercost (trans. H. Maxwell), Glasgow, 1913
Peter of Langtoft: *Metrical Chronicle* (ed. T. Wright), Rolls Series, London, 1866
Robert Mannyng of Brunne: *Metrical Chronicle* (ed. F. J. Furnivall), Rolls Series, London, 1887
Chronica Monasterii de Melsa (ed. E. A. Bond), Rolls Series, London, 1867
Political Songs of England (ed. T. Wright), Camden Society, London, 1839
William Rishanger: *Chronica et Annales* (ed. H. T. Riley), Rolls Series, London, 1865
Nicholas Trivet: *Annales* (ed. T. Hog), London, 1845
Matthew of Westminster: *Flores Historiarum* (ed. H. R. Luard), Rolls Series, London, 1880

SCOTTISH CHRONICLES
Walter Bower: *Scotichronicon* (ed. W. Goodall), Edinburgh, 1759
Blind Hary: *Wallace* (ed. M. P. McDiarmid), Scottish Text Society, Edinburgh, 1968–9
John of Fordun: *Scotichronicon* (ed. T. Hearne), Oxford, 1722
Sir James Fraser: *Historical Works*, Edinburgh, 1824
John Major: *Historia Majoris Britanniae*, Edinburgh, 1740
Liber Pluscardensis (ed. F. J. Skene), Edinburgh, 1877
Andrew of Wyntoun: *Original Chronicle* (ed. F. J. Amours), Scottish Text Society, Edinburgh, 1907

Collections of Documents

J. Bain: *Calendar of Documents Relating to Scotland*, Edinburgh, 1884
H. Gough: *Scotland in 1298*, London, 1888
F. Palgrave: *Documents and Records Illustrating the History of Scotland*, London, 1837
F. Palgrave: *Kalendars and Inventories of the Treasury of the Exchequer*, London, 1836
Rotuli Scotiae, London, 1814
J. Stevenson: *Documents Illustrative of the History of Scotland*, Edinburgh, 1870
J. Stevenson: *Documents Illustrative of William Wallace*, Edinburgh, 1841
E. L. G. Stones: *Anglo-Scottish Relations, 1174–1328*, Oxford, 1970

Modern Works

E. M. Barron: *The Scottish Wars of Independence*, Inverness, 1934

G. W. S. Barrow: *Robert Bruce*, London, 1965

G. W. S. Barrow: *The Anglo-Norman Era in Scottish History*, Oxford, 1980

J. G. Bellamy: *The Law of Treason in England in the Middle Ages*, Cambridge, 1970

A. A. M. Duncan: *The Nation of Scots*, Historical Association Pamphlet, London, 1970

J. E. Morris: *The Welsh Wars of Edward I*, Oxford, 1901

R. Nicholson: *Scotland, The Later Middle Ages*, Edinburgh, 1974

List of Maps

The maps were drawn by Anthony Barton

Sources of Illustrations

TEXT ILLUSTRATIONS

Numbers refer to pages

8, 94 Battle scene. From *Old England,* vol. I, London, 1845

30 A captive wearing a torque. From *Old England*, vol. I, London, 1845

64 The large seal of Colchester, part of the Borough Regalia. Engraving by J. Greig, 1824. Photo Colchester and Essex Museum

105 King Alfred being abused for letting the cakes burn. Engraving published by Thomas Kelly, 1813. Mansell Collection

118, 148 Battle of Hastings from the Bayeux Tapestry. From *Old England*, vol. I, London, 1845

125 Hereward slaughtering the Normans in his father's hall. Engraving after H. C. Selous. Mansell Collection

171 Egfrid offering the Bishopric of Hexham to St Cuthbert. From *Old England*, vol. I, London, 1845

172 William Wallace. Engraving, 1819. Mansell Collection

189 Scottish Badge, the *Thistle Floral*

PLATES

1 Celtic head-trophy from Roquepertuse, France. Musée Borely, Marseilles

2 Coin of Caratacus, found near Guildford, Surrey. British Museum, London

3 Coin of Claudius. British Museum, London

4 Brecon Beacons, Powys, Wales. Photo Cambridge University Collection: copyright reserved

5 Caer Caradoc, near Clun, Shropshire. Photo Cambridge University Collection: copyright reserved

6 A 'testudo' from Trajan's Column, Rome. Photo Alinari

7 Head of Claudius, found near Saxmund-

ham, Suffolk. British Museum, London

8 Snettisham hoard from Hunstanton, Norfolk. British Museum, London. Photograph as found, from Castle Museum, Norwich

9 Relief of Brigantia from Birrens, Dumfries and Galloway. National Museum of Antiquities of Scotland, Edinburgh

10 Tombstone of Longinus from Colchester. Colchester and Essex Museum

11 Skulls from the Walbrook stream, London. Museum of London

12 Statue of Boadicea, sculpted by Thomas Thornycroft (1815–85), erected 1902, Thames Embankment, London. Photo British Tourist Authority

13 Charred dates from Colchester. Photo Colchester Archaeological Trust

14 Coin showing Helena. British Museum, London

15 Bronze head of Constantine. National Museum, Belgrade. Photo Hirmer, Munich

16 The initial of the Colchester Charter, 1413. Borough Archives, Colchester. Photo Colchester and Essex Museum

17 Hadrian's Wall, near Housesteads, Northumberland. Photo Peter Chèze-Brown

18 The Mote of Mark, Galloway. Photo Dr L. R. Laing

19 The Danish Great Army landing, from the *Life, Passion and Miracles of St Edmund,*

King and Martyr, mid-12th-century manuscript, M. 736, Pierpont Morgan Library, New York

20 The Alfred Jewel. Ashmolean Museum, Oxford

21 King Cnut, from the *Liber Vitae* of the New Minster, Winchester, *c.* 1031, Ms Stowe 944, f 6r, British Library, London

22 The death of King Harold from the Bayeux Tapestry. Musée de la Ville de Bayeux. Photo Giraudon

23 Norman knights from the Bayeux Tapestry. Musée de la Ville de Bayeux. Photo Giraudon

24 Croyland Abbey, Lincolnshire. Photo Edwin Smith

25 Coin of William the Conqueror. National Portrait Gallery, London

26 Wicken Fen, Cambridgeshire. Photo The National Trust

27 The Wallace Monument on Abbey Crag at Stirling. Photo British Tourist Authority

28 Letter from William Wallace and Andrew Moray, 1297. Photo Archiv der Hansestadt Lübeck

29 Battle scenes from the Holkham Bible Picture Book, *c.* 1327–35, Ms Add 47 682 f 40, British Library, London

30 Hexham Priory church, Northumberland. Photo Edwin Smith

31 Stirling castle, central Scotland. Photo Edwin Smith

Index

Figures in italics refer to illustrations